HISTORY
LESSONS

HISTORY

How Textbooks from Around the World
Portray U.S. History

LESSONS

Dana Lindaman and
Kyle Ward

THE NEW PRESS

NEW YORK
LONDON

Published in the United States by The New Press, New York, 2004
Distributed by W. W. Norton & Company, Inc., New York

LIBRARY OF CONGRESS CATALOGING-IN-PUBLICATION DATA
Lindaman, Dana.
History lessons : how textbooks from around the world portray
U.S. history / Dana Lindaman and Kyle Ward.
p.   cm.
Includes bibliographical references and index.
ISBN-13 978-1-56584-894-8 (hc) 978-1-59558-082-5 (pbk)
ISBN-10 1-56584-894-2 (hc) 1-59558-082-4 (pbk)
1. United States—History—Textbooks—Evaluation.
2. United States—History—Study and teaching—Foreign countries.
3. Textbooks—Foreign countries—Evaluation.   4. United States—
Foreign public opinion.   I. Ward, Kyle Roy, 1969-   II. Title.
E175.85.L56   2004
973—dc22   2004042595

The New Press was established in 1990 as a not-for-profit alternative to
the large, commercial publishing houses currently dominating the book
publishing industry. The New Press operates in the public interest rather
than for private gain, and is committed to publishing, in innovative ways,
works of educational, cultural, and community value that are often
deemed insufficiently profitable.

www.thenewpress.com

Book design by Kathryn Parise
Composition by dix!

Printed in the United States of America

2   4   6   8   10   9   7   5   3   1

CONTENTS

PART I I I
A World Power

PART I V
World War I

PART V
The Great Depression and World War II

PART VI
The Cold War

PART VII
Modern Times

ACKNOWLEDGMENTS

We would like to thank the following people who contributed their time, expertise and resources to this project. This project owes a great debt to their efforts and support. Our apologies for any names we have absent-mindedly omitted:

Ludmila Guslistova, Dale Cook, Mary Beth Clack, James Loewen, Roger Paré, David Nancekivell, Emilia Beatriz Ribeiro Rocha Laranjeira, Regine Jean-Charles, Anna Skubikowski, Junior Damaceno, Jérôme Viala-Gaudefroy, Tom Conley, Dr. David Landhuis, Caroline Cresp, Greg Cohen, Lia Brozgal, Roger Kim, Dr. Daniel Fried, Paul Humber, Dr. Tim Harte, Ben Wilkinson, Nam Nguyen, Mark Farha, Snjesana Koren, Takura Nyamfukudza, Raymond Womberai Shana, Dara Ogunlesi, Ursula H. Wuttrich-Vare, Dr. Dennis Hart, Jonathan Keltner, Dr. Sonia Zaide, Michael Hersrud, Scott Hersrud, Dr. Richard Lewis, Dr. Ken Smemo, Daniel Aguirre-Oteiza, Juan de Dios Vázquez, and Mirit Lerner-Naaman.

The names associated with the following institutions provided us with research opportunities, direction, feedback, and many of the textbooks used in this project:

Columbia University's Reid Hall in Paris, Mary Beth Clack at Harvard University's Widener Library, Dr. Rebecca Bennette at Harvard University's Center for European Studies, Dr. Hanna Schissler and Gisela Teistler from the Georg Eckert Institute, André Marcus and Marlene Mossek from the Center for Monitoring the Impact of Peace (CMIP), All-Nations Publishing Co., and, of course, our ever-patient editor at The New Press, Marc Favreau.

*To my parents who taught me to think critically
and to my wife, Elise, who keeps it sharp.*

To the Wards—Joe, Kenny, Karen, and Jodie

EDITORS' NOTE

Although we cannot reproduce the pages from the various texts exactly, we have attempted to keep each text and its format as close to the original as possible, in order for our readers to more thoroughly compare these varying renditions of history. Beginning with layout, we've attempted to reproduce the original style and format in each of the selections when possible, from the titles and subtitles to the italicized and boldface text. As for the Anglophone selections, we have left them in their original English: i.e., with their Anglicized spellings, vocabulary, and syntax. On occasion we were able to acquire an English version of the original text put out by the original publishers. We noted this in the citation for the text since in these cases we were assured of the original authors' intent. For the remaining texts, we sought out competent translators to render them into accurate and readable English. We expressly requested that they strive to keep the language as close to the original as possible, in syntax and vocabulary, so that the reader of English could get a sense of the respective foreign language. For example, most languages have passive constructions that allow them to speak of something without assigning blame. They also have special idiomatic expressions that have come out of their various histories. To the extent possible and according to the norms of the English language, we have preserved these details. When necessary, we have included editors' notes to assist the reader. Otherwise, we have followed this project's guiding principle and have let the texts speak for themselves.

When possible, we have made every effort to have the translations checked for accuracy by other translators. Should our readers find any errors in translation, we, the authors/editors, take full responsibility for them and apologize for any ensuing misunderstanding that may result. The goal of this project is to enlighten our readers, not confuse them. We gladly welcome any criticism that helps us render a more accurate portrait of U.S. and global history.

It is also necessary in such a vast project dealing with U.S. history to explain our liberal use of certain terms that have posed problems in U.S. history textbooks in general. Few U.S. textbook publishers willingly include the terms *America* or *American* in their textbooks anymore since they are considered by many to be too ethnocentric. The United States is, after all, but one of many countries that inhabit the American continents.* Therefore, the designations given to the United States by foreign textbooks are numerous and varied. In general, most countries outside North and South America do not hesitate to use the title *United States* for the country and *Americans* for its citizens. They frequently use the adjective *American* to describe something pertaining to the United States: e.g., *American policy, American president*. However, Latin American countries are far more reluctant to grant the title of *American* to those things having to do with the United States. Consequently, terms like *North American* and *Yankee* are often used instead. These we have translated with their direct English equivalent. Conveniently enough, the Spanish language has a very good alternative for the adjective *American: estadounidense*. But this expedient solution in Spanish translates literally to "United States-ian" in English—hardly an agreeable option.

In this special case and in our own writing, we have substituted *U.S.* for *American* as an adjective because it is even more precise and loses nothing in translation. For the citizens of the United States we have retained the

---

*Already here there is a difference of opinion. Geography textbooks in Europe point to one American continent divided into North and South, whereas textbooks in the United States speak of two distinct continents, North America and South America.

usage of *Americans* since the term is common, immediately understandable, and widely recognized as referring to the citizens of the United States. The United States is the only country on the American continent that uses the term *America* as a part of its official appellation. It is therefore hardly unreasonable that the United States should find the simple term *American* more agreeable and accessible than some other term. Other countries call their citizens by the nationalized version of their country name (i.e., Brazil—Brazilians; Mexico—Mexicans; Canada—Canadians; Peru—Peruvians; etc.). It is simply too cumbersome to read the terms *U.S. nationals, U.S. citizenry,* or *U.S. people* at every turn—history and convenience have convinced us on this issue.

To designate the broader sense of the Americas, we have employed the terms *North American* and *South American* when necessary. Otherwise, we have used the terms specific to the countries being discussed.

A few remarks on the nature of textbooks in the U.S. and abroad are called for here.

There are few countries with an education system as decentralized as that of the United States. The United States Department of Education has absolutely no say in textbook production or adoption. Twenty states have a textbook adoption process, in which a state board establishes a list of acceptable textbooks approximately every five years and leaves the individual decisions to the districts or local school boards. The remaining states do not have even that system in place. When there is no state oversight, textbook publishers market directly to the individual district or local school boards. Most textbooks run in five-to-seven-year cycles, meaning every five to seven years, a new round of textbooks will be published with the hope of being adopted in the main markets (Texas, California, and New York). If any of these markets do adopt them, they are in effect assured of being adopted elsewhere across the country. As for the history textbooks themselves, the U.S. Department of Education has worked toward the establishment of voluntary norms or standards, but these serve as mere suggestions and not as any sort of fixed national curriculum. In the U.S. model, the market drives textbook production.

Some countries have a more regionalized version of this arrangement (e.g., Germany), and others are far more centralized, with the state determining a national curriculum (e.g., France and Japan). Here, the textbooks are published by private companies who must conform to standards set by state or regional government. Others control textbooks from production through distribution (e.g., South Korea, Nigeria, and Cuba), with the respective governments setting the curriculum and publishing the history textbooks themselves. This was also the case in Soviet Russia, but since the end of the Cold War Russia has privatized textbook publishing and now several textbooks are offered on the Russian market. (All of the Russian textbooks excerpted here are post-Soviet texts.) State production is still the case in most Middle Eastern countries and in North and South Korea. Students in these countries use the same textbook in every village, hamlet, and city; there is simply one history textbook available to all. The state sets the standards, prints the textbooks, and makes them available to the schools and students.

INTRODUCTION

We live in extraordinary times. Through our televisions, computers, radios, and newsprint we have access to what seems like the entire world. At almost any moment we can turn on the television and instantly see news dealing with hunger in developing nations, terrorism in the Middle East, and the economic situation in Japan and Western Europe. We can view documentaries that show us the daily routine for Aborigines in the Australian outback, life in a small Norwegian village, and work for people in the mountains of Peru. And as if these were not enough, we can search the Internet to research nearly any group, country, or society, past or present, in the world. One can check the daily news coming out of the Philippines, learn about the trials of the Tiv people in Nigeria, or simply get an update on the British Parliament and its next appearance on C-Span. What this instant access reveals to us is that people and groups around the world are very unique. The great variety of languages, dress, customs, diets, and beliefs all demonstrate the singularity of these different and distinctive societies throughout the world. One way to begin to understand these societies and their diversity is to look at their history, how time has formed them and made them who they are. History, then, is one possible avenue toward better understanding.

What makes this day and age so extraordinary, though, is the irony that, while we marvel at the exotic customs of distant peoples, the very media that provide this information also brings us closer to these distant cultures than we have been at any other time in our collective history. The Internet, e-mail, satellite and cellular telephones, advances in the speed of travel, and a global economy have brought all these unique cultures into almost constant contact with one another. Certain societies that could have more easily ignored the United States fifty years ago find themselves today dealing with U.S. corporations, fashion, food, entertainment, and U.S. foreign policy on a daily basis. And this is hardly a one-way street. However, there is one distinct advantage that these other countries have over the United States in this relationship: They are constantly exposed to the U.S., receiving a daily dose of information on the U.S. and Americans, studying English at school, and in some cases continuing their studies in this country. Americans, in sharp contrast, seem to know relatively little about other countries and cultures. This isolationist tendency is nowhere more apparent than within our own educational system.

One of the few constants in history courses both in the U.S. and abroad is the use of textbooks to teach national history. These national histories are typically written by national authors with a national audience in mind, leading to a sort of insularity on any given historical topic. While this is an understandable initial approach to learning about history, in a diverse, global society, people must move past the bias of national history. One practical way to begin this approach is to examine the way our national texts approach the study of other nations. It is here, on this two-way street, that our project has taken shape. Our research lies at the intersection of national histories and identities, where U.S. history has encountered other national histories.

History textbooks are an especially useful resource, because they typically represent the most widely read historical account in any country, and one encountered during the formative adolescent years. Unlike independently authored historical accounts, textbooks are a quasi-official story, a sort of state-sanctioned version of history. In nearly all countries the government takes some role in setting the standards for an acceptable cultural, political, and social history—i.e., what the authorities want the next generation to learn about its own national heritage—enfolding them, as it were, into a collective national identity. The fundamental contribution of any textbook is, of course, the story, an account that reveals much about a nation's priorities and values. Because history textbooks contain national narratives written by national authors for a national audience, they model the national identity in a very profound and unique way.

There are important cultural elements that surface when working with textbooks. U.S. history textbooks, for example, typically deal with national history from a political perspective, explaining events according to a chronology governed by presidential terms or political eras (i.e., Reconstruction, Progressive Era, Cold War, etc.). The French, *au contraire*, avoid this political history in favor of a more social or economic history, one in which the history of ideas figures prominently (the American Revolution and the French Revolution are discussed more as the end of authoritarian regimes than as political events). Formats, too, vary: The British, for example, are more inclined to include citations from authors and important figures in the text itself, whereas other countries include their primary source materials separate from the text. Furthermore, one finds a single story thread more prevalent in the Anglophone countries, whereas French textbooks eschew a long written narrative in favor of short summaries and pages of primary source materials. These may seem like small differences, but they inculcate a way of seeing the world and of seeing history. The simple fact that U.S. history textbooks contain a master narrative of more than 1,000 pages encased in a cover often emblazoned with a patriotic title is significant. It means something. It also means something that American students study the Declaration of Independence, the Constitution and the names of the Founding Fathers. In order to more fully compare historical perspectives, we must be willing to reflect on these cultural and political elements that underlie any text.

Cultural misunderstandings are often the result of our inability to read these cultural elements or cues. If we wish to move beyond judgment and toward understanding, we must honestly consider other perspectives. It is useless to say that a country is ridiculous or backward simply because its version of an historical event does not agree with the U.S.'s account. It is important, however, to ask why, and then to consider what is included and/or excluded, the language employed, and the educational context in which the book is used. Do the authors use the first-person *we* and speak of *our* nation, or do they use an impersonal construction? Does the text pass judgment on other nations, including the United States? Is there more than one account available in any given country? Since our goal is to provide readers with foreign perspectives on U.S. history, we have included only foreign material. Of course, the project that follows on these pages is best read with a U.S. history textbook in mind, if not next to, the reader. A few notes on these U.S. textbooks may prove useful.

Despite the generally attractive layout of the text with its graphics, charts, and dazzling pictures, one quickly notices that the content of U.S. history textbooks is rather bland. Over the last 20 to 30 years, textbook publishers have become averse to bold historical narratives for fear of being labeled as too liberal, too conservative, too patriotic, or too sexist and rendering themselves unattractive to buyers on the textbook market. Instead, they have become encyclopedias of historical names, places, and timelines. In order to meet the market's demands, they are doing away with what is most interesting about history: perspective, interpretation, historiography, bias, debate, and controversy. By reducing history to a series of inoffensive facts and figures, no matter how attractively packaged, textbook publishers are effectively judging students incapable of discussing and debating important topics and issues.

Instead of avoiding these difficult issues, this work embraces them, with the intention of bringing back to the study of history those very things that make it so interesting and important. Instead of just reading about specific events, our readers have the opportunity to develop their own historical perspective and discover how individual biases, perspectives, and interpretations from around the world have shaped our understanding of specific historical events.

It is ironic that, today, many history classes in the United States are taught from an isolationist standpoint, where events in U.S. history are portrayed as if they occurred within a historical vacuum. If other nations are mentioned in American textbooks, it is often only within the context of the impact of the United States' foreign policy or from the viewpoint of U.S. interests.

The United States developed in a global context. The U.S. received the majority of its population through immigration; it participates in a global economy, and rose to world supremacy within the context of an interwoven global system. Why not, then, consider these historical intersections as essential elements of U.S. history and examine the impact these events have had on both the U.S. and the other nations involved?

This book represents four years of research into what other countries are teaching their youth about the United States. The premise is simple: It looks at historical events and issues that are taught in U.S. history textbooks, but from the perspective of the other nations involved. We have restricted ourselves to the use of history textbooks—and some ancillary material—used in history classrooms at the secondary school level. Because this project is intended for American readers, the foreign selections are arranged according to the chronology of a U.S. history textbook. We have provided short paragraphs in our own words (these are set in italics) to introduce the selections and to set them in context.

Comparative history is relatively new in the United States and, certainly now, more than ever, is relevant in our current political climate. In the minds of many Americans, the rest of the world suddenly matters again. Of the many things September 11, 2001, taught Americans about ourselves, one of the most pressing is that, despite all the opportunities we're given to learn about other cultures and societies, we still understand relatively little about the rest of the world and how they view us. This book is meant as one step forward in that effort.

HISTORY LESSONS

PART I

The New World and
A New American Nation

I

Viking Exploration

In the 10th and 11th centuries, the Vikings were considered the most powerful force throughout Europe and the North Atlantic. Through raids and exploration, Viking ships traveled deep into Russia, the Mediterranean, and across the North Atlantic to North America. They are usually given credit for being the first Europeans to set foot on what would be known as the "New World." Most American history textbooks today either briefly mention the Viking exploration of the North Atlantic or, as is more than likely, have completely dropped it from their books. When they are mentioned it is usually within the context of the history predating Columbus, with little attention being given to the actual power they once held.

★

NORWAY

In the history of the world the period of the Vikings is arguably Norway's great shining moment on the world stage. Even though Norwegian textbooks spend a great deal of time discussing the Vikings within the context of Norway's history, the Vikings' westward exploration is given relatively little attention.

According to the sagas, some Vikings who had been driven off course went to Iceland in the latter half of the 800s. There they met some Irish monks who left the island when settlers from the Western Sea islands and Norway began to settle there from the 860s. One reason that many Norwegian chieftains emigrated to Iceland could have been that they didn't want to submit to Harald Fairhair as overlord, but for most of them another motivation was probably decisive: On the island they could clear new farms without bloody conquest.

Under the leadership of Eirik* the Red from Rogaland, Greenland was colonized by Icelanders in the 980s. In the time that followed, over 250 farms were built in the Eastern Settlement and almost 80 farms in the Western Settlement. The Nordic societies lasted until about 1500 when the population died out.

Eirik's son Leif was the first European to land in North America. In the 1960s Norwegian archaeologists found remains of Viking houses in L'Anse aux Meadows on the northernmost tip of Newfoundland. That could have been the place where Leif Eiriksson wintered. The land was given the name of Vineland and several Greenlanders went west to settle there. Attacks by Indians or Inuits is the most likely reason that they were not successful.†

★

CANADA

Probably because of the assumed geographical location of the Vikings exploration, some Canadian textbooks not only include the story of the Vikings but also go into far greater detail than their American or Scandinavian counterparts.

The First Intruders

As every schoolchild knows, Norsemen made the first documented European visitations to North America. There is contemporary evidence of

---

* Eirik is the Scandinavian spelling of Eric or Erik.

† Emblem, Terje. *Norge 1: Cappelens historieverk for den videregaende skolen.* Oslo: Cappelens, 1997, 49.

these visits in the great Icelandic epic sagas, confirmed in our own time by archaeological excavations near L'Anse aux Meadows on the northern tip of Newfoundland. The sagas describe the landings to the west of Greenland made by Leif Ericsson and his brother Thorvald. They also relate Thorfinn Karlsefni's colonization attempt at a place Leif had called Vinland, an attempt that was thwarted by hostile Aboriginals labeled in the sagas as 'Skraelings'. It is tempting to equate Vinland with the archaeological discoveries, although there is no real evidence for doing so.

Later Greenlanders may have timbered on Baffin Island. They may also have intermarried with the Inuit to such racial mixings. But Greenland gradually lost contact with Europe, and the Icelandic settlement there died away in the fifteenth century. For all intents and purposes, the Norse activities became at best part of the murky geographical knowledge of the late Middle Ages.

In our own time the uncovering of a world map executed in the mid-fifteenth century, showing a realistic Greenland and westward islands including inscriptions referring to Vinland, created much speculation about Europe's geographical knowledge before Columbus. This Vinland map has never been definitively authenticated, and many experts have come to regard it with considerable scepticism. Like the Vinland map, none of the various candidates for North American landfalls before Columbus—except for the Vikings in Newfoundland—can be indisputably documented.*

---

* Bumsted, J.M. *A History of the Canadian Peoples.* Toronto: Oxford University Press, 1998, 7–9.

2

Columbus

Contact between the New World and Old Europe was virtually inevitable given the European desire for riches during the Renaissance period and the advances in navigation and cartography. Although Columbus has become an often maligned figure in contemporary textbooks, nobody fails to mention his contribution to the first lasting contact between the new world and old.

★

CUBA

Although most U.S. textbooks place "discovery" in quotations, this Cuban textbook does so for the "new world." The terms may be controversial in some circles, but there is little debate that Columbus is the key figure.

Christopher Columbus and the "new world." The existence of Cuba, and of the American continent, remained practically unknown to Europeans until the end of the 15th century. It is true that stories were being told of Norman incursions into territories west of Europe, beyond the cold

Northern Sea, and that names like Eric the Red and his son Leif were being mentioned as the protagonists of those adventures. But in practice nothing was known about those lands, and much less about their inhabitants.

So when Christopher Columbus, an experienced sailor from Genoa, set about organizing a voyage across the Atlantic, his purpose was not to discover a new world but to find a shorter, less dangerous route to India, an important market of spices and other items in great demand in countries of Western Europe.

In his journey Columbus could of course come across territories not yet occupied by any European power, so in accepting the project, the Catholic King and Queen of Spain, Fernando and Isabel, not only agreed to share with Columbus the commercial benefits resulting from the undertaking but also appointed him Admiral, Viceroy, and Governor General of the lands he might discover.

This is how, authorized by the Capitulations of Santa Fe, and with supplies provided by the Spanish Crown, Columbus began his voyage. His three ships—the *Santa María,* the *Niña,* and the *Pinta*—set sail from palos de Moguer harbor, in the southern Spanish province of Huelva, on August 3rd, 1492.

Columbus sailed for 72 days. Longer than expected, the voyage created panic among the ever more restless sailors, who feared Columbus might have gone insane, and pressed him to return to Spain. But before the agreed 3 day term expired, in the early morning of October 12th, 1492, Andalucian sailor Rodrigo de Triana sighted land. Columbus' intrepidity, willpower, and skills had paid off. They had arrived at an island the indigenous inhabitants called Guanahaní—presently Watling—in the Lucayas or Bahamas, and which the Admiral called San Salvador, since it had saved his efforts from disaster. Columbus did not know it then, but he had discovered a new continent for Spain.

Advised by the native inhabitants through signs and gestures that there was more land nearby, he continued his voyage southeast. Fifteen days later, on October 27th, Columbus arrived at the coasts of Cuba, which he called Juana in honor of Prince Juan, the first born of the Spanish royal couple. Later, in 1515, the island would be renamed Fernandina by a decision of King Fernando, although all along it would retain its primitive name of Cuba.

This is how Europe arrived in Cuba, a land whose pristine natural scenery prompted Columbus to call it "the most beautiful land the human eye has beheld".

Columbus found in Cuba a hospitable, industrious, and peaceful civilization whose members he called *Indians,* in the belief he had arrived in India, the legendary Asian peninsula he had originally set off to find.*

★

CARIBBEAN

This Caribbean text is meant for students of the English-speaking Caribbean. There is insufficient demand in each island country to merit publishing separate textbooks. Consequently, these countries typically look to British or U.S. publishers for one general edition to be used across the various islands. The text spends a considerable amount of time recounting the destructive results of this initial contact.

Columbus's First Voyage

The fears of the seamen grew daily as the trade winds steadily blew their ships further and further west. By mid-September they were on the point of mutiny. Even Columbus began to doubt the wisdom of his plan. According to his earlier reckoning they should have already reached Japan. For a while he quietened his men's fears by showing them a log book in which he had underestimated the true distance they had travelled. A week later the seamen were once again talking about throwing their stubborn admiral into the sea and turning back. Columbus avoided mutiny by telling his men that they were sailing between two islands and could at any time turn towards land. On 10 October Columbus himself promised that the voyage would be abandoned if land was not sighted within forty-eight hours. As the deadline was drawing to a close, on Friday 12 October 1492, Rodrigo de Triana, keeping watch on the Pinta, sighted land.

Columbus went to bed convinced that the island was one of the Far

---

* Navarro, José Cantón. *History of Cuba: The Challenge of the Yoke and the Star.* Havana: SI-MAR, 2000, 15.

Eastern spice islands. A closer look in the morning showed that the island had no exotic spices, jewels, rich clothes or gold. The natives he met had no trade goods at all, except a little inferior cotton. He could not learn where he was or what they called their island. Columbus gave it a new name, San Salvador (Holy Saviour), and pointed out to his men that the natives were willing to please and were nonbelievers. Their souls could be won for the Christian Church and that was sure to please Queen Isabella. Besides, the 'Indians', as Columbus mistakenly called the Arawaks, might be taught to cultivate cotton to export to Europe. In the meantime he took several Arawaks on board to guide him to the real spice islands.

Hispaniola

The Arawak guides led Columbus along their own trade routes between San Salvador, Cuba and Hispaniola. They continually told him—as they did all later European explorers—that there were mountains of gold further inland, or on 'just' the next island. For three months Columbus unsuccessfully looked for the fabled wealth of Asia. The search continued until one day just before Christmas when the Santa Maria ran aground on the north shore of Hispaniola, and sank. Thirty-nine seamen who couldn't find a place on the remaining two ships unhappily became the first European settlers in the West.

The Amerindians and the Spanish

THE RETURN TO HISPANIOLA

Columbus returned to Spain in 1493 convinced that he had discovered one of the islands of the Indies. He wrote to Queen Isabella with plans for making Hispaniola the centre of a great trading empire. The first step would be to build towns from which Spaniards could trade with the Indians. The island could also be used as a base for exploring other parts of the Indies.

Isabella gave the task of collecting stores, men and ships to Juan de Fonseca, who was a priest, like most of the officials at her court. He and Columbus gathered seventeen ships and 1,200 men. Among them were builders, masons and carpenters with the materials to start work on the first towns in the 'Indies'. To organise the trade there were merchants and clerks as well as map-makers who would be useful for voyages beyond Hispaniola. To provide food for the colony there were farmers with animals and stocks of seed. An important part of the expedition was a party of priests for the work of converting the Indians to Christianity.

Columbus led his fleet back to Hispaniola through the islands of the Lesser Antilles, where he saw many Carib settlements. He wrote that the Caribs were a savage people but that they seemed healthy and intelligent and would make good slaves.

At Hispaniola the fleet landed at Navidad. Columbus found that the fort built a year before had been destroyed and the Spaniards he left behind had all been killed in fights with the Arawaks. He ordered a new trading post to be built and named after Queen Isabella, but he chose a site far away from supplies of fresh water. Plants soon wilted in the salty soil and men died from fevers carried by mosquitoes in the nearby swamps. He sent expeditions to seek gold but his men found that the Arawaks were farming people with no riches to trade. Some gold could be panned from rivers but there were no mines.

These setbacks did not stop Columbus' belief in the wealth of the Indies and he took three ships to explore further west. They sailed to Jamaica but passed quickly on to Cuba. For a month the ships explored its south coast before they returned to Hispaniola.

DESTRUCTION OF THE ARAWAKS

While Columbus was away from Hispaniola, the Spaniards had abandoned work on the buildings and farms at Isabella. Instead they forced the Arawaks to provide them with food. They had also robbed them of trinkets and assaulted their women. The Arawaks were a peaceful people who had treated the Spanish with courtesy. Now they decided to resist and came together to fight the invaders who had made themselves unwelcome. Columbus immediately organised expeditions to overcome the Arawak forces. A one-sided struggle followed.

The Arawaks had only simple bows and arrows, stone clubs and wooden spears. The Spaniards were armed with steel swords, metal-tipped pikes and cross-bows. They used fierce dogs and armour-covered horses which terrified people who had never seen animals larger than a rabbit or

coney.* Horses gave the Spaniards the advantage of quick attacks and re-
treats, while the Arawaks suffered dreadful casualties by rushing headlong
at the enemy. In a very short time tens of thousands of them were killed.
The fighting marked the end of any pretence that the Spaniards would
trade fairly. Instead, Columbus forced the people of the island to pay a tax.
Every three months each male over fourteen had to hand over enough gold
to fill a hawk's bell and every other Arawak had to supply 25 pounds (about
12 kilograms) of spun cotton. Arawaks who failed to pay were forced to
give several weeks' free labour. Hundreds of Arawaks who resisted the tax
were captured and sent back to Spain for sale as slaves. They were given no
extra clothing and half died from cold on the voyage.

In 1496, Christopher Columbus returned to Spain, leaving his brother,
Bartholomew, in charge of Hispaniola. The wars against the Arawaks continued and led to Spanish control of the whole island. In 1493 there had
been between 200,000 and 300,000 Arawaks on Hispaniola. By the end of
1496 perhaps as many as two-thirds of the Arawaks were dead. They were
killed not only by Spanish weapons but also by the smallpox brought to the
island on Columbus' ships. The Arawaks had no immunity to the disease
and it raced through the island, weakening and killing whole tribes. Within
a few years great herds of European cattle, swine and goats were roaming
the island destroying the Arawaks' maize and cassava crops.

In three years the Spanish plan for a trading base in Hispaniola had
given way to a conquest of the whole island. Bartholomew Columbus built
a line of forts from the abandoned Isabella to a new Spanish headquarters
which he started at Santo Domingo. Hispaniola had become the first
Caribbean colony of Spain and Santo Domingo its capital.

THE THIRD VOYAGE

On his return to Spain Columbus found himself out of favour with
Queen Isabella. She was disappointed with the way he had governed Hispaniola and annoyed that he had not found the wealth of the Indies. She
had sent back the Arawak slaves and turned down Columbus' idea that
Caribs might be made slaves for the same reasons. The cold would kill
many of them on the voyage. Spain had no use for slave labour and as a

* A coney is a fish common to the West Indies.

Christian queen it was her duty to protect the Indians, not enslave them. It was only in 1498 that Isabella agreed to let Columbus make a third voyage. This time Columbus sailed far to the south through the Gulf of Paria. He saw a huge volume of fresh water pouring out of the Orinoco River. There seemed so much that he was sure that the river must run through an entire continent and not just an island. He sailed on to Hispaniola where he found that a revolt had broken out against his brother Bartholomew. Columbus had five ringleaders hanged and tried to buy the support of the other Spanish by allowing them to take over parts of the island as private estates. This did not stop a steady stream of complaints to Spain against the Columbus brothers and, in 1499, Isabella sent Francisco de Bobadilla to Hispaniola with special powers to act on her behalf. His first act was to have the Columbus brothers arrested and sent back to Spain.

THE FOURTH VOYAGE

Isabella forgave Columbus and after a while allowed him to make a fourth voyage to the Caribbean to explore the coastline he had sighted across the Gulf of Paria. She warned him to stay clear of Hispaniola. Columbus did not heed the warning but sailed directly to Santo Domingo to claim his share of the taxes which had been so cruelly taken from the Arawaks. He was not allowed to enter Santo Domingo but had to take on fresh water and supplies at a nearby natural harbour.

Columbus left Hispaniola and sailed west to the coast of Honduras. Between January and May he sailed along the coast before turning his worm-eaten ships north again to Hispaniola. The ships were not fit for the voyage and sank near St Ann's Bay, Jamaica. Columbus sent Diego Mendez by canoe to Hispaniola to beg for a rescue ship. It was almost a year before he could hire a vessel to collect Columbus and the survivors of his crew. Columbus finally arrived back in Spain in 1504 and died there in 1506, probably still believing that he had discovered part of the Indies.*

* Claypole, William, and John Robottom. *Caribbean Story, Bk. 2: The Inheritors.* Kingston: Carlong, 1994, 24–26.

3

British Exploration

Only after their victory over the Spanish Armada in 1588 did Great Britain have the opportunity truly to begin to explore and colonize the New World. Though they came late to the North American table, the British carved out a nice piece for themselves after establishing only two colonies of their own, Plymouth and Jamestown. While the French and Spanish pushed farther inland in pursuit of El Dorado for more furs, the British contented themselves with establishing some semblance of a new society on the shores of the Atlantic.

★

GREAT BRITAIN

Exploration

English involvement in exploration before the 1550s had been minimal. Henry VII did sponsor voyages by the Cabots to the Americas but Henry VIII, despite his reforms of the navy, was little interested in the world beyond western Europe. The English, it seemed, were content to focus their trade and thus their voyages on western Europe and even more closely on the Netherlands and the port of Antwerp.

From 1551 this situation changed and changed drastically. Antwerp's prosperity was shaken by the devaluation of the English currency in 1551 that depressed trade. In 1557 France and Spain declared themselves bankrupt, having piled up heavy debts in the Netherlands. More dramatically, the Dutch revolt (1572) against Spain disrupted trade and finally (1585) closed the port to traders. English merchants perforce had to seek markets elsewhere. Thus the 1550s saw voyages to Morocco and the Gold Coast and, most significantly, to Russia. [. . .] Under Elizabeth the need to diversify trade became ever more important but other motives were also present. Increasing patriotism and nationalism as a result of Protestantism and the war with Spain demanded that England should not stand back and take second place. Attacks on Spanish ships and colonies led easily onto the idea that the English had every right to establish their own colonies. Anxieties about over-population and attendant problems of disorder also led some to see colonization as a useful way of reducing social pressures at home.

Under Elizabeth voyages of exploration thus reached a significant level for the first time and the first attempts to establish colonies were made. How successful were these ventures? In terms of their objectives they were singularly unsuccessful. Explorers hoped to find either a north-west or north-east passage to Asia and to build England's share of that trade that was both lucrative and mythical in its proportions. Of course no such passage was found and many lives and much money were thrown away in the attempt. Another objective was the discovery of the 'southern continent', a land believed to lie across the southern edge of the world. Discovery and exploitation would balance the Spanish dominance of America but Drake, deputed to discover this new land in 1577, followed a more traditional course, attacking Spanish ships and colonies and ultimately becoming the first Englishman to sail around the world.

The fates of the first colonies were equally dismal. In 1585 Sir Walter Raleigh settled colonists in Virginia but they swiftly returned home after suffering food shortages and failing to establish good relations with the local peoples. In 1587 Raleigh established another colony. The 150 settlers simply disappeared. Raleigh returned in 1590 to find a deserted site. Their fate has never been discovered. These failures brought a temporary end to colonizing ventures, to be recommenced when the Virginia Company was established in 1606. Overall the resulting lack of enthusiasm for colonies is not surprising. Elizabeth's foreign policy was dominated by events in Europe. Her overwhelming need, right through to the end of her reign, was security and exploration and colonies made no direct contribution to security. Too great an involvement might even have prejudiced security if royal finances had been drained by expenditures on unnecessary projects. Thus there was little practical royal backing for these ventures even if Elizabeth did perceive the propaganda value of success. Drake's circumnavigation won him a knighthood, received at the Queen's hands on board his ship in 1580. Voyages also provided experience and testing ground for ships and sailors. In the long term the importance of exploration and colonization under Elizabeth was not what was achieved but that a start had been made that would lead to the development of much wider-ranging trade in the seventeenth century.*

☆

CANADA

The Thirteen Colonies

While the French were establishing settlements at Port Royal and Quebec early in the seventeenth century, their European rivals, the British, were also busy establishing colonies, on the Atlantic coast of North America. In 1607, a year before Champlain came to Quebec, a group of British merchants supported the creation of a small settlement at Jamestown on Chesapeake Bay in what would be the colony of Virginia. Much like the French, the residents of Jamestown had to survive disease, starvation, and resistance, but the original settlers managed to persevere. As was the case with the French colonies, Virginia was able to secure its future by producing a single crop that was much in demand in Europe, but instead of fur it was tobacco.

Virginia was the first of 13 British colonies that eventually became the United States. Each colony was different—settled by different groups of people, at different times, and for different reasons. Historians often classify the 13 colonies into three groups:

---

* Dawson, Ian. *Challenging History: The Tudor Century*. Cheltenham: Thomson, 1993, 322, 325, 326.

1. *New England.* These most northerly colonies were Massachusetts, New Hampshire, Connecticut, and Rhode Island. Settled by Puritans, a religious sect whose beliefs were under attack in England, they developed a mixed economy of farming, fishing, and logging. They exported many goods to Europe and the West Indies, including livestock, grain, and timber, but the most important export was rum, which was manufactured from molasses brought from the West Indies.

2. *The Middle Colonies.* These colonies included New York, New Jersey, Pennsylvania, and Delaware. They enjoyed great prosperity in the eighteenth century, principally because the Delaware River valley developed into a rich agricultural area, producing grain, hemp, flax, and livestock. Quantities of timber and iron contributed to the growth of manufacturing as well.

3. *The Southern Colonies.* These were Maryland, Virginia, the Carolinas, and Georgia. The economic mainstay of these colonies was tobacco and rice, which were grown on large plantations worked by Black slaves imported from Africa. This huge work force of slaves produced the wealth that supported a small group of white landowners.*

---

* Francis, Daniel, and Sonia Riddoch. *Our Canada: A Social and Political History.* Scarboroug: Pippin, 1995, 91–92.

4

Puritans

The treatment of Puritans as a subject in U.S. textbooks begins with their arrival in the British colonies. This selection, however, gives more of the background information regarding who the Puritans were and what led them to leave England for the New World.

★

GREAT BRITAIN

'wonderful presumptuous and bold'
—THE PURITAN CHALLENGE (1568–1585)

The idea of a Catholic threat is easy to comprehend, even if there is disagreement about the degree of danger. The idea of a Puritan threat is more problematical. There was no Puritan country poised to invade England. No armed Protestant rising threatened to depose Elizabeth. During the 1570s and 1580s Puritans came to fill more places in Elizabeth's government. So how could there be a Puritan threat?

In the beginning 'Puritan' was just another insult. Presumably Puritans irritated their neighbours and fellow church-goers by behaving in a 'holier than thou' manner, convinced that they knew the true path to God. Although members of the Church of England, they believed that the Church did not yet quite follow that true path, being in their eyes a compromise or 'mingle-mangle'. Their intention was to purify the church [. . .] hence their nickname which developed during the 1560s.

These critics of the church did not like their odious name of Puritans. They spoke of each other as 'true gospellers' or the 'godly'. Others, including Archbishop Parker, also called them 'precise folk' or 'precisians', a telling name for they would not rest content with the vagaries of Elizabeth's church. They wanted the one, true, precise way and that certainly involved expunging any vestiges of 'Romish superstition' from the church. There was no better way for a Puritan to spend his or her time than in bible-reading, listening to a rousing preacher or zealously seeking improvement in the church. Perhaps the simplest way to define Puritans is to say that what separated them from fellow-Anglicans was their willingness to challenge openly Elizabeth's settlement, criticising her church in words and by example in their own services. Unlike the acquiescent majority they agitated, sometimes desperately, for reform. Having said that, they were seeking reform from within the church in order to strengthen it. In a sense their striving for reform only became a challenge because they were so strongly resisted.

What did the Puritans want to reform? The answer comes in two parts—the liturgy (the form of worship) and the administration of the church. For Puritans the liturgy was still far too close to Roman Catholic practices. They objected to kneeling at communion, elaborate music, decorated vestments, celebration of saints' days and signs of superstition, such as making the sign of the cross on a child's head at baptism. Such things were sinful to Puritan minds, likely to lead the unwary and unlearned into error and damnation. If people were to be saved for heaven reforms were needed and urgently. Thus the vestments ordained by Elizabeth could be described as the 'rays of anti-Christ' but perhaps the worst vituperation was reserved for theatres and plays which not only 'maintain bawdry, insinuate foolery, and renew the remembrance of heathen idolatry' but, worst of all, 'call thither a thousand whereas an hour's tolling of a bell brings to the sermon a hundred'.

Puritans feared that, with such temptations in view, people could not hear God's word. Hence the importance of preaching clearly and loudly, showing people the route to salvation. Here was another major frustration for Puritans. Far too few priests were zealous preachers. Many had been ordained under Mary and were only too happy to maintain the trappings of Catholicism. Others were dismissed as 'dumb dogs, unskillfully sacrificing priests, destroying drones, or rather caterpillars of the world'. Too few were 'diligent barkers against the Papish wolf' and if they did not bark, said Puritans, how could they help ordinary people join God's elect?

Thus, in Puritan eyes, the liturgical compromise of 1559 and the poor quality of the clergy threatened every individual's chance of salvation. The second grave issue of concern was the church administration which, with its hierarchy of bishops and others, seemed almost identical to the Catholic church. For Puritans their religious leaders should be enthusiastic preachers whose first duty and personal commitment was to spreading the word as laid down in the Bible. Bishops seemed to be mere administrators, little different from government officials. There was also no place in their ideal scheme for church courts and fines. Sinners should make their peace and do their penance in the heart of their own congregations. The most extreme Puritan sub-group was the Separatists (also known as Brownists after one of their leaders, Robert Brown) who rejected the idea of a national church, believing that each congregation should control its own affairs.

Elizabeth saw Puritanism as a challenge to her authority. This challenge was both indirect, implicit in Puritan distaste for church hierarchies, and direct in the demand for reform of the 1559 settlement. They demanded change. Elizabeth had no intention of changing. In Elizabeth's eyes Puritan ideals were 'dangerous to kingly rule', and through their sermons 'great numbers of our people . . . otherwise occupied with honest labour for their living, are brought to idleness . . . divided amongst themselves with a variety of dangerous opinion'. Puritans wanted people to think about religion for themselves. Elizabeth wanted conformity and obedience.

Given the queen's attitude it is surprising to find so many staunch Puritans at the very centre of her government. But their presence there did a great deal to maintain the momentum of Puritanism. Elizabeth's own favourite, Leicester, and his brother, the Earl of Warwick, were noted

Puritans. So too were the Earls of Huntingdon and Bedford and Francis Walsingham. Other councilors and many MPs* were Puritans or sympathetic to their cause. Such great figures and many gentlemen appointed puritan preachers to parishes or to university posts and protected them from investigations. Puritanism was strong in the universities and London, everywhere except amongst the poor whose illiteracy effectively excluded them. Puritan emphasis on reading and study meant that it could not be a mass movement but that it would have influence out of proportion to its numbers.

Puritanism developed as the critics realized that firstly Elizabeth would not permit change and that secondly, in her drive for conformity, she would enforce the liturgical compromises they detested. The first clash came over vestments in the 1560s. In the next decade criticism intensified as frustration grew and a new generation of Puritan leaders emerged. The new, younger men were more impatient, believing that the bishops had given in too easily to Elizabeth's demands. The most notable figure in this group was Thomas Cartwright, Professor of Divinity at Cambridge University, until deprived of the post in 1570.

Parliament was an important pressure point used by Puritans. In 1571, 1573 and 1576 MPs sought reforms in the words of Walter Strickland in 1571 'so as to have all things brought to the purity of the Primitive Church'. This was to no avail. Elizabeth declared in 1572 that 'Thenceforth—no bills concerning religion should be received into this House unless the same should first be considered and liked by the clergy'. She anticipated that the bishops were unlikely to approve of radical demands. This was certainly true of the key issue that developed in the early 1570s— Presbyterianism. Presbyterians, led by Cartwright, argued that there was no support in the scriptures for a hierarchy of bishops acting as a church government. They said that each congregation should choose its minister, who would lead that congregation with the aid of a small group, the presbytery. Thus the whole Roman apparatus of bishops would be swept away. Thomas Wilcox, a Presbyterian, wrote 'Either must we have right ministry of God and right government of his church, according to the scriptures . . . (both of which we lack) or else there can be no right religion'.†

---

* Member of Parliament.

† Dawson, Ian. *Challenging History: The Tudor Century.* Cheltenham: Thomson, 1993, 363, 365.

5

French and Indian War

Because of their ongoing strife in Europe during the 18th century, it seems inevitable that British and French colonies would eventually come to blows in the New World. The two rival colonies grew alongside one another, but under vastly different philosophies. The French were mostly Catholic, and the British were Protestant. The French were also more independent, living with the Indians to profit from trapping furs, whereas the British settlers tended to enclose themselves in forts to protect themselves against the natives. The two camps encountered and grew irritated with one another over many decades. By the mid-1700s, the growing annoyance had broken out into all-out war on the North American continent. It is worth noting that this political rivalry receives little or no mention in recent French history textbooks.

★

GREAT BRITAIN

This British textbook places the fighting in North America within the context of an ongoing struggle for power in Europe between themselves and the French. This text

also demonstrates the British propensity for anecdotes and personal narratives. No-
tice the long quotations and short stories illustrating the narrative.

The British and French in North America

While British and French merchants competed for trade in India, British and French settlers competed for land in North America [. . .]. The French first settled along the banks of the River St Lawrence, then explored the Great Lakes. From there they moved south along the eastern bank of the River Mississippi. The settlement which has become the great modern city of Detroit was founded in 1701. By 1718 the French had reached the Gulf of Mexico where they founded New Orleans, much later famous as the birthplace of jazz.

But the towns were not important. What really interested the French settlers was the fur of the bear, the seal and the beaver. The fur trade for clothes was very profitable. This huge area of North America, which was claimed by France, was in fact only sparsely occupied by trappers, who roamed over very great distances. There were fewer than 100,000 settlers, which is not a lot when you compare this with the population of France at the time—20 million!

Despite the hardships and difficulties, some British people went to the northern part of America, now known as Canada. Why? There were profits to be made there in the fur trade. They settled round Hudson's Bay. A report from the Hudson's Bay Company in 1753 shows the great problem of transport: 'The Indians cannot carry large quantities . . . because their canoes, deeply loaden, are not able to withstand the waves and storms they may meet with upon the Lakes'. Another explains that: 'A good hunter among the Indians can kill 600 beavers in a season, and can carry down *(transport)* but 100'.

Most British colonists settled in a coastal strip between the Atlantic Ocean and the Appalachian Mountains [. . .]. By 1733 these settlements had been organized into thirteen colonies. These colonies were more densely occupied than the French areas. By the middle of the eighteenth century the population of the thirteen colonies was as much as one quarter of that of Britain (1½ million compared with 6 million).

Despite the great expanses of land available, the British and French came into conflict:

1) To the north there were quarrels between the fur trappers and traders.

2) To the south of the Great Lakes the British wanted to settle on land which the French claimed was theirs.

The French were determined to stop the British from advancing. To defend their lands the French started to build forts. In 1754 they built the strong Fort Duquesne on the River Ohio. In hilly and thickly-forested land the best way of traveling is along rivers. The River Ohio was very important to the French as a link between their settlements on the Great Lakes and on the Mississippi. It was also the obvious route for the British to use to expand westward. The British felt hemmed in. The scene was set for war.*

Fighting in Canada, 1754–60

We left the story of the quarrel between the British and French in North America with the French building the great Fort Duquesne. It was finished by the summer of 1754. The British colonists in Virginia were particularly worried by this. A small force under the command of a young man named George Washington was sent to attack the fort. The expedition was easily beaten back by the French. In 1755 a stronger British army was sent. It was ambushed by a large force of French and Indians. Nearly two-thirds of the British, including their commander General Braddock, were killed. The massacre was horrific. One survivor later wrote:

> 'I cannot describe the horrors of the scene; no pen could do it. The yell of the Indians is fresh on my ear, and the terrific sound will haunt me till the hour of my dissolution *(death)*.'

When war was declared between Britain and France in 1756, it went badly for Britain at first. The French Governor of Quebec, Montcalm, started to advance southwards towards the British colonies of New England.

But by 1759 the British were better organized. Pitt was now the British Prime Minister and taking personal control. The French fleets were block-

---

* Heater, Derek. *Presenting the Past, Bk. 3: Reform and Revolution.* Oxford: Oxford University Press, 1991, 9, 10.

aded in the harbours of Toulon and Brest, and when they tried to break out, were pursued and defeated. This meant the French could not send reinforcements across the Atlantic to Canada. Pitt ordered attacks on the French colonies in North America from several directions. The most important and famous was the expedition sent up the River St Lawrence. It is worth telling the story in some detail.

Pitt chose his commanders carefully. In charge of the army was Major-General James Wolfe; in charge of the navy was Vice-Admiral Sir Charles Saunders. Both were courageous and daring commanders. They assembled their forces at Louisbourg, a fort and harbour captured from the French only the previous year, 1758. Wolfe described the force in a letter to his Uncle Walter:

'The fleet consists of twenty-two sail-of-the-line and many frigates, the army of 9,000 men—in England it is called 12,000. We have ten battalions, three companies of grenadiers, some marines (if the Admiral can spare them) and six new raised companies of North American Rangers— not complete and the worst soldiers in the universe; a great train of artillery, plenty of provisions, tools and implements of all sorts.'

You can see what he meant. Although he was well equipped, he did not have the number of troops he was promised. And they were not good enough for the job. His task was formidable—to capture Quebec, strongly defended by the French commander Marquis de Montcalm.

During the winter the St Lawrence was blocked by ice. They had to wait for summer. On 6 June 1759 they set sail. They made first for the island of Orleans in the river opposite Quebec. From this island Wolfe scanned the northern bank of the river to find the easiest way of attacking Quebec.

There was no easy way. There were 106 cannon projecting from the walls of Quebec itself. In front and to the west of the town were steep cliffs, called the 'Heights of Abraham'. Down-river the French had built strong defence-works. Behind these Montcalm had concentrated 14,000 men. At first Wolfe launched attacks below these defence-works to try to bypass them. But Montcalm's troops beat off the British soldiers.

Time was running short. If Quebec were not taken by the autumn, the British ships would be frozen in the iced-up river. Wolfe made a desperate and bold decision. He moved his troops up river. In the early hours of the morning of 13 September Wolfe led a band of men in boats to a little cove under the Heights of Abraham. A midshipman who was with them later told how Wolfe quietly recited Gray's poem, 'Elegy in a Country Churchyard'. It had to be in a low voice for fear the French sentries might hear. The poem is still famous: it starts with the line, 'The curfew tolls the knell of parting day' and contains the line particularly relevant to Wolfe: 'The paths of glory lead but to the grave.' Wolfe leaped on shore at 4:00 a.m.

Wolfe and his soldiers clambered up the cliff. The small contingent of French guarding the heights were taken by surprise. Soon after dawn a force of 4,500 British troops clambered up the cliffs and even cannon were hauled up. Montcalm was horrified when the news reached him. He marched a force round from the other side of Quebec. At 10 a.m. he attacked. The British held their fire, then they let loose a withering stream of musket-shot. The French broke ranks and fled. But in the battle both Wolfe and Montcalm were killed.

The British took Quebec. The following year they took Montreal. The French were completely defeated. Britain now had Canada. Wolfe was a hero. Or was he? Was he really so brilliant? He seemed to waste a lot of time in the summer. Wasn't he foolish, though extraordinarily lucky, to risk climbing the Heights of Abraham? Perhaps his success was mostly due to Admiral Saunders' control of the river with the navy.

The Treaty of Paris

In 1763 a peace treaty was signed bringing the Seven Years War to an end. Britain now had the most powerful empire in the world:

1. She gained some extra West Indian islands where there had also been a lot of fighting. They were important for producing sugar.

2. She gained control of north-east India. The French were allowed to keep three trading posts in India but were forbidden to fortify them.

3. The French were driven from North America. Britain gained Quebec and the land to the west of the Appalachian mountains. And the French sold Louisiana to Spain.*

* Heater, Derek. *Presenting the Past, Bk. 3: Reform and Revolution.* Oxford: Oxford University Press, 1991, 14–16.

★

CARIBBEAN

Although much of the fighting in the French and Indian War took place in or near present-day Canada, this Caribbean text reminds the reader that the West Indies was an important venue as well—both as a theater of the war and as booty afterward.

France and Britain Compete for Empires

THE SEVEN YEARS WAR

After 1750 the main conflicts between European powers in the Americas were concerned more directly with rivalry between Britain and France. The first matter to be decided was ownership of North America. Here Britain had thirteen colonies on the eastern seaboard. Between 1700 and 1775 their population grew from under a third of a million to nearly two million. They had become the most important markets for goods made in Britain. In return, their products such as tobacco and timber were in great demand in Britain. In the 1750s the French began to build a line of forts starting in Canada and running behind the narrow strips of English colonies. This threat was matched by French pressure on English trading settlements in India. In 1756–63 the two countries fought the Seven Years War to decide these questions of empire.

By 1759 the British had gained the upper hand over the French on the American mainland. The British Prime Minister then ordered that the French West Indian islands should be captured so they could be kept to bargain with when the time came to make peace. The French were almost powerless to stop this. By 1761 the only French colony which Britain had not seized was St Domingue and even that was cut off from France by the British navy.

In the peace the most valuable islands were used as bargaining counters. The British handed them back in return for the whole of Canada. Britain also kept the French colony of Grenada and the Grenadines as well as three neutral islands, Tobago, St Vincent and Dominica. France took over the fourth neutral island, St Lucia.

In the Seven Years War, Britain had driven the French armies from

India as well as Canada. At the peace in 1763 she ruled a world-wide empire with lands in India and the Far East as well as the Caribbean and North America. Only twenty years later this 'first British empire' had lost its thirteen colonies on the coast of America. It was a story in which the Caribbean sugar colonies* could not escape being involved.†

★

CANADA

How does one explain the differences that led to the conflict between the French and the British in their new colonies? This Canadian text has several ideas.

New France and the Thirteen Colonies were established at about the same time. Yet population figures for the two regions indicate a wide disparity in the rate of development. [. . .]‡ The reasons for this disparity are complicated. One reason was simply the different landscapes that the French and British inhabited. The British settlements were farther south and were not confined to relatively small area of fertile land as were the French in the St. Lawrence valley. Another reason was the importance of fur in the economy of New France. The fur trade did not require large numbers of settlers, unlike the mixed economy of farming and fishing in the Thirteen Colonies, which afforded more opportunities for immigrants to get established. Yet another reason was that the British were less wedded to the theory of mercantilism. While New France was discouraged from producing almost anything but furs, the Thirteen Colonies produced a variety of crops and carried on substantial trade with Europe and the West Indies. Finally, the British colonies were much more open to immigration of all sorts than were the French colonies. Dissident religious groups were among the founders of the colonies, and in the eighteenth century Dutch people, Germans, Scandinavians, and French Protestants

---

* The islands of Guadeloupe and Martinique.

† Claypole, William, and John Robottom. *Caribbean Story, Bk. 2: The Inheritors.* Kingston: Carlong, 1994, 120.

‡ 1660: New France—3000; 13 Colonies—90,000. 1760: New France—64,041; 13 Colonies—1,593,625 (Francis 1995, 92).

were just a few of the non-British settlers who were welcome. In New France only pious Catholics were encouraged to settle.

War and Conquest

The final battle for control of New France took place in 1760, but France and Britain were at war almost constantly after 1743. In part the reasons for this conflict were rooted in North America. The expanding Thirteen Colonies were spreading inland and threatening France's control of the fur country. The French believed that to protect the fur trade, and ultimately to preserve New France itself, they had to confine the British to their coastal territories. However, just as important as the territorial rivalry was the commercial rivalry between France and Britain on a global scale. Both these countries were growing rich on overseas trade, and their desire to dominate world shipping and commerce led inexorably to open warfare. New France was expected to contribute to French war aims by harrying the British colonies, thus drawing British troops to America and giving the French greater freedom of action in Europe.*

---

* Francis, Daniel, and Sonia Riddoch. *Our Canada: A Social and Political History.* Scarboroug: Pippin, 1995, 92–93.

6

Government in Colonial America

GREAT BRITAIN

This British excerpt focuses on the economic agreements that dictated the relationship between the Empire and her colonies. It also takes a longer look at how politics developed within the thirteen colonies and also alludes to problems on the horizon.

British Imperialism

THE SEVEN YEARS WAR AND CRISIS IN NORTH AMERICA

Centered on North America, Britain's first empire had grown as a result of English migration rather than conquest. By the mid-eighteenth century, nevertheless, North America had become the scene of mounting Anglo-French conflict, which soon merged with a wider European and global struggle known as the Seven Years War. Although Britain emerged victorious, the long years of war had the effect of irrevocably altering her relationship with the American colonies: while British statesmen resolved to assert imperial supremacy, the colonists were equally determined to maintain and extend their freedoms. The differing, and eventually mutually exclusive, notions of imperial authority lay at the heart of the conflict which led to the Declaration of American Independence in 1776.

THE NATURE OF IMPERIAL AUTHORITY

Early attempts at settlement in the late sixteenth century had foundered due to lack of metropolitan support. Chartered in 1606, the Virginia Company represented the first systematic attempt to colonise North America. Despite a hazardous infancy, Virginia prospered as a result of the commercial cultivation of tobacco. Economic dislocation, political upheaval, and religious strife in the middle decades of the seventeenth century encouraged further emigration from England to North America. By 1759, the 13 mainland colonies which later rebelled had a population of around one and a quarter million, in addition to some 340,000 Africans, mostly slaves.

Economic relations between Britain and the colonies were governed by a series of Trade and Navigation Acts, the first of which was introduced in 1651. With the central aim of maximising profits from North America, these acts restricted the carrying trade within the empire to British or colonial ships, prohibited the import into the colonies of any goods which had not first passed through England, and listed colonial commodities which could not be shipped to foreign countries. The economic system which resulted became known as mercantilism. In order to protect imperial markets for domestic industries, the home government also placed a series of restrictions on colonial manufacture. In 1699, the Wool Act forbade the export of raw wool, woolen yarn, or cloth, while the Hat Act of 1732 limited the number of apprentices a hatter could employ to two. The Iron Act of 1750 sought to stifle the growth of the colonial metalware industry by placing restrictions on further expansion. While establishing its authority over colonial trade, parliament was more circumspect when it came to taxing the colonies for revenue.

Three distinct categories of colony existed by the mid-eighteenth century: charter, proprietary and royal. Connecticut and Rhode Island, on account of their charters, enjoyed especial freedoms. In addition to fully elective legislatures, the two charter colonies chose their governors by a popular vote. With the exception of Massachusetts, where the council was elected, the other colonies, royal and proprietary, possessed similar forms of government. The governor and his council were appointed by the crown or the proprietor. Each colony also had an elected assembly which by the early eighteenth century had established the right to give assent to laws and taxes, and to initiate legislation. Despite the general acceptance of these arrangements, there existed real differences about the constitutional standing of the assemblies. On the one hand, the colonists perceived their elected legislatures as true parliaments which they enjoyed in virtue of their rights as Englishmen. On the other, the home government thought of them as subordinate agencies which derived their authority from the crown. In the first half of the eighteenth century, the potential for conflict was masked by the British government's relative lack of interest in the political and constitutional structure of the colonies. In these circumstances the principal rivalry was played out between the governor and the assembly.

In the battle between governor and assembly, the former found himself at a distinct disadvantage. The assembly's legislative functions made it an essential component of government in each colony. Moreover, its revenue-raising powers allowed it to refuse to vote funds until its demands were met. Further leverage was provided by the fact that in most colonies the governor's salary was dependent on an annual allocation from the assembly. The governor's freedom of action was also limited by the paucity of patronage at his disposal.

In eighteenth-century Britain, political stability was in part maintained by the government's distribution of patronage, principally in the form of appointments to offices. This practice was extended to the selection of officials in colonial administration. The home government's invasion of the governor's prerogative to appoint other officials within his colony had the effect of limiting the amount of patronage with which he could attract possible American supporters. Domestic political stability, therefore, was bought at the price of diluting British authority in the colonies.

The weak position in which many governors found themselves can be illustrated by a number of examples. Lewis Morris' governorship of New Jersey (1738–46) was characterised by legislative stalemate: in one session the only public act passed was for the destruction of crows, blackbirds, squirrels and woodpeckers in three counties. Morris' successor, Jonathan Belcher, fared little better, bitter conflict with the assembly depriving the government of tax revenues for several years. In New York, crown instructions to grant the governor a regular salary were ignored by the assembly and had to be abandoned in 1755. At the time of the outbreak of the Seven Years War, therefore, the assemblies had attained a vitality and independence which belied their theoretical subordination to imperial authority. All the time that Britain chose not to interfere in the internal structure of the colonies an uneasy peace was maintained. The prolonged struggle with the French, however, led to a more intrusive approach by Britain which set colonial rights and imperial authority on a collision course.*

* Smith, Simon C. *British Imperialism, 1750–1970.* Cambridge: Cambridge University Press, 1998, 4–6.

7

The American Revolution

Long considered the key period in the founding of the American nation, the Revolutionary War gives U.S. students such historical terminology as the *Founding Fathers*, the *Declaration of Independence*, the *Minuteman*, the *U.S. Constitution*, as well as the concept of *liberty*, all of which are often used as the basis for understanding American history, culture, society, and politics.

★

GREAT BRITAIN

In the seventeenth century a number of people, mainly from Britain, sailed across the Atlantic, and settled in America. By the middle of the eighteenth century, these settlements were organized into thirteen colonies. The total population in 1776 was 2.5 million.

The colonies flourished. The northern colonies developed ship-building and trading; the middle colonies, farming; and the southern colonies, tobacco and rice plantations. The American colonists were also very proud of the way they arranged their government and laws. They were meant to be ruled by Britain. But the journey across the Atlantic took so long that the colonies had to be allowed to run most of their own affairs. Each colony had its own assembly (or parliament). And in many towns decisions were made by gathering all of the citizens together.

Thomas Jefferson, one of the most brilliant of the American colonists, and later President of the USA, wrote a pamphlet in 1774 in which he summed up what many in America were thinking: that they had a right to live their own lives. He wrote:

> 'America was conquered, and her settlements made and firmly established, at the expense of individuals, and not of the British public. Their own blood was spilt in acquiring lands for their settlement, their own fortunes expended [spent] in making that settlement effectual [successful]. For themselves they fought, for themselves they conquered, and for themselves they have a right to hold.'

As the colonists became stronger and more prosperous they became more self-confident. A letter written by a farmer in 1764 ends with the following words:

> 'For my part I am resolved to contend [fight] for the liberty delivered down to me by my ancestors: but whether I shall do it effectually or not, depends on you, my countrymen. "How little soever one is able to write, yet when the liberties of one's country are threatened, it is still more difficult to be silent." '

They became irritated that they were 'bossed about' by the British Government. Then, in the middle of the eighteenth century the British Government tried to tighten its control. It sent out governors to each of the colonies to overrule the assemblies. It tried to force the colonists to trade only with Britain and only in goods the British wanted.

We saw in Chapter 1 how the British took Canada from the French in the Seven Years War. This had important effects on the thirteen colonies:

1. They no longer needed British help to defend themselves from French attack.

2. The war had cost the British Government a great deal of money. It thought that the American colonists should help to pay for it.

The Seven Years War ended in 1763. During the next few years the British Government kept on introducing new taxes. Each new tax roused the Americans to fury. The cry went up, 'No taxation without representation'. In other words, why should the Americans pay taxes imposed by a parliament in London where there were no American MPs? There were angry demonstrations, particularly in New England and British troops were sent to keep order. In 1770 British soldiers opened fire on some Boston townsfolk who had taunted and jostled them. Five Bostonians were killed. News of the 'Boston Massacre' angered the Americans even more.

In the same year the British Government decided to abolish all the unpopular taxes—except the tax on tea. But by now the colonists were too angry to be satisfied by this. In December 1773 three tea-ships put in to Boston harbour. Many townspeople, disguised as Indians, clambered on to the ships.

[. . .]

This 'Boston Tea Party' was an important act of defiance. The Americans would *not* drink tea whose price included a tax. The British Government hit back: the port of Boston was closed and public meetings in the town were forbidden.

This was too much for the Americans. Representatives from twelve of the thirteen colonies met at Philadelphia to organize protest and resistance against the British. This meeting was called a 'Continental Congress'.

The situation was tense. In April 1775 General Gage, Governor of Massachusetts, sent troops to take control of a depot of arms and ammunition at Concord. This was to prevent the colonists from taking weapons. A man called Paul Revere galloped round the countryside warning that British troops were on the march. Some local farmers formed up with their muskets on the village green at Lexington to meet the British troops on the morning of 19 April. Firing started and fighting lasted throughout the day as the British 'redcoat' soldiers pushed on to Concord. As an American poet, Emerson, wrote much later:

'Here once the embattled farmers stood, And fired the shot heard round the world.'

The American War of Independence had started. It was also to become, for the colonists, the American Revolution.

The war started as a struggle by the Americans for fairer treatment from the British Government. On their side, the British Government of George III and his ministers thought that the Americans were being unreasonable. Some Americans soon came to believe that there could never be agreement—the colonies had to break free of all British control.

Many colonists wished at first to be loyal to Britain. But some were won over to the idea of independence by a pamphlet called *Common Sense*. It was published in January 1776, and during that year it is estimated that a million copies were sold! It was written by Tom Paine. Paine was born in England, where he earned a living first as a maker of ladies' underwear, then as a customs official. But he was much more interested in politics. In 1774, at the age of 37, he decided to emigrate to America, where he wrote his popular pamphlet and as a result earned the title 'Godfather of America'.

Meanwhile the Continental Congress was meeting again in Philadelphia. After emotional discussions, it was decided to make a formal statement of independence. It was composed mainly by a brilliant young man called Thomas Jefferson. It is known as 'The Declaration of Independence'. It is written in rather difficult language. However, it is so important that we must quote some parts.

It starts by declaring 'that all men are created equal' and that 'their Creator' has given them the 'Rights' of 'Life, Liberty and the Pursuit of Happiness'. It goes on to state that if any government tries to take away these rights, 'it is the Right of the People to alter or abolish it'. The Declaration claims that the aim of 'the present King of Great Britain' has been 'the establishment of an absolute Tyranny' over the colonies. There follows a list of the ways in which the British Government treated the Americans as if they were not equals and deprived them of life, liberty and happiness. It concludes by declaring 'That these United Colonies are, and of a Right ought to be Free and Independent States'. The Declaration was announced by the ringing of the famous Liberty Bell, which can still be seen in Philadelphia.

[...]

THE FIGHTING

The war lasted for six years from 1775 to 1781 and became quite complicated, involving other countries as well as Britain and the American colonies.

The man appointed to be commander of the American army was George Washington. But first he had to form an army, which would be far from easy:

1. the colonies did not have uniforms, weapons or money;
2. the motley bands of men who joined him did not have proper military training:
3. the men had great distances to travel to join the army: the colonies covered 800,000 square miles (sixteen times the size of England).

A writer described the army with which Washington vainly tried to defend Philadelphia in 1777 as 'ragged, lousy, naked regiments'. But the Americans did become good at what we today call 'guerrilla warfare': they used speed and knowledge of the country to outwit their enemy. By contrast, the British army and commanders were slow and blundering.

This is how one famous American historian has described the two sides:

'The British could beat or scatter the Americans in battle but could not round them up wholesale or prevent their gathering again quickly to renew the struggle. They could make marauding [destructive] expeditions into the back regions of South Carolina, North Carolina, and Virginia, but they could not occupy those regions and hold them in subjection [under complete control] against the bands of American troops skilled in guerrilla warfare.'

In the first year of the war the British General Howe missed a splendid opportunity of a decisive victory in New England. Washington wrote: 'All winter we were at their mercy'. But Howe allowed Washington's army to retreat intact.

Still the Americans suffered many defeats. And Washington's ragged army suffered dreadfully in its primitive camp in the winter of 1777–1778 in Valley Forge. Many, in despair, deserted.

But meanwhile, the British made another mistake which gave the colonists a vitally important victory. The British General Burgoyne collected in Canada a large army of British and German soldiers (mercenaries, hired for the purpose) and Indian warriors. He started to march south. General Howe should have marched north from New York to meet him. He did not. American troops under General Gates caught Burgoyne's army in the forests and forced them to surrender at Saratoga.

Saratoga was a great blow to British pride. But more than that, Britain's old enemy, France (and later, Spain and Holland), now agreed to join in the war to help the Americans. The French supplied money and soldiers and their navy made it increasingly difficult for the British to supply their armies across the Atlantic.

The British now tried to take control of the southern colonies. In his home state of Virginia, Washington trapped a British army under General Cornwallis at Yorktown at the end of a long peninsula. And there were no British ships available to rescue them. Cornwallis surrendered on 19 October 1781.

At the surrender ceremony at Yorktown, Cornwallis ordered the British band to play mournful music. In particular he asked for an old nursery rhyme called *The World Turned Upside Down*. Some of the lines are as follows:

> *'If buttercups buzz after the bee;*
> *If boats were on land, churches on sea;*

> *If summer were spring*
> *and the other way round*
> *Then all the world would be upside down.'*

If a collection of American colonists could defeat the British, the world *must* be upside down!

The British Prime Minister, Lord North, realized that the Americans had won. He resigned. In 1783 a peace treaty was signed in which Britain officially recognized American independence.

Many people in Britain believed that the thirteen colonies had been lost because of incompetence. The army had been incompetent in not defeating Washington at the beginning; and the Government had been incompetent in ever allowing the quarrel to break out into war at all. Some

Americans wished to be loyal to Britain. Many of these loyalists even fought on the British side, and after the war many fled to Canada and Britain. [. . .]

On the other hand, most Americans believed that the British had lost all claims to loyalty by their actions. Before the war started, they thought the British were unfair. During the war, they were outraged by the savage brutality of the British troops (especially those from the German state of Hesse). This point is made in the Declaration of Independence in connection with loss of life. King George III is accused of 'transporting large armies of foreign mercenaries to complete the works of death, desolation and tyranny, already begun'. The strength of feeling once the war had started, is illustrated in this comment by a British writer in South Carolina: 'Even in their dresses the females seem to bid us defiance; . . . they . . . take care to have in their breast knots, and even on their shoes something that resembles their flag of the thirteen stripes. An officer told Lord Cornwallis not long ago, that he believed that if he had destroyed all the men in North America, we should have enough to do to conquer the women.'

However, most modern historians believe that the American colonies were bound to demand their independence whatever policies the British Government used. They had become too developed and prosperous—too grown up to be kept under the control of Britain.

WAS IT REALLY A REVOLUTION?

The Americans had won independence from Britain. But were the changes enough to call them a 'Revolution'? For example, there were still many poor people in America and there were still slaves, especially on the southern plantations. But even so, the separation from Britain was used as an opportunity to introduce many reforms (changes).

Some states now allowed more people to vote in elections. The property of the loyalists, many of whom were wealthy, was taken by other people. Class differences between people steadily became less. The freedom of people to worship as they pleased was proclaimed. In particular, the listing of rights and freedoms in the Declaration of Independence and the Bill of Rights was a very important step—and not just for the Americans. The idea that people could live in equality and freedom was exciting for people in other countries too, especially in Europe where these rights were not enjoyed. Thousands of Frenchmen fought in America: many were present at Yorktown. They helped Americans to enjoy rights which they did not have in their own home country. These comparisons helped prepare the way for the next major revolution, this time in France. Only two and a half months after Washington became the first President of the USA, the people of Paris stormed the Bastille. The French Revolution had begun.*

★

FRANCE

French textbooks include the American Revolution for several important reasons. First of all, most French historians consider the war the indirect result of the ideas that circulated in the Parisian salons and among the many French philosophers of the 18th century. Second, the war provides an example of the period's dissatisfaction with the established order, the ancien régime. Finally, the war offers an example of a government based not only on fresh ideas, but on written documents such as the Declaration of Independence and the Constitution, as well.

The American Revolution

The influence of the "Lumières" was felt far and wide. A simple revolt by the British colonies of North America against the taxes imposed by the homeland became a veritable political revolution. These same colonies not only obtained independence from England, they also provided the first written constitution the world had seen.

The Revolt

Aside from Canada, Great Britain possessed thirteen colonies on the Atlantic coast of North America. Beginning in 1763 there arose a conflict which saw the colonists oppose the British government for having raised their taxes without consulting them. Since they did not participate in the parliamentary elections in London they refused these scandalous measures and put the problem in political and institutional terms: "no taxation

* Heater, Derek. *Presenting the Past, Bk. 3: Reform and Revolution.* Oxford: Oxford University Press, 1991, 46–54.

without representation." The situation deteriorated in 1773 when the Crown forced them to buy tea from the Indian Tea Company. On December 16, in the Boston Harbor a group of youth dressed as Indians climbed aboard three vessels and threw cargo overboard into the sea; the so-called **Boston Tea Party.** The British authorities reacted quickly: closing the port, raising a surtax on the city, and sending troops. The general rebellion of the colonists had begun.

The War

Volunteers from amongst the colonists came together to form militias. Each colony called its own "governing body" (convention) from which certain representatives periodically met together in Philadelphia at the Continental Congress beginning in 1774. The first skirmishes took place in 1775 the year George Washington was named Chief General by Congress. July 4, 1776, Congress voted the Declaration of Independence of the United States of America.

The war took on an international dimension when European volunteers like the Marquis de Lafayette poured in to aid the *rebels* in this the first war for freedom. In 1778, Louis XVI decided to act on behalf of the Americans. The Franco-American victory at Yorktown in 1781 was decisive. In 1783, through the Treaty of Versailles, the British recognized the independence of the United States.

The Constitution

Congress asked each state to send its representatives to a special convention entrusted with the task of writing a constitution. This document, adopted on September 17, 1787 and modified and completed by a series of amendments is still in use today.

The thirteen states (there are fifty today), which regulated their own police, justice and education, joined together in a sort of **Federal State** for their diplomacy, army and finances. Influenced by Montesquieu, the authors of the Constitution were careful to **separate the three branches of power.** George Washington was elected President in April of 1789. This republic was not yet completely democratic: there was no universal suffrage (it would arrive little by little during the 19th century) and slavery would endure until 1861. But even so, the American winds of change blew through Europe and inspired those who were excited about changing the established order: the American example had an international impact.*

★

CANADA

The American Revolution, like so many other North American conflicts, spilled over into the neighboring British colonies to the north. These Canadian texts put the conflict in a broader context and spell out its effect on the British in Canada as well as the Loyalists in the 13 colonies.

In early April 1775 British troops, attempting to raid clandestine colonial arms depots in Massachusetts, were fired upon by the Americans. A long-festering imperial political crisis turned into a shooting war. From the vantage point of the American leadership, they were involved in a 'revolution' to secure their rights against the arbitrary authority of the British Crown. From the vantage point of the British government, the Americans were engaged in a 'rebellion' against duly constituted authority. Whatever its label, for many of the inhabitants in British North America the event meant involvement in an extended civil war in which brother fought brother, friend opposed friend, and many were eventually pushed into exile. Indeed, the proportion of exiles from the new United States (relative to population) exceeded that from France after 1789, from Russia after 1917, and from Cuba after 1955. Instead of seeing the people of the northernmost colonies as important victims of the American Revolution taking place to the south, it makes far more sense to view them as participants (although often at a distance) in a great civil war that affected the whole transatlantic region of Britain's vast empire.

The Americans moved quickly in 1775 to organize an alternative government and raise an army, under the command of George Washington of Virginia. While that force was still in embryo, the Second Continental Congress authorized an invasion of Quebec as a move to bestow 'the coup de grace to the hellish junto' governing Great Britain. Washington was

---

* Frank, Robert and Zanghellini, Valéry. *Histoire: 2de*. Paris: Bélin, 1996.

somewhat more enthusiastic about this plan than he was about subsequent proposals to invade Nova Scotia. One army was ordered to proceed to Quebec by way of Lake Champlain and the Richelieu River. Another was authorized to travel across northern Maine and along the Chaudière River to the St. Lawrence.

[. . .]

Fortunately for the British, the Americans were neither as well organized nor as lucky as Wolfe's expedition had been in 1758–9, and the Quebecois were not as enthusiastic about 'liberation from tyranny' as the invaders had hoped. General Richard Montgomery (1736–75), struggling to bring an invading army up the Lake Champlain route, wrote that 'the privates are all generals' and that those from different colonies did not get along together. Benedict Arnold (1741–1801), bringing his army across what is now Maine under horrendous late autumn conditions, lost nearly half his troops in the process. On 11 November, Montgomery and his troops arrived near Montreal and pressed on to Quebec, although his soldiers were constantly deserting. At the same time, the habitants were hardly rushing to enlist in the American army. In Quebec, Colonel Allan Maclean (1725–84), who had earlier organized two battalions of disbanded Highland soldiers, had stiffened resistance. Montgomery joined Arnold at Pointe-aux-Trembles on 3 December. He quickly determined that he lacked the force and the supplies to besiege Quebec. Instead, he decided to storm the town. The assault on 31 December was a desperate move by the Americans, who were suffering from smallpox as well as problems of logistics and morale.

The garrison held. The result, wrote one British officer, was 'A glorious day for us, as complete a little victory as ever was gained'. General Montgomery's frozen body was found not far from the barricade against which he had led the charge. He was subsequently buried with military honours, with Guy Carleton, who had known him from earlier campaigns, as chief mourner. General Arnold took a ball through the left leg at the first battery, and over 300 Americans were taken prisoner. The American forces, now under Arnold's command, remained in military occupation of more than fifty parishes over the winter of 1775–6. Their desperate seizure of foodstuffs, sometimes paid for with worthless Continental currency, according to one American, cost the occupying army 'the affections of the people in general'. In May 1776 British reinforcements arrived at Quebec, and by mid-June the Americans had completely retreated, never to return. Quebec became an important center for the British army, later serving as the staging point for a counterinvasion of the United States (equally unsuccessful) in 1778, led by General John Burgoyne.

The Americans had desperately wanted Quebec. George Washington wrote to Benedict Arnold early in 1776: 'To whomsoever it belongs, in their favour, probably will the balance turn. If it is ours, success, I think, will most certainly crown our virtuous struggles; if it is theirs, the contest, at least, will be doubtful, hazardous and bloody'.*

Loyalists

In 1775, thirteen British colonies broke away to form the United States of America. The colonies that now form Canada, as well as about a third of the inhabitants of the thirteen southern colonies, remained loyal to Britain. The American Revolution (1775–83) and its aftermath meant great hardships for those in the American colonies who remained loyal to Britain. These Americans, known as Loyalists to Canadians, but Tories to the Americans, were treated harshly by the break-away rebels. Their homes were burned and looted, their properties and businesses taken away and many were arrested.

Although most of these Loyalists returned to Britain, many immigrated to Canada. In the years following the American Revolution, about 50,000 Loyalists moved to Canada.†

★

CARIBBEAN

The American Revolution caused great economic suffering in the Caribbean isles. Their loyalty to the British crown cost them dearly, but it wasn't offered without reason: They had strong economic and personal incentives to keep their close ties with Great Britain, according to this selection.

* Bumsted, J.M. *A History of the Canadian Peoples.* Toronto: Oxford University Press, 1998, 80–83.
† Barr, Janis, et al. *Twentieth Century Canada.* Calgary: Wiegl, 1996, 19.

France and Britain Compete for Empires

[...]

THE THIRTEEN COLONIES AND THE SUGAR ISLANDS

Between about 1700 and 1775 the Caribbean had many close links with the mainland British colonies, which were governed in a similar way to the islands with governors, councils and elected assemblies. But the closest connection was through trade. The mainland colonists made their living as timber-cutters, farmers, manufacturers, ship-builders, and traders. A large part of the goods they produced were sold as estate supplies to the sugar plantations in the Caribbean.

The key to the trade was the huge quantities of molasses which were left after the cane had been milled for export to Europe. On most plantations it was simply stored in large tanks. Merchant ships from the mainland toured the islands, calling in at plantations and filling hogs-heads with molasses from the tank. With the money they earned by selling the molasses, planters bought goods for their estates.

In 1771 New York imported over two million litres of molasses and Boston about a million. Much of this was turned into rum and sold throughout the American colonies or exported to England. [...] Apart from Boston and New York, traders set out for the Caribbean from about a dozen other important American ports.

COLONIAL REVOLT

After the Seven Years War the British government tried to make the American colonists pay a share of the costs of defeating the French. They aimed to do it by taxing legal documents. In the future they were to be written on paper which had a stamp to show that the tax had been paid. The American colonists refused to pay, saying that their assemblies alone had the right to demand new taxes. On this point the Caribbean settlers agreed with the Americans. In St Kitts and Nevis, British colonists rioted against the tax duties and destroyed the stamped paper. The British government gave way over the stamp tax and tried to collect the money through import duties on all lead, paper and tea imported by the colonies.

The colonists still objected and rioted against the duties. The British withdrew them, except for the one on tea. When the British East India Company tried to unload tea at Boston, the citizens dumped the cargo into the sea. The British decided to punish the people of Boston by closing the assembly of their colony, Massachusetts, and ruling it directly. Again the Caribbean colonists supported the Americans. The Barbados and Jamaica assemblies sent protests to the English king.

THE ASSEMBLIES CHANGE SIDES

But in 1775 the British government sent an army to force the Americans to obey the regulations. The colonists decided to fight for independence. This move brought about a change of opinion in the Caribbean colonies. More West Indians had family or trading connections with England than with America. The planters also feared to lose their special position within the British Empire. Their prosperity would collapse if rebellion in the thirteen colonies meant they could not sell sugar to Britain.

The island colonists also faced the unpleasant fact that their white population was much smaller than the mainland's. They felt they needed British soldiers and warships to protect them from foreign invasions and from their slaves. So, instead of protests, the island assemblies rushed to send petitions to England, stating their loyalty. The Jamaican assembly's petition made their reasons clear:

> Weak and feeble as this colony is from its very small number of white inhabitants, and its peculiar situation from the encumbrance of more than two hundred thousand slaves, it cannot be supposed that we now intend, or ever could have intended, resistance to Britain.

The planters were forced to admit that they needed the protection of the British army and navy. Yet the islands paid a heavy price for their loyalty during eight years of war that followed.

THE WAR OF AMERICAN INDEPENDENCE, 1775–83

France, Spain and Holland joined the war on the side of the Americans. Several other European nations objected to British attempts to stop and search all ships which might be carrying arms to the Americans. They signed an agreement of 'armed neutrality' to fight back when ordered to stop by the British.

In the Caribbean these forces were joined by American privateers who attacked British shipping from bases in the Dutch, Danish and French islands. Their activities caused great hardship to the British islands. In the first year of the war the quantity of sugar shipped to Europe fell by a half. Estate supplies, which had come mostly from North America, quickly became scarce and their prices rose. The cost of grain is said to have risen by 400 per cent by the end of 1777. Insurance rates on British ships in the Caribbean rose from 7 per cent of their cargo's value to over 20 per cent. After France joined the war, it became safe only to travel in convoys.

Planters tried to grow local provisions to replace those which fell into the hands of the enemy, but most of the crops failed after hurricanes ripped through the islands in 1780 and 1781. In the **Leewards** there were long droughts in the periods between the hurricanes.

Several islands were captured in the war. Dominica was taken by the French in 1778. The British replied by taking St Lucia in the same year, but in 1779 they could not stop the French capture of St Vincent and Grenada. In 1780 Sir George Rodney was put in charge of British operations in the Caribbean. He had quick successes against the Dutch, capturing their poorly defended island colonies and their Guyana settlements. Then, in 1781, the British army under General Cornwallis surrendered at Yorktown. Britain was now powerless in North America, and both the Spanish and French fleets opened full-scale war in the Caribbean.

The French fleet quickly retook St Eustatius and the Guyana colonies, following this with the capture of Tobago in 1781 and St Kitts, Nevis and Montserrat in 1782. Meanwhile the Spanish had taken Florida and some of the Bahamas. The two allies were then ready for a joint expedition to capture Jamaica. The island was saved by Admiral Rodney, who caught up with the joint fleet as it passed by the Saintes Islands between Dominica and Guadeloupe. Only seven of the Spanish-French ships were taken, but the rest of the invasion fleet was scattered. The Battle of the Saintes saved the West Indies from further attack. In the following year, all who had taken part in the war signed the Treaty of Versailles (1783). The treaty recognised the independence of the thirteen colonies which became known as the United States of America. In the Caribbean, all the territories were returned to their pre-war owners except that France kept Tobago and gave St Bartholomew to Sweden in return for an agreement that French ships could trade in Swedish ports.*

⋆

GERMANY

References to Germany and the Revolutionary War typically revolve around the British use of German mercenaries, the infamous Hessians. However, Hessians were in fact poor farmers from the region of Hesse who were loaned (or sold) to the prince of England to pay off debts. They were not professional soldiers, as is often indicated in U.S. history textbooks.

Origin and End of the Revolutionary War

The "patriots" won their freedom in a war lasting almost eight years. They had to fight not only against the English and the approximately 30,000 soldiers from German lands—the so-called "Hessians"—but at the same time against approximately a third of the colonists, who continued to hold to the British crown. In this respect the war of independence was also a civil war. The intervention of the French, who supported the rebellious Americans against the "arch rival" England first with weapons and money, then with troops from 1778 onward, was militarily decisive. In the *Peace of Versailles* (1783) England had to acknowledge the sovereignty of the thirteen colonies and let them have the area between the Appalachians and the Mississippi. The remaining loyalists to the king, numbering over 80,000, were expelled or emigrated freely, mostly to Canada. In not a few cases their possessions were confiscated and divided up. Almost half of the colonial upper class was replaced in this manner.†

---

* Claypole, William, and John Robottom. *Caribbean Story, Bk. 2: The Inheritors.* Kingston: Carlong, 1994, 131–134.

† Golecki, Von Anton, et al. *Deutsche Geschichte Zwischen 1800 un 1933—Geschichte der Supermächte.* Bamberg: C.C. Buchners Verlag, 1998, 164–165.

PART II

Westward Expansion

8

The War of 1812

Often seen as a minor war or the "Second War for American Independence," U.S. textbooks focus on how Britain caused the War of 1812 by their actions on the high seas and their backing of Indian attacks on the frontier. Through their system of naval impressments, the blocking of American ships from trading on the continent of Europe, many Americans began to clamor for war. What rarely receives mention in U.S. textbooks is the broader European context out of which the war's conflict had sprung. Napoleon was dominating Europe at the time. His armies controlled much of the European continent, and he was locked in a battle on land and sea with England, France's traditional enemy. Many British students have never even heard of the War of 1812, simply because its significance pales in relation to the conflict with France: 1812 means little; 1814 means everything (Waterloo).

★

GREAT BRITAIN

Great Britain's treatment of the War of 1812 is characteristic of its view of this war, as a side note to history.

Another area of increasing importance for British policy was the United States. Relations with the ex-colonial Americans were always fraught with difficulty. British assumptions about her maritime rights, and especially her use of blockades against those with whom she was in dispute, led to clashes with the Americans who resented what they saw as a high-handed and arrogant British attitude. In 1812 this led to a war which lasted until 1814 and included the famous defeat of British forces at New Orleans which, bizarrely, occurred after peace had actually been signed without the knowledge of the combatants. In the course of the war much had occurred to stoke up bitter feelings for the future. The British burned the President's official residence in Washington—the white-wash repairs giving rise to its future popular name; the Americans burned Toronto. Little was resolved for the future by the Peace of Ghent which ended the official hostilities. Fishing rights remained in dispute. The territorial boundary between the USA and Canada was still undefined. Many Americans still harboured grudges against Britain going back to the War of Independence. Andrew Jackson, the victorious general of New Orleans, who became President in 1828, hated the British because his brother had been killed and his home destroyed by British forces when he was 11-years-old.*

Grievances, arising from British conduct of the maritime war against the French, led the United States to declare war on Britain on 19 June 1812. An American plan for a threefold attack on Canada failed, and a British force under General Brock forced the surrender of Detroit on 16 Aug. 1812. In Apr. 1813 the Americans captured and burnt Toronto, and in Sept. defeated the British in the battle of Lake Erie and recaptured Detroit. In Aug. 1814 a force of 4,000 British veterans landed in Chesapeake Bay, defeated the Americans at Bladensburg and burnt parts of Washington. A peace treaty was signed at Ghent in Belgium on 24 Dec. 1812 [sic], largely restoring the pre-war situation. Before news of the peace reached America, General Pakenham was killed on 8 Jan. 1815 leading an unsuccessful British attack on New Orleans.†

---

* Scott-Baumann, Michael (ed). *Years of Expansion: Britain 1815–1914*. London: Hodder and Stoughton, 1999, 192.

† Cook, Chris, and John Stevenson. *The Longman Handbook of Modern British History, 1714–2001*. London: Longman, 2001, 275.

★

CANADA

This Canadian textbook attaches a special significance to the War of 1812, a war in which they were "invaded" by their southern neighbor.

After some years of worsening relations, the Americans declared war on Great Britain on 18 June 1812. There were several *casus belli*. One was British highhandedness in searching American ships on the high seas during the Napoleonic blockade, removing British subjects aboard them and recruiting them into her navy. Another was the British failure to abandon the Ohio Valley, where military posts continued to monitor the fur trade. Most of all, the Americans coveted Canada, which they proceeded again to invade in 1812 and 1813. A succession of invading armies were thrust back through the major entry points: the Detroit-Windsor corridor, the Niagara peninsula, and Lake Champlain. A relatively small number of British regulars, assisted by colonial militia and Native peoples, held the province against American armies, which were neither well trained nor well led. A number of Canadian heroes emerged from the war, their reputations to be further mythologized after it was over: General Isaac Brock, Tecumseh and Laura Secord.

The appearance of invading American armies posed a crisis of allegiance for many of the American settlers in Upper Canada. Most remained silently on their farms, although some supported their countrymen and retreated across the border with them. A handful of Americans were arrested and tried for treason at Ancastern in 1814. Before the war ended, York (Toronto) was burnt, the American capital at Washington was sacked in retaliation, and Fort Michilimackinac (on western Lake Huron) was captured and held by Canadian voyageurs.

The Americans treated the War of 1812 as a second War of Independence, a necessary struggle to complete the process of separation from the mother country. National survival was taken as victory. From the British perspective, the war had been little more than a sideshow to the major struggle, which was against Napoleon in Europe. Only in the Canadas did the War of 1812 have any great impact. The great struggle between British and American allegiance was played out internally in Upper Canada between 1812 and 1815, and the British won. After 1815 the overt American influence on Upper Canada would gradually decline.*

New England is presented as less than enthusiastic about the war by another Canadian textbook:

When war was officially declared between Britain and the United States in 1812, the Atlantic colonies, buffered by a neutral New England were spared military invasion. In 1814 Maritime pride and purses swelled when Sir John Sherbrooke's forces occupied part of the coast of present-day Maine. Under the cover of occupation, trade between the Maritimes and New England flourished. Many New Englanders welcomed the British forces and a few even considered applying for reentry into the British Empire.†

The Legacy of the War of 1812

Hostilities ended in 1814, by which time both sides were heartily sick of the fighting and ready to talk. The results of the peace negotiations were summarized by the Treaty of Ghent. A major portion of the boundary between the United States and British territory was clarified. Between the Lake of the Woods and the Rocky Mountains, it was set at the forty-ninth parallel of latitude; beyond the Rockies the area would be jointly occupied for ten years. In 1817 an agreement known as the Rush-Bagot Convention limited the number and type of armed vessels the Britain and the United States were permitted to have on the Great Lakes. The myth of the "undefended border," which is often mentioned in the story of Canadian-American relations, dates from this time. Like other myths, it was only partly true, since both Britain and the United States did erect fortifications along the boundary at different times in the nineteenth century. It is true, however, that no war was ever fought after 1812.

Because of the war, large scale American immigration into the colony came to an end. After 1815 Americans could not get land grants, and though this regulation was relaxed, new rulings still made it difficult for

* Bumsted, J.M. *A History of the Canadian Peoples.* Toronto: Oxford University Press, 1998, 100–102.

† Finkel, Alvin, et al. *History of the Canadian Peoples: 1867 to the Present, v. 2.* Toronto: Copp Clark Pittman, 1993, 334, 335.

them to obtain titles of property. Official British policy now favoured the British Isles as a source for the immigrants needed to build up the colonies. Thousands were encouraged to come, and their presence reinforced the connection with the mother country.

There was yet another outcome of this war, and that was the growth of Canadian nationalism. As historian George F. Stanly has said, the war gave Upper Canada a history, and in this history anti-Americanism was a dominant ingredient. During the Revolutionary War Loyalists had suffered at the hands of uncontrolled mobs, who burned and looted their possessions, finally driving them into exile. Now once again, they were victims of American aggression. But this time they stood up and confronted the enemy. Led by the stalwart hero Sir Isaac Brock, innocent people rose up to defend their homeland, and through superior courage they repelled a much stronger invader conveniently ignoring the role played by British regulars and Aboriginal fighters. Their brave deeds proved that the Upper Canadians were loyal and worthy subjects of the British Crown. Americans, by contrast, were not to be trusted. Memories of the war were revived from time to time and fuelled anti-American sentiment in colonial and Canadian society for decades to come.*

★

CARIBBEAN

The Caribbean nations had a unique vantage point on the conflict that arose between the United States and Great Britain. Many of the islands were still British colonies and were trading regularly with her as well as with the U.S. Here, American and Latin American markets are seen as causes for war.

The U.S. to 1865

RIVALRY WITH BRITAIN

The United States became an independent nation after the thirteen American colonies had defeated British forces in the War of Independence from 1775 to 1783. For many years after independence, the Ameri-

* Francis, Daniel, and Sonia Riddoch. *Our Canada: A Social and Political History.* Scarboroug: Pippin, 1995, 423–24.

can people occupied only the eastern part of their huge territory. In the southern states small numbers of white Americans controlled the lives of the slaves who worked their tobacco and cotton plantations. In the northern states, there was a much larger population of European peoples who were active traders, ship-builders and manufacturers. They hoped that freedom from British rule would make it possible to replace Britain as the main trading and shipping power in the American hemisphere.

Up to the early nineteenth century, however, British ships and traders still sold twice as many goods to Latin America as the Americans did. British ships sailed across the Atlantic with manufactured goods, especially textiles and iron products. They sold these in the Caribbean islands or mainland and then sailed north to pick up cotton and other produce for shipping back to Europe.

Between 1812 and 1814 Britain and the United States fought a war over this trade. It began when the British claimed the right to stop and search American ships which might be supplying goods to their enemy, the French Emperor Napoleon. After the war there were further quarrels when the British government tried to prevent American goods carried in American ships being sold to her Caribbean colonies. In reply, the United States closed American ports to British ships sailing from Canada or the West Indies. The British then gave way and allowed American goods into their Caribbean islands, provided they paid extra duties of 10 per cent. The 10 per cent duties caused a second round of arguments. They were settled in 1830 when the two countries finally allowed each other's ships to move freely. By then, the United States had made her attitude to European activities in the western hemisphere quite plain.*

---

* Claypole, William, and John Robottom. *Caribbean Story, Bk. 2: The Inheritors.* Kingston: Carlong, 1994, 167.

9

The Monroe Doctrine

The Monroe Doctrine is mentioned in nearly every textbook that deals with the growth of the new nation in North America. It is often viewed as the United States' first attempt at imperialism. As with the War of 1812, there is a larger European and Latin American context in which to see this moment.

★

GREAT BRITAIN

This British textbook offers a slightly different take on who should get credit for Latin American security. It is interesting to note that Great Britain still refers to "security," while most Latin American texts refer to "economic interests."

The French, firmly established in Spain after 1823, possessed the only fleet capable of transporting an invasion force. An attempt at Anglo-American co-operation floundered because of United States suspicion of Cannings' motives. In December 1823 the American President Monroe declared the American continent closed to further European colonization.

This was directed against Britain and her Canadian claims as much as in defence of the South American states.

Canning had already obtained assurances from Polignac (the French ambassador) that France had no intention of assisting a Spanish assault on South America. The record of these conversations was made public as the Polignac Memorandum. Since the meeting preceded the Monroe Doctrine by two months, the Latin Americans were reminded that they owed their security to Canning and the Royal Navy, not the United States.*

★

BRAZIL

In the following excerpts, the authors use the Monroe Doctrine to explain U.S. growth, U.S. interests in Latin America, and even U.S. recognition of Brazil's independence.

Consolidation and Expansion of the New State

The Napoleonic wars and the continental blockade in Europe indirectly affected the North-American trade with Latin America and some European countries, particularly with France. England, the main enemy of the French Empire, and also an American rival in the conquest of new markets, started to cause problems in order to block the commercial relations between the US and the European and Latin American countries.

Those commercial quarrels added to the North American expansionist ideas, which aspired to take Canada from England, leading to the **Second War of Independence** (1812–1814). The British wars in Europe and the North-American desire for a commercial rapprochement made possible the signing of the **Lasting Peace of Ghent,** confirming the Great Lakes region as a neutral zone and defining the borders between the US and British Canada.

The war led to the rise of American nationalist feeling related to terri-

---

* Martin, Howard. *Challenging History: Britain in the Nineteenth Century.* Surrey: Thomson, 1996, 212.

torial unity and also caused concern about the European threat to American commercial interests. One of the main US concerns was related to the growth of trade between the US and the independent Latin America countries, now threatened by a revival of colonization due to the intentions of the Holy Alliance. Those feelings were expressed by the **Monroe Doctrine** (1823) through US President Mr. James Monroe (1817–1825) in his address to Congress, the message of which can be summarized as "America for the Americans".

The Monroe Doctrine shaped, from the political point of view, an international economic expansion for the US. That policy would be essential for its commercial development. The internal expansion, through the conquest of territories in North America led to the **race west.** From the Atlantic coast, where the original 13 colonies started, the pioneers moved forward to the interior until they reached the western coast, the Pacific Ocean.*

The Independence of Latin America

What mattered for the Spanish American elites, represented by the *criollos* (Spanish descendents born in America), was breaking up the ties with the monopolist *métropole,*† which made trade difficult, especially trade with England, the main economic power at the time. In its colonies the Spanish crown reserved the most productive sectors for itself, besides limiting access to administrative and political positions to its own appointments. But England was interested in the colonies' independence which would eliminate the commercial barriers imposed by the Iberian monopolists thus activating new markets, indispensable for its industrial progress. *Criollos* and the British had intersecting interests that lead them to the same goal: the independence of the Spanish America.

Britain's support was decisive for Latin America's emancipation. With the Napoleonic defeat in 1815, the Iberian metropole returned to the old style colonialism, but they did not succeed because of the British support for the *criollo's* fight for independence from 1817 to 1825. The **Monroe**

---

* Vicento, Cláudio. *História geral.* São Paulo: Scipione, 2002, 329–31.

† Editors' note: *Métropole* in the European sense means the homeland or the home country. Thus, for Latin America, Spain or Portugal is meant. For the British colonies, Great Britain would be the *métropole.*

Doctrine, established by the US, also helped to consolidate Latin America's independence, aiding the *criollo*'s war of independence.*

Recognition of Brazil

Another serious problem that Brazil had been facing was the recognition of its independence. The Latin American governments delayed the recognition of Brazil's independence because they were suspicious of the real intentions of the Brazilian monarchic government. They saw it as a typical European system, which was not compatible with the republican regime adopted by all the other newly independent Latin American countries. They also questioned the legitimacy of Brazilian sovereignty over the Cisplatina Province (now Uruguay) and the insistence of the Brazilian Emperor D. Pedro I on keeping it Brazilian.

The United States and the main European powers took their time in recognizing Brazilian independence since they wanted to take advantage of the situation to serve their interests. The United States was the first country to recognize Brazilian Independence in 1824. Although the recognition would have been coherent in the context of the Monroe Doctrine, the North Americans declared that they intended to amplify their international markets. Brazil would be a strong ally in a future anti-European commercial bloc. Thus commercial hegemony was the main aspiration for the North Americans.†

★

CARIBBEAN

The Caribbean text is very explicit regarding the reasons for including such a warning in Monroe's speech: economic interests.

The Monroe Doctrine

The United States and Britain were both pleased at the revolt of Spain's colonies in South and Central America. The new countries set up

* Vicento, Cláudio. *História geral.* São Paulo: Scipione, 2002, 323.

† Silva, Fransisco de Assis. *História do Brasil: Colônia, Imperio, República.* São Paulo: Moderna, 2002, 126.

by the Liberators were no longer bound to obey trading regulations made in Spain and they bought increasing amounts of goods from British and American traders. So Britain and the USA were both alarmed when the King of Spain called on the rulers of other European countries to supply him with ships and troops to win back his colonies.

In 1823 the British Foreign Secretary, George Canning, asked the Americans to join in a warning that the United States and Britain would resist the scheme to reconquer Spain's colonies. The American President, Monroe, however, went further and issued an independent warning which also applied to Britain. It was delivered in his annual message to Congress in December 1823. The part of the speech which became known as the Monroe Doctrine said:

> The American continents by the free and independent conditions which they have assumed and maintained are henceforth not to be considered subjects for future colonisation by European powers.

He went on to say that any European attempt to interfere in 'any portions of this hemisphere' would be seen as 'the manifestation of an unfriendly disposition to the United States'. In other words, the Americans were making it clear that they were the major power in the American hemisphere—not any other European country, including Britain.*

★

MEXICO

This Mexican text is decidedly more critical of the ambition of the U.S. government.

The Monroe Doctrine and the Thesis of Manifest Destiny

Within the first few decades of the 19th century, the US system had all the economic and political problems of a complete society that had grown from 4 million people in 1790 to 10 million in 1820, and was still growing. With such growth came the frequently heard slogan in the political discourse of the era, "The March West."

* Claypole, William, and John Robottom. *Caribbean Story, Bk. 2: The Inheritors.* Kingston: Carlong, 1994, 167–168.

The territories of Kentucky, Tennessee, Ohio, Indiana and Illinois were quickly incorporated into the new nation by means of despoiling the indigenous populations. In order to continue this expansion, certain people like Moses and Stephen Austin penetrated Mexican territory under agreements of colonization, in which they promised to respect the sovereignty of the Mexican government in the province of Coahuila and Texas. Then, the senior administrators of the North American government went into action, playing their expansionist ambitions against the diplomatic slowness of the European powers.

In Europe in the meantime, Russia, Prussia and Austria, under the direction of the Chancellor of the latter, Clemente de Metternich (1815), had agreed to unify their interests under the so-called "Sacred Alliance," hoping to fortify the absolutist monarchies and, consequently, to combat the ideas of liberalism. For its part, Spain, led by Fernando VII, relied on the armies of this reactionary coalition and sought to defeat the Spanish liberals, defenders of the Constitución de Cádiz (1812). This same political strife tried to implant itself in the newly liberated ex-colonies of Spain.

In 1822 events occurred that brought about, as a consequence, the need for the North American government to take a position with respect to the power of the Sacred Alliance, over which France now ruled, led by Louis VIII. In August, the plenipotentiary ministry of the United States communicated the following: "The English government has invited us to make a joint declaration against the powers of the Sacred Alliance."

At the insistence of the Secretary of State, John Quincy Adams, the fifth president of the United States, James Monroe, included in the annual message delivered to Congress the second of December, 1823, the following statement: "With the existing colonies or dependencies of any European power we have not interfered and shall not interfere. But with the Governments who have declared their independence and maintained it, and whose independence we have, on great consideration and on just principles, acknowledged, we could not view any interposition for the purpose of oppressing them, or controlling in any other manner their destiny, by any European power in any other light than as the manifestation of an unfriendly disposition toward the United States."

The political and military events of the American continent demonstrated how such a declaration could be manipulated in order to justify the imperialistic comportment of the United States, itself. The principal manifestation of this tendency was to assume the role of protector of the young Hispano-American nations, and under this pretext, to intervene in their politics and determine their destinies. Along with this political act that helped the United States to obtain in practice its recognition as a capitalist power at the international level, it's worth mentioning the governing character that the Monroe Doctrine has held ever since in the relations of this great power with the Hispano-American nations.*

★

FRANCE

French textbooks rarely, if ever, mention the Monroe Doctrine. By 1823, France had lost its North American colonies. The following text comes from a supplemental history book used by many students and teachers in French classrooms.

In 1819 Spain was in the midst of colonial revolt. Taking advantage of the situation, the US, using both threats and persuasion, convinced Spain to cede the portion of the coast that they still possessed reaching from the Atlantic to the mouth of the Mississippi, including Florida. Through this action they achieved new, direct access to the Gulf of Mexico. President Monroe had Spain in mind, or more precisely, her rebelling colonies, when he gave his famous speech outlining the position of the United States and setting the new tone from America: the end justifies the means. A French expedition had just reestablished the authority of Ferdinand VII over Spain. The circumstances gave credibility to the rumors that the European powers intended to intervene in the Americas in order to reestablish their dominant authority over the rebelling colonies. What would the United States do? Everything about the situation begged for their intervention. Their sympathies were with the rebelling colonies that were only following in their footsteps. Their own proper interests certainly didn't include the return of European imperialistic powers in the near vicinity, but instead the maintenance of weaker states as neighbors. President Monroe decided then to recognize the insurgent governments and to give a warning

* Palacios, Mario Alfonso Rodriguez. *México en la historia: tercer grado, educación secundaria.* Mexico City: Editorial Trillas, 1992, 50–51.

to Europe. In a message to Congress he defined the principles of his administration, what would come to be known as the Monroe Doctrine. It reaffirmed the principle of neutrality put forth by Washington while providing more detail and extending its application to all the New World. The United States wished to remain on good terms with Europe and restated its desire to remain uninvolved in her internal conflicts. In return, they asked that Europe not interfere in any of the affairs in the American sphere. They refused to allow European colonization in areas previously untouched by European domination. Specifically, they would consider any action against a government having proclaimed its independence as an unfriendly act. The European governments hardly took notice of this declaration by the United States assuming it unsupportable. They considered it a bragging tool to be used as propaganda for some internal politics. But the text was not without value. It was the first attempt at a national doctrine formulating the motto or idea: Hands off the American Hemisphere! Through its broad definition of this new hemisphere, it also marked the beginning of a certain American hegemony over the larger American space.*

---

* Rémond, René. *Histoire des États-Unis.* Paris: PUF—Que sais-je?, 1992, 40–41.

10

Manifest Destiny

Beginning in the 1830s and 1840s, many Americans came to view the U.S.'s westward expansion as ordained by God. Today, "Manifest Destiny" is often associated with imperialism and portrayed in a negative light in many history textbooks. The countries that give it the most coverage tend to be those most affected by it historically, i.e., Mexico, Canada, the Caribbean, and Latin America.

★

CANADA

This Canadian text refers to "manifest destiny" in terms of the threat felt by Canadians toward their American neighbors to the south.

Political Developments to 1867

The expansionary goals of the United States provided a catalyst for British North American union. In the first half of the nineteenth century, the Americans had swept aside the Indians and Spanish to extend their borders to the Pacific. They argued that it was their God-given right, or "manifest destiny," to do so. If the belligerent statements of politicians and pundits following the Civil War could be believed, the boundaries of the United States would soon extend to the North Pole as well. Most British North Americans had little interest in becoming American citizens. In the 1860s they were proud members of the British Empire and intended to stay that way. It was true that the mother country was tired of pouring money into the defence of the struggling North American colonies, but by adopting a tighter political framework, they could arguably better repel American aggression and serve the interests of Great Britain as well as their own.*

This textbook details how the U.S. obtained the state of Washington.

In 1842 the Webster-Ashburton Treaty had sorted out the complex eastern boundary issues along the Maine-New Brunswick border. The western boundary west of the Rocky Mountains was settled in 1846. Under the Oregon Boundary Treaty the border across the Rockies to the Pacific continued from the Great Lakes at the 49th parallel to the Pacific (excluding Vancouver Island). This 'compromise' allowed the Americans to possess the state of Washington, in which they had virtually no nationals and which had been occupied chiefly by the Hudson's Bay Company. While the geographical interests of British North America may have been sacrificed by the Oregon settlement, entente was good for business.†

Although the rush for gold in California is a common theme in U.S. textbooks, what was taking place north of the border is not discussed.

Canadian Gold Rush

Meanwhile on the West Coast, sheer serendipity brought the region to the attention of the world. In 1857 the discovery of gold on the mainland,

---

* Finkel, Alvin, et al. *History of the Canadian Peoples: 1867 to the Present, v. 2.* Toronto: Copp Clark Pittman, 1993, 12.

† Bumsted, J.M. *A History of the Canadian Peoples.* Toronto: Oxford University Press, 1998, 148.

along the Thompson and Fraser rivers, brought fortune-hunters scurrying from around the world. The amount of gold easily available was quite small by earlier California standards. The ensuing rush was a pale imitation of the American one. Nevertheless, hundreds of miners, mainly from California, made their way to the Fraser River in the interior of British Columbia in the spring of 1858. The quiet village of Victoria was transformed overnight into a major port. South of the 49th parallel, talk of American annexation spread rapidly. The British government rushed legislation putting New Caledonia under the direct jurisdiction of the Crown. [. . .] The miners, however rough in appearance, were not really badly behaved and accepted British authority readily enough.*

This text further explains how American interest in British Columbia drove this region to seek union with Canada.

While the question of Rupert's Land dragged slowly to its conclusion, the Canadian government was presented with an unexpected (although not totally unsolicited) gift. It consisted of a request from British Columbia—to which Vancouver Island had been annexed in 1866—for admission into the new union. The initiative from the Pacific colony had originated with the Nova Scotia-born journalist, Amor De Cosmos (William Alexander Smith, 1825–97), a member of the colony's legislative council. As early as March 1867 he had introduced a motion that the British North America Act, then about to be passed by the British Parliament, allow for the eventual admission of British Columbia. Entry into Confederation would introduce responsible government, as well as resolving the colony's serious financial difficulties, which resulted partly from the interest on debts incurred for road building during the gold rushes. Union with Canada received an additional impetus when—conterminously with the passage of the British North America Act but quite independent of it—the American government purchased Alaska from the Russians. The purchase touched off demands in the American press for the annexation of British Columbia as well. Officially the British notified the colony in November 1867 that no

---

* Bumsted, J.M. *A History of the Canadian Peoples.* Toronto: Oxford University Press, 1998, 158–59.

action would occur on its relationship with Canada until Rupert's Land had been duly incorporated into the new nation.*

★

MEXICO

Mexico lost a considerable amount of land to the U.S. in the 19th century, a fact which is given prominent treatment in Mexican textbooks.

The Expansionist Tendencies of the United States of America

The process of expansion of the USA intensified in the first half of the 19th century. The country appropriated Louisiana in 1803, West Florida in 1810, East Florida in 1819, Texas in 1845, New Mexico, California and Arizona between 1845 and 1848 and Oregon in 1847. In the second half of that century it incorporated into its territory La Mesilla (1853) and Alaska (1867).

The methods that this country utilized in the process of expansion were some of the following:

- The purchase or annexation of territories and the incorporation of certain regions in the USA.
- The negotiation of borderline treaties.
- The financing of separatist movements.
- Bribery and conspiracy, war, displacement, extermination and relocation of indigenous populations to reservations.

With all these strategies, the territories of the United States of America grew more than triple of what the country possessed in 1783. The US expansionism was based on the content of the **Monroe Doctrine** and **Manifest Destiny.** The former proclaimed that any intervention of the European powers in the independent countries of the American continent would be considered as a threat to the security of the USA and that Amer-

---

* Bumsted, J.M. *A History of the Canadian Peoples.* Toronto: Oxford University Press, 1998, 193–95.

ica would no longer be a territory of colonization or conquest for said powers. In this way, the USA reserved for itself the right to intervene in the American continent when it felt its interests were threatened. Manifest Destiny consisted in the belief that the USA was the "country chosen by providence" to inhabit the American continent and that the US people had been chosen by divine will to cultivate and benefit from the land.

The USA demonstrated its expansionist politics toward our country from the beginning of the 19th century, and put it into practice through various strategies. For example, they tried to buy Mexican territories on several occasions. Then in 1821 and 1822, they obtained the means by which to populate Texas through the concessions granted to Moses and Stephen Austin. In 1825, the USA began a politics of intervention with Joel R. Poinsett, the representative of that country in Mexico. Anthony Butler, successor to Poinsett, tried to negotiate a new border treaty with the Mexican government and eventually to buy from our country the territory of Texas. For their part, the southern slave states of the American Union tried to seize some of the Mexican territory along the border, and founded in them other states with systems based on slavery. In such a way, they hoped to gain political predominance over the free-states in the US Congress.*

The Thesis of Manifest Destiny

In 1830 the Sacred Alliance was fading and its ideological principles were swept away in nearly all of Europe. In America, the process of expansion of capitalist North America required an ideological and political justification. It was a lawyer named John L. O'Sullivan who, in a series of newspaper articles which appeared in 1845, tried to justify the increasingly aggressive politics of the North American government concerning the territorial annexations, making them appear legal by "divine right."

The name given to this new application of Monroe-ism was *Manifest* or *Revealed Destiny*, a name which invoked Providence in an act similar to the feudal crusades. One phrase became well-known and symbolic for the success of its intentions: "The view of the map captivates the North Americans." It referred ever after to the American continent.

* López, José de Jesús Nieto, et al. *Historia 3*. Mexico: Santillana, 2000, 108–109.

The briefest recounting of the interventions and actions of the United States, in America in the 19th century, would fill several pages of this unit. Let us limit ourselves to only the most general cases which were, unfortunately, neither the only nor the last.

Interventions in Mexico:

a) Open help for the Texan colonies in their separatist activities (1836).

b) Invasion of Mexican territories (1846) in order to obtain, by means of war, more than 2 million km² as booty.

Interventions in Central America and the Caribbean:

a) Separation of Panama from the Republic of Colombia, to which it belonged, with the intent of opening an inter-oceanic canal.

b) Occupation of Puerto Rico and Cuba under the pretext of freeing them from Spain who kept them as colonies.*

★

BRAZIL

Brazil offers a concise summary of U.S. expansion after independence. This text is careful to highlight the economic benefits of the expansion as well.

In the middle of the 19th century, the country reached its continental dimensions through expropriation of lands from the native Indians and neighboring people, or by buying colonial possessions from European powers:

1803—bought the territory of Louisiana which had belonged to France.

1819—bought Florida, a Spanish possession, which gave to the US access to the Antilles (Caribbean).

---

* Palacios, Mario Alfonso Rodriguez. *México en la historia: tercer grado, educación secundaria.* Mexico City: Editorial Trillas, 1992, 51–52.

1848—war against Mexico, in which Mexico lost 2 million Km² of its territory (treaty of Guadalupe-Hidalgo). From that new land were created the states of Texas, California, New Mexico, Arizona, Utah and Nevada. With those annexations, the US reached the Pacific Ocean.

1867—bought Alaska from Russia.

The North-America territorial expansion was mainly justified by the Doctrine of Manifest Destiny, in which the US carried out the annexation of areas between the Atlantic and the Pacific Oceans. The North Americans were chosen by destiny to dominate America. In reality the territorial advancement was in fact due to the international capitalist goals of expansion. The conquest of the West to the Pacific Ocean gave the US direct access to the Western world and gave the US access to and a strategic position in the sought after markets of China and Japan. The annexation of Florida opened a way to the Mexican Gulf, the Antilles Sea and also to Latin America.*

* Vicento, Cláudio. *História geral.* São Paulo: Scipione, 2002, 329–31.

11

Texas and the Mexican-American Wars

Through a combination of political diplomacy and military might, the U.S. was able to expand its own borders at the expense of its Mexican neighbor during the 19th century. U.S. textbooks speak of the "annexation" of Texas, but Mexican texts view the loss of territory as a chapter in the history of American imperialism.

★

MEXICO

The Republic of Mexico lost more than half its nation in the final Treaty of Guadalupe Hidalgo.

The Separation of Texas

There were many causes for the separation of Texas from the Mexican Republic. Among the most important the following stand out:

- The discontent of the Texan colonies for the neglect of the Republican government; for the high taxes that hindered the importation of machinery and goods; for the outrages and abuses from both military and government officials; for the lack of roads and schools and the disinterest instead of defense on the question of Indian attacks.

- The expansionist policy of the USA, that tried since before 1821 to establish the boundaries toward the mouth of the Rio Bravo in order to seize Texas, New Mexico, Nuevo Santander, Coahuila and part of the provinces of Nueva Vizcaya and Sonora.

- The depopulation of the frontier on the border shared with the USA and the sale of land at extremely low prices promoted by the state of Coahuila since 1824.

- The erroneous politics of the Mexican government that permitted the uncontrollable colonization of Texas until the US population outnumbered the local Mexican population. This fact alone resulted in the US settlers being granted vast expanses of land and controlling the political power by designating their own authority.

- The separatist tendencies of Texas favored and financed by the government of the USA.

In January of 1821, eight months before the completion of Mexican Independence, the authorities of New Spain granted to Moses Austin a concession in order to found in the territory of Texas a colony of US immigrants. One year later, Agustín de Iturbide, who represented the independent government, authorized Stephen Austin, the son of Moses, to expand the colony from the Rio Brazos to the Colorado. In September of 1835, Stephen Austin and Lorenzo de Zavala called a meeting of the most prominent Texans who agreed to organize an army to defend Federalism and to form its own government independent from that of Coahuila. That same month, Samuel Houston, ex-governor of Mississippi, organized a meeting with the purpose of accelerating the Texan insurrection.

In November of 1835 appeared the Texas Act of Independence in which the Texan colonists demonstrated a desire to remain separate from the Mexican Republic while Santa Anna's centralist regime endured. In November of this same year, the first Texan government was organized in which only one representative was of Mexican origin.

In December of 1835 the Texan insurgents attacked the garrison of the

Mexican Army. They expelled the authorities representing Santa Anna's government and defeated General Martín Cos at San Antonio Béjar. At the end of 1835, the Texan separatists approved the Declaration of Independence of Texas. They established a provisional government, designated a commission to represent themselves to the USA, and elected Houston as Commander-in-Chief of the Texan Army. Houston called on US volunteers to fight against the Mexican army with the promise of land at the conclusion of the conflict. With the complicity of the US government, hundreds of adventurers, well-armed and well-prepared, responded to Houston's call.

Texas finally declared its independence on March 1, 1836, calling itself a "free and independent" republic. David Burnett and Lorenzo de Zavala were designated president and vice-president, respectively. The Mexican government intended to be finished with the Texas separatists; in order to do so, it organized an army of 6000 soldiers, led by Santa Anna. The Mexican troops did not succeed in finishing off the separatists due to a lack of human resources and materials, the great distance that separated Texas from the center of the country, the constant civil strife, the lack of a disciplined and professional army, the ineptness of both politicians and military officers, the collaboration of certain sectors of the dominant class in Mexico with the separatists, the disrepute of the generals, and the scarcity of public funds.

In San Jacinto, Texas, Santa Anna was surprised, defeated and captured by Houston's troops. In exchange for his life, he signed the Treaty of Velasco in which he promised to recognize the independence of Texas and to remove his troops to the banks of the Rio Bravo. In 1837, the USA recognized the independence of the Republic of Texas.

The Annexation of Texas to the United States of America and the War of 1847

On March 1, 1845, the US Congress approved an initiative to annex Texas envisioned by the President John Tyler (1790–1862). Originally the Texas borders came to the Rio Nueces, but the US settlers enlarged the territory up to the Rio Bravo. Due to the annexation of Texas and the modifications to the Texas border, between our country and the USA there began a series of political claims that led to mutual accusations.

The increase in US population in certain border regions of Mexico and the intent of the USA to buy or acquire Mexican territories constituted the principal antecedents and causes of the US intervention in Mexico in 1846–1848. One could also mention as causes of the intervention the support of the US settlers living in New Mexico, California and other border territories who incited the rebellion against the Mexican government, declared themselves independent and solicited their own annexation to the USA.

Another factor that influenced the military invasion of Mexico was the interest on the part of the southern slave states of the USA in expanding their territories in order to control the US Congress, especially when it came to divisive issues that pitted northern states against south states. And finally, the support of the government of the USA which encouraged the incursion of Indians, adventurers, or US military soldiers into the territories of California and New Mexico aggravated the tensions between both countries. At the same time, in certain southern cities of the USA public opinion was provoked to provide weapons, munitions, boats and money for the invaders.

Mexico broke off diplomatic relations with the USA because of the annexation of Texas. At the end of 1845, the US government's representative arrived in our country with the intention of negotiating the renewal of diplomatic relations, the acceptance of Texan independence and the purchase of New Mexico and California. However, the government of Mexico strongly rebuffed any such proposals. Because of the Mexican rebuff and without a declaration of war, President James K. Polk ordered his troops to invade the Mexican territories. Meanwhile, the USA proclaimed that Mexico was the aggressor. The US Congress declared war against Mexico on May 13, 1846.

In August of 1846, while the Americans [*estadounidenses*] invaded Mexico, the government of Mariano Pardedes Arrillaga was defeated by the Federalists who reestablished the Federal Constitution of 1824. Antonio López de Santa Anna and Valentín Gómez Farías were named President and Vice-President, respectively, in the new government of the Republic. The former, at the head of the Mexican army, led his troops to the north of the country to fight the US, while Gómez Farías stayed in Mexico City to attend to the affairs of the government.

At the end of 1846, the invading army had already occupied Monterrey, Saltillo, Tampico, Upper California and New Mexico; Veracruz was threatened. In February of 1847, Santa Anna confronted the forces of General Taylor in the cañón de la Angostura, near Coahuila, without a decisive result for either side. Gómez Farías intended to pursue resources in order to sustain the military campaign against the US, but the wealthy and the Church refused to help the government. In order to solve the problem of resources, Gómez Farías was granted the authority by Congress to seize and sell up to 15 million pesos worth of Church goods. The Church responded with excommunications for those seizing her goods and supported any conspiracy to overthrow the government.

While the US invaded the national territory, in the streets of Mexico City a series of scandalous fights broke out between Mexicans. Soldiers from select battalions sent by Gómez Farías to defend the Veracruz gate, known as "polkos" for their complicity with President Polk, put themselves in the service of the clergy and instead of defending the country, rebelled against the government.

Santa Anna returned to the capital of the Republic, dismissed Gómez Farías, reversed the decree calling for the seizure of clerical goods and returned to fulfill his function as president of the nation. In March of 1847, the invaders, after occupying Veracruz, advanced toward Mexico City. They defeated the Mexicans in Cerro Gordo, Padierna and Churubusco.

On August 20, 1847, Generals Manuel E. Rincón and Pedro María Anaya, with 650 poorly armed Mexicans, defended the convent of Churubusco. They made the US troops withdraw with a considerable number of dead and wounded before they were finally defeated.

The battalion of St. Patrick, formed of Irish soldiers, participated heroically in the defense of Churubusco alongside the Mexican people. The majority of this battalion was killed in the fighting but the survivors were exchanged for arms after being tortured. After many hours of spirited defense, the Mexicans came to the end of the park and had to give up the plaza. The head of the invading forces demanded of General Pedro María Anaya that he give up his weapons. His response has become famous, "If I had the park, you wouldn't be here."

The result of the battle of Churubusco was the US proposed armistice. The Mexican government would have to cede the territories of Texas, New Mexico and upper California, along with a large part of the states of Tamaulipas, Nuevo León, Coahuila, Chihuahua, Sonora and Lower California. Moreover, it included the concession of perpetual and free transit by the Isthmus of Tehuantepec. Such conditions were refused by the government of Mexico; the armistice was declared invalid and the war continued.

The US, in its advance on Mexico City, attacked Molino del Rey and el Castillo de Chapultepec, which succumbed after three days of attack. The Battle of San Blas was led by Felipe Santiago Xicoténcatl and included officers and cadets from the Military College, among whom several were known as the "Boy Heroes." They resisted the enemy offensive at Castillo de Chapultepec but died defending their homeland. On September 14, 1847, Mexico City fell into the hands of the invaders despite the valiant resistance of the Mexican troops and population.

The Mexican Resistance and the Defense of the Capital

In the war against the USA, the Mexican people assumed an attitude of bravery and great heroism. On the other hand, President Santa Anna, the high military command and the ecclesiastical hierarchy gave in while surrendering to the invaders or helping the foreigners. For its part, the troops, made up of roughly half the army and workers principally from the capital, rose up to fight and resist with great heart and courage against the US invasion.

In Mexico City, the invading troops were welcomed with a hail of stones, sticks, boards, machetes, and other projectiles that the people threw from balconies, roofs, and plazas. From the windows and roofs came the first musket and rifle shots aimed at the invading armies. The desperate resistance of the population lasted several days, resulting in the installation by the invaders of a regime of terror and abuse.

The Treaty of Guadalupe Hidalgo: The Sale of La Mesilla

The Treaty of Guadalupe Hidalgo put an end to the war between the USA and Mexico. The accord was signed February 2, 1848. The treaty granted occupation rights to the USA in the territories of Texas, New Mexico, Upper California and the northern part of Tamaulipas, Coahuila and Sonora. The northern frontier of Mexico would be the Rio Bravo. Moreover, the US government agreed to pay the claims of its citizens against the Mexican government. It would not demand any compensation for the expenses of war. It would pay 15 million pesos for the territories obtained and would prevent incursions by barbaric Indians. Mexico remained plunged in a crisis that unleashed new internal conflicts. The country lost an area of 2.4 million km², more than half its territory, in signing the Treaty of Guadalupe Hidalgo.

The demands of the USA did not end. In December, 1853, they demanded the cession of the Baja California territory, at the northern border of the country, and the Tehuantepec Pass, but the Mexican representatives rebuffed such aspirations. However, Antonio López de Santa Anna sold the territory of La Mesilla (109,574 km²) for 10 million pesos, of which the US Congress only agreed to pay seven.*

---

* López, José de Jesús Nieto, et al. *Historia 3*. Mexico: Santillana, 2000, 110–14.

12

Slavery

Slavery is a major subject for U.S. history textbooks today. Most treat it as primarily a North American phenomenon, justly highlighting the close relationship of slave labor to the development of the American economy, and the centrality of slavery to American politics in the nineteenth century. Slavery's international context is rarely discussed at length, if at all. In fact, its history touches the whole of the Atlantic world and beyond.

★

NIGERIA

Nigeria had one of the most active slave ports serving Western Africa. It not only lost many of its inhabitants to the slave trade, but profited from it as well. This text is explicit about its role in the trade and the benefits derived from it.

The Trans-Atlantic Slave Trade

The Atlantic slave trade began from about 1480. It began when the Portuguese made contacts with the coast of West Africa. At the time cheap labour was needed for the Portuguese sugar plantations on the island of Saõ Tomé, which is situated close to the coast of Africa. The Portuguese, therefore, bought some slaves and sent them to the island. At first the need on the island was not great and, consequently, the number of slaves demanded was small. But soon there were some developments in the 'New World'. The 'New World' was the name given by Europeans to North America. In American and the West Indies, sugar plantations had been created. At first Red Indians were used on the plantations. Later, poor whites were brought in when the Red Indians failed to make adequate impact. The Portuguese discovered that the black slaves could also be used. So from Lisbon, which is the capital city of Portugal, they began to supply African slaves. The number of slaves obtained from the west coast therefore increased from about 200 a year in the year 1500 to about 1000 a year in 1515. By 1527 the number had increased to about 6000.

By 1532 the trade had become more lucrative as the Portuguese began to make a direct shipment of slaves to the West Indies. During the second half of the sixteenth century the English and Dutch entered the trade. In the Caribbean islands the Portuguese, Spanish, English and Dutch had all established colonies. All these colonies had sugar plantations and all the sugar plantations needed slaves. This was why the demand for slaves from Africa was so big. The demand for slaves increased in the eighteenth century as cotton plantations were established in the southern states of America and cotton production was greatly increased to meet the demand for textiles in Europe.

The trans-Atlantic slave trade was different from domestic slavery in many ways. For example, while domestic slavery involved a few people, the trans-Atlantic trade involved large numbers of people. Secondly, slaves were treated very cruelly both in the ships which took them across the Atlantic and on their arrival in the New World. They had no rights whatsoever. Instead, they were tied up with ropes and chains. They were sent to distant places among totally strange people. Many thousands of slaves died in the process. They had no opportunities to distinguish themselves in these strange new environments. This contrasted with the humane treatment given to domestic slaves.

Where did the supply of slaves come from? First, the Portuguese themselves kidnapped some Africans. But the bulk of the supply came from the Nigerians. These Nigerian middlemen moved to the interior where they captured other Nigerians who belonged to other communities. The middlemen also purchased many of the slaves from the people in the interior. These people in the interior sold war captives or those condemned to die for committing offences. Many of the slaves were social undesirables who had been condemned as thieves, adulterers or stubborn children. Many of the purchases were obtained after inter-village and inter-ethnic battles. Some agencies also began to specialize in the recruitment of slaves.

We do not know the exact number of Africans who were victims of the trade in human cargo. This is because no accurate census figures were kept. One historian has suggested a figure of 9 560 000 exported slaves for the entire period of the trade. This historian has also argued that the total number was not less than 8 000 000 and not more than 10 000 000. It has, however, been argued by other historians that these figures are grossly underestimated, and therefore inaccurate. It is likely that more people were exported. One source has in fact stated that in 1749 alone more than 8110 Nigerians were taken captives in 23 vessels from Benin, Bonny, and Calabar. Another source has claimed that the English ships carried about 123 000 slaves from West Africa to the sugar islands of the West Indies in the thirty nine years from 1672–1711. In view of these facts it seems that the number of slaves taken from Africa would have exceeded ten million people.

Organization of the Trade

The European traders arrived on the coast of Nigeria. The Portuguese made contacts with the Oba of Benin and proceeded to build the port of Ughoton. From the port slaves were carried to the ships and sent to the island of São Tomé. When slaves were first exported right across the Atlantic to America they were sent via Lisbon, the capital of Portugal. However, it was not long before they were sent direct to the West Indies and the Americas from the West African coast. A pattern had emerged in the organization of the trade by this time. The Portuguese founded a settlement at São Tomé from where they purchased slaves at Benin and the Nigerian ports. The English, the Dutch and the Spaniards also arrived at the Nigerian ports to purchase slaves who were then transported to Lisbon and the European ports from where many of them finally made their destinations after a voyage across the Atlantic. This system has been called the 'triangle trade' because three ports were involved. The triangle trade was later modified to allow for a direct trip across the Atlantic from Nigerian ports to the New World in America and the West Indies. In both situations the trade in human cargo was oppressive and harsh, and the forced migration of people was on a scale that had never before been witnessed in history.

Effects of the Trade

The Europeans sold Nigerians certain articles in exchange for the slaves taken away. Many of these articles, such as umbrellas, swords and guns became status symbols and were greatly desired by important chiefs and families. Some food crops also found their way to the country. Among these were cassava, maize, citrus fruits and rice. The crops made an impact on the feeding habits of Nigerians. Nigerians also began to learn how to cultivate these new crops.

A merchant class grew up in Nigeria. Their business was to serve as middlemen. They became very rich and powerful. They also owned exotic goods. Some communities benefited from the trades. For example, the Ijaw profited from the traffic. They increased their salt production in order to provide currency for exchange with the interior contacts. The attraction of guns and gunpowder also led to greater economic incentives for the people.

The slave trade led to the development of new settlements. The city states of the coast were mainly a response to the slave trade. The slave trade also led to the final expulsion of those that were considered social undesirables in the society as such people were shipped with the other slaves to North America.

However, the slave trade brought much ill to the society. The impact on the morale of the people is not yet known. But certainly a people who did not care about what befell their victims were unlikely to develop much feeling for strangers outside the community. As people engaged in more trade in human cargo, the Nigerian society was robbed of the services and contributions of those able-bodied and intelligent people who would have assisted the society. It is suggested that many of those sold to slavery were men and women who were intelligent and independently minded. Because they were seen as a threat by the rulers they were got rid of. Yet it is such men who are able to make an impact on every society by their will and independence of mind. Homes and families were hit by tragedy as husbands and wives disappeared. Children suffered from the disasters. The trade also led to a drain on manpower. Agriculture and other professions were bound to suffer from the loss. It has been suggested that the thin population of the Middle Belt region can be explained by the active slave trade that affected that region.

Many Nigerian middlemen began to depend totally on the slave trade and neglected every other business and occupation. The result was that when the trade was abolished these Nigerians began to protest. As years went by, and the trade collapsed such Nigerians lost their sources of income and became impoverished.

As the Europeans insisted on talking to representatives of communities, a class of Nigerians emerged with powers which were not part of the traditional practices. The result was that individuals began to lose their personal freedom within society as some Nigerian societies became more authoritarian.

Perhaps the greatest evil was one which was not immediately recognized by the traders. In the New World the Africans faced many difficulties. They were seen as belonging to a slave class and were consequently treated as second-class citizens. Far away from his home country, the African slave lost touch with his language and people. Instead he was made the victim of all kinds of racial prejudice. Even when slavery was abolished blacks in America were given the worst jobs, the poorest housing and were denied access to political power. It was these injustices that the civil rights movement attacked in the 1960s. The movement asks that black people be given respect and dignity as equals in the society. The slave became a 'wretched of the earth'. His masters and owners took everything from him: his language, his family, his skills, his dreams.*

★

ZIMBABWE

Zimbabwe's historical relationship with Great Britain—as a former British colony—may explain the blame the British receive for the slave trade in this text.

* Omolewa, Michael. *Certificate History of Nigeria*. Lagos, Nigeria: Longman Group, Ltd., 1991, 96–103.

Beginnings of the Slave Trade

During the first half of the 18th century, Portuguese merchants as well as other foreign traders, were heavily involved in the slave trade. This was in response to the internal demand for labour in the sugar plantations of the French island colonies of Mauritius and Reunion in the Indian Ocean; the Portuguese cocoa plantations on the island of Saõ Tomé and coffee plantations of Brazil; and the clove and coconut plantations of the Arab islands of Zanzibar and Pemba.

By taking out of the region active human beings in exchange for perishable consumer items such as cloth, beads and guns, the slave trade deprived African societies of a major factor of production.*

The Slave Trade

During the 18th century, Britain became a leading industrial country in Europe. Many factors contributed to give her such a leading industrial position in Europe. Although Europeans usually refuse to acknowledge slavery as one of such factors, we would like to recognize that factor here and now. There were, of course, other factors. There was the agricultural revolution of the same century. There was also the inventiveness of many Britons such as Richard Cartwright, William Caxton, and the creative capacity of those who guided government along a direction that inspired the industrialists to fulfill their fullest potential.

The Impact of the Slave Trade

The history of the slave trade is generally an unpleasant record of man's savage behaviour. As such, historians have tended to shy away from discussing its contribution to the rise of British industrial development during the 18th century. [. . .] Eric Williams† demonstrates by the use of statistics and other data how the trade in humans gave Britain enormous

---

* Sibanda, Dr. M., and Dr. H. Moyana. *The African Heritage, Book 3.* Harare: Zimbabwe Publishing House, 1999, 23.

† Authors' note: Dr. Eric Williams (1911–81) was born in Trinidad, educated at Oxford, taught at Howard University, and eventually became prime minister of his native Trinidad and Tobago. He was a renowned historian who wrote extensively on slavery in the West Indies.

resources in the form of money, which was responsible for the rise of major industrial towns and ports such as Southampton, Liverpool and many others. The shipping industry developed dramatically as a result of the slave trade. Again, ports such as Liverpool developed extensive ship building yards in order to meet the rising demand for ships which the slave traders used to travel to Africa, to the Americas and back to Britain. The more the trade in slaves, the bigger the demand for ships grew. These port cities became wealthier with the growth of the slave trade. The traders needed to insure their ships and their slaves. So insurance companies got a boost and grew rapidly in England during the 18th century.

The enormous wealth generated by the slave trade also led to the rise of many banks which financed the activities of traders. [. . .] Britain came to amass enormous wealth, more than any other European country and so had the resources to be the leading European nation in the industrial revolution. *

★

PORTUGAL

Portugal has a special relationship with the history of slavery. Portuguese and Dutch ships fueled the slave trade between Europe, Africa, and the Americas.

The Progression of the Slave Trade

Slavery was one of the pillars of the African societies. The prestige and power of the great lords was evaluated by the number of slaves one had. The practice of slavery in Africa would facilitate the entry of Europeans in the process.

In Africa, a person could become a slave through war, but there were other means that led to a similar end, like the paying off of a debt. The fact is that someone could simply be sold as a slave. These transactions occurred in times of great famines caused by natural disasters like droughts, floods, insect plagues, etc.

* Sibanda, Dr. M, and Dr. H. Moyana. *The African Heritage, Book 3.* Harare: Zimbabwe Publishing House, 1999, 121, 122.

Since the XV century, some Portuguese accounts tell of markets where Africans traded their products, including their brothers in race.

To try to interpret the slavery trade as a unique form of colonial exploitation is to forget that it was a practice perpetrated by the indigenous. The slave traders operated directly with the local slave masters or through intermediaries—white, black, mixed or half castes like the 'lançados' (the bonded ones). Generally the advantages to both parties were equal: the African obtained manufactured products from Europe and military help he needed to defend himself against his enemies both local and foreign.

In 1529, D. João III wrote to the king of Congo saying that the slave trade would not contribute to the depopulation of the kingdom, because 'Congo was so full of people that it seemed that no slave had come out of it at all'. This letter shows that a few people had started to condemn the slave trade.

The experience would profoundly transform not only the demographic situation in Africa but also the economic and human geography of America and parts of Europe as well.

In the beginning of the XVI century Garcia de Resende considered already, though with a poetic emphasis, that the slaves in Lisbon superseded the locals. In those days the slaves were 10% of the Lisbon population.

The development of the slave trade became part of the process of exploitation of the American continent. In comparison with the India slavery, the blacks had a better physical capacity and resisted better to the climate, two important factors to justify the successive migratory waves that since the middle of the XVI century left Africa towards America.

Cabo Verde and São Tomé became centers for the slave trade from Guinea, Congo and Angola. Various testimonies from that time praise the blacks from that territory, as being the strongest and having more ability and adaptation to work.*

Movement of the Slave Trade

[. . .] The time between the moment the slaves were bought and when they arrived at the port was very dangerous not only for the Europeans

---

* Mendes de Matos, Margarida, et al. *História, 10° ano, 2° volume*. Lisbon: Texto Editora, 1994, 197–98.

traders but for the slaves as well. Revolts and disturbances occurred frequently. The Africans found the new scenario very disturbing: foreign scenery, the sea and white men. They were frightened thinking maybe that they were going to be eaten by cannibals or be offered as a sacrifice to some foreign god. Many of them refused to eat, finally forced to do so under torture. Many in desperation threw themselves in the sea or became mentally disturbed.

The traders tried to convince them that they were taking them to a better life in a better land, but it was not easy to convince the slaves because the spectacle that preceded the boarding was confusing to them. The baptism that they all had to go through frightened them. No less terrifying was the act of the 'marking'. The Europeans branded the slaves with a hot iron on their chest or the left arm. This marked the African as a slave for life.

The crossing of the Atlantic was extremely difficult for the slaves. First, there was not enough room in the boats. They suffered from the heat, thirst and lack of hygiene. There was not enough food for everyone. The slaves suffered from many infectious and epidemic diseases and were afraid of the sea. Even the whites could not face these things. Some blacks committed suicide and many became depressed, which could lead them to a mental distress that most of the time was irreversible.*

[. . .]

Some religious individuals in the XVI century condemned slavery, mainly the Dominicans. Those who defended the practice, like Padre Fernando de Oliveira, were actually very few in number.

Theologians, missionaries and people in power, pointing to the existence of the slave trade in Africa and preaching about the rebellious character of the blacks, did little to change the situation. But at the end of the XVII century the royal power demanded measures of hygiene, nutrition, medical, and religious care in the slave trade.

At the time the European States and the slave traders didn't recognize the catastrophic consequences of these massive migrations. The demographic situation in the African regions colonized by the Europeans in

---

* Mendes de Matos, Margarida, et al. *História, 10° ano, 2° volume*. Lisbon: Texto Editora, 1994, 199–200.

those days became extremely fragile since the slave traders preferred the young and strong and also the women.

On the other hand on the American continent there originated a new ethnic-cultural situation as a result of the multiplicity of mixed races and cultural expressions. The marks of these contacts, more or less distant, persist in the physical characteristics of the various societies and in elements of acculturation and syncretism. Brazil became the most expressive model of the process conveyed by the Portuguese as it melted Indian, white and black in a complex mix of ethnicities and cultures.*

★

GREAT BRITAIN

British textbooks frequently point out that, although Great Britain played an important role in the slave trade, it was also one of the first countries to outlaw slavery.

Between 1526 and 1870, 10 million people were captured in West Africa, mainly by the British, and shipped across the Atlantic to work as slaves on plantations in the various colonies of North and South America and the West Indies. The effects of the slave-trade on the black people were horrific. Families and communities were broken up. Conditions on board ship were appalling. Hundreds were crammed side-by-side and head-to-toe for many weeks. Here is an extract from a description of a typical voyage by the captain of the slave-ship 'Hannibal' in 1693:

> 'We spent in our passage from St Thomas to Barbados two months eleven days . . . in which there happen'd much sickness and mortality. 320 [negroes died] which was a great detriment [loss] to our voyage, . . . whereby the loss in all amounted to near 6,560 pounds sterling.'

Those who survived were sold to plantation-owners, who branded them so that they could identify their slaves if they tried to escape. It was not until 1807 that the slave-trade was abolished in Britain. Even

* Mendes de Matos, Margarida, et al. *História, 10° ano, 2° volume.* Lisbon: Texto Editora, 1994, 201.

then slavery itself remained for many years in the West Indies and the Americas.

All this trading activity is important because it helps us to understand how the European empires developed. The merchants and then the governments of several European countries came to realize how profitable it was. They also realized it was important to control those parts of the world where the profits lay.*

★

MEXICO

This Mexican text is decidedly more interested in the lives of slaves once they arrived in the United States than with the international slave trade itself.

The Problem of Ethnic Integration in the United States

Of all the ethnic groups that have conformed to the demographic mosaic of the United States in the last three centuries, none have had as much sociopolitical relevance during the 19th century as that of African origin. The peoples that founded the North American colonies, right from the start, brought slaves with them in order to burden them with the most difficult jobs and of their productive work. As the economy of the colonies grew more robust, the number of slaves increased considerably, such that during the period of US independence, the black population counted 600,000 persons.

Between 1807 and 1808 the slave trade was abolished in the United States; that is to say, their public introduction and/or sale was forbidden at the demeaning auctions. This did not prevent the illegal activity of both from continuing. By 1820, in the southern territories alone, the black population exceeded a million and a half. In 1860 it grew to 4 million in this northern nation, the southern territories claiming 80% of the population itself. Most of the black slaves could be found on the large southern plantations.

* Heater, Derek. *Presenting the Past, Bk. 3: Reform and Revolution.* Oxford: Oxford University Press, 1991, 6, 7.

What was it like, the life of a slave? There is no easy response; it must first be understood that the living conditions depended upon the region where they lived. For example, in the area known as Louisiana, particularly in the city of New Orleans, they enjoyed certain liberties as a result of the changes implemented as a consequence of the French Revolution. In the rest of the southern states, about 200,000 black slaves had succeeded in seeking protection under the Statute of Free Men; they had to wear an insignia which identified them, register with the authorities and live in designated areas (the forerunner of the ghettos). Moreover, they lacked any and all civil rights. With great difficulty, they might acquire some property, but it was common for them to fall back into slavery.

On each plantation, the average number of slaves fluctuated between 75 and 100 persons; however, there were cases of landowners holding more than 1000 blacks in their service. Within these demeaning conditions, there were different levels of exploitation. The highest level was reserved for those who were chosen for domestic service (cooks, chambermaids, nannies, washers, seamstresses, gardeners, drivers, blacksmiths, millers, carpenters, shoemakers, and other maintenance work). The majority, however, were destined for agricultural work and suffered the most inhuman treatment imaginable, including marking them with hot iron to identify them should they flee. They frequently endured corporal punishment and were placed in metal neck, wrist or ankle irons for life. They even received corporal mutilations as a form of intimidation or repression.

From the beginning of the 19th century, the government of the United States of America had to address the question of the right to use slave labor. In the decade beginning in 1850 the sociopolitical differences became more pronounced between the north and the southern states that systematically refused to abolish the system of slavery at the heart of their legal structures. The resistance movement against slavery began to form organized demonstrations. Among those who had the strongest influence on public opinion in the United States, let us look briefly at the two most famous figures.

John Brown, a black leader [sic], led his followers into confrontations with the authorities in Kansas, organized the transfer of an important group of slaves to Canada, crossing northern states that gave him more or less discreet help. Captured in December of 1859 and executed, he became a martyr and symbol for the freedom of his race [sic]. A notable woman of African origin, Harriet Tubman, also led many slaves to freedom using the collaboration of progressive white farmers and free blacks that formed a "trail" to Canada, known as "the underground railroad." Her activity in favor of civil rights continued until her death in 1913.*

---

* Palacios, Mario Alfonso Rodríguez, et al. *México en la historia.* Mexico: Trillas, 1992, 52–56.

13

The Civil War

In most U.S. history textbooks, the American Civil War constitutes a chapter unto itself, and makes for a natural dividing point in survey history courses. The Civil War, for American readers, raises important questions about race, states' rights and the Constitution. U.S. textbooks overwhelmingly treat it as a distinctly American event. Apart from the usual anecdote about the Confederacy seeking the support of England and France, little interest is paid to how this war might have affected other nations.

★

CANADA

The context for this discussion of the U.S. Civil War is the larger subject of Canada's road to unification.

Canada's Road to Confederation

Neither the bind of the double majority nor the beginnings of national sentiment was alone sufficient to propel British North Americans to national unification. As so often was the case, events in the United States provided the catalyst. The American federal union broke apart with surprising suddenness in 1861. The southern states seceded into their own Confederacy. The American Civil War began. Many Canadians quietly rooted for the Confederacy despite its maintenance of slavery. Britain adopted an official policy of neutrality. The British watched warily while public opinion in the northern states, whipped up by American newspapers, talked openly of finding compensation for the lost Confederacy by annexing British North America.

Britain could hardly leave her North American colonies unprotected. Defending them at great expense was not something the British faced with relish, however. By the 1860s the British ruling classes believed that colonies like British North America would inevitably separate from the mother country. Why not hasten the process and save money? An independent British North America could organize its own defences.*

[. . .]

In 1861 a fierce civil war broke out in the United States. Fought over the issue of slavery between the northern and southern states, the war lasted for four bloody years. During the conflict many people in Britain supported the South, mainly because the British cotton industry relied on imports from the southern slave plantations. The South also had its supporters in British North America, not necessarily because the colonists agreed with slavery, but because some of them feared that a victorious North might unleash its army on Canada.

This fear continued after the war, with good cause. Americans were angry because Great Britain had supported the slave states, and they considered seeking revenge by invading British North America. Cooler heads prevailed, but the threat of invasion was an incentive for Canadians to believe that their best defence was in unity. Certainly the British believed this. They did not want to be called in to defend their colonies against the

---

* Bumsted, J.M. *A History of the Canadian Peoples*. Toronto: Oxford University Press, 1998, 176–77.

Americans. They much preferred a strong, united British North America that would be prepared to fight its own battles.*

The defence issue was driven home to British North Americans by the American Civil War, which pitted the slave-holding South against the industrial North. Although many British North Americans were sympathetic to the Northern cause, the Southern Confederates also had their supporter in the colonies, especially among elite circles in cities such as Halifax and Montreal. Public opinion in Britain was also divided over the conflict. There were important interests in Britain, especially those involved in the importation of such southern products as cotton and tobacco, who would have been happy to see the Confederacy gain independence. As the war dragged on, a number of incidents on the high seas and along the border helped to increase tensions between Britain and the North and exposed the vulnerability of the British North American colonies.

In late 1861 a Northern naval ship seized the *Trent,* a British steamer en route from Cuba to Britain, and arrested two Confederate agents aboard. Although the North eventually yielded to Britain's protests and released the two agents, the British responded to the threat of an eventual war with the United States by reinforcing the existing 3000 troops in British North America with an additional 15000 men.

During the war British-built destroyers purchased by the Confederacy, including the *Alabama,* the *Florida,* and the *Shenandoah,* sank over one hundred vessels. The North in turn pursued Confederate ships into British waters: in December 1863 they chased the *Chesapeake* into Nova Scotia waters and arrested the men aboard. Border raids also increased tensions. The government was livid in 1864 when a Montreal magistrate set free Confederate agents who had robbed three banks in St Albans, Vermont, and then crossed back into Canada.†

---

* Francis, Daniel, and Sonia Riddoch. *Our Canada: A Social and Political History.* Scarboroug: Pippin, 1995, 127–28.

† Finkel, Alvin, et al. *History of the Canadian Peoples: 1867 to the Present, v. 2.* Toronto: Copp Clark Pittman, 1993, 593.

★

GREAT BRITAIN

From a British point of view, there was much to be said for a break-up of the United States. The cotton industry's dependence on the South and an initial sympathy with the Confederate States predisposed the Cabinet to favour the seceders. [British MP] Gladstone's impolitic statement in his Newcastle speech, October 1862, that Jefferson Davis and the other southern leaders 'have made an army . . . are making, it appears, a navy, and they have made . . . a nation', brought him a hail of criticism but it did reflect ministerial thinking. The previous year Britain had declared its neutrality, recognizing the South as belligerents not as rebels. [Prime Minister] Palmerston gained some popularity by the firmness with which his government responded to the seizure of two southern politicians, on mission to London, from a British ship by Union warships. A strong letter was sent to Washington, toned down by Prince Albert, and troops were moved to the Canadian border. The Confederate representatives were released. Confederate commerce raiders were built on Merseyside, although the government eventually intervened once it became clear that the North would win. Palmerston had had a life-long hatred of slavery, but the Emancipation Declaration, which so strongly influenced public opinion, did not have the same impact on official policy.*

The treaty still did not create a new climate in Anglo-American relations such as [former British Prime Minister] Aberdeen was hoping for. Fears about American encroachments further west remained and the slavery issue was too emotive a problem on both sides of the Atlantic to allow for an easy solution as long as the institution remained in existence. Even so, in the years before the American Civil War, relations did improve to the extent that the young Prince of Wales was allowed to make a visit to the USA in early 1860, following a trip to Canada. The Civil War, however, put new stresses and strains on Anglo-American relations. Opinions in Britain were divided between those who supported the Union and those who wished to see the Confederacy succeed in its attempt to set up a new na-

---

* Martin, Howard. *Challenging History: Britain in the Nineteenth Century.* Surrey: Thomson, 1996, 227.

tion. With hindsight it is too easy to see the issue primarily as a matter of freeing slaves and abolishing the institution of slavery. At the time the situation was far more complex. To begin with, the issue of slavery was very much played down by the American President, Abraham Lincoln, in the immediate period before hostilities commenced. He continued to enforce the Fugitive Slave Law which meant the return of runaway slaves to their masters even when they had taken refuge in 'free' states; he repeatedly denied, during the first 18 months of the war, that it was being fought on the issue of slavery; he did not abolish slavery until the Emancipation Edict of January 1863.

Palmerston was sympathetic to the claim of the Confederacy that individual states which had entered the Union freely had a legal right to leave it freely. He did not wish to go to war with the Union over the issue, but he suspected that certain elements in the US Government, led by William H. Seward, the Secretary of State, were intriguing to heal the internal divisions in the country by trying to involve the US in a war with foreign powers. Seward was notoriously anti-British and Palmerston sent reinforcements to Canada as a precaution. As soon as the Civil War began in 1861, Palmerston and [Foreign Secretary] Russell agreed to recognise the Confederacy as a belligerent and to receive, unofficially, Confederate representatives. This fell short of recognising the Confederacy as a sovereign power, but it was a clear enough sign of preference. When the Union suffered an unexpected reverse in the first major battle of the war at Bull Run, Virginia, in July 1861, Palmerston indulged in some witticisms at Lincoln's expense. However, although by the end of 1861 he was feeling fairly certain in his own mind that Lincoln would not be able to compel the seccessionist states to return to the Union, he still made no official move to recognise the Confederacy.

The main crises of the war, from the British point of view, came over two separate incidents. First, the removal, by the Union Navy, of two confederate envoys, Mason and Slidell, from a British mail steamer, the Trent, off the coast of Cuba, late in 1861, nearly led to disaster. It was fortunate perhaps, on this occasion, that communications across the Atlantic took sufficiently long for tempers on both sides to subside. In the end the Union Government, declaring that the naval officer who had seized Mason and Slidell had exceeded his authority, agreed to release the two men. The second incident involved the building of a warship for the Confederacy at a shipyard in Birkenhead. The Union Government found out about the project and protested to Palmerston that this was a breach of neutrality. The Government carried out an enquiry but could find no proof for the accusation. Palmerston and Russell therefore decided to allow the order to be completed. Just before completion, the Union's Ambassador in London, Charles Adams, received concrete proof of the Confederate involvement and submitted it to Russell. By the time the new evidence had been evaluated and a decision made it was too late. On 31 July 1862 orders were sent to Birkenhead to impound the ship, but she had already sailed two days before and, as soon as she was outside British territorial waters, she raised the Confederate flag and assumed the name Alabama.

The Alabama was eventually sunk by the Union Navy in the summer of 1864, but not before she had done considerable damage to Union shipping. The Union Government, suspecting that the British Government had secretly connived at the escape of the ship in the first place, demanded compensation. Palmerston treated this claim with contempt and the matter remained a bitter bone of contention until 1872 when, following Gladstone's decision to accept international arbitration in the case, Britain paid $15 million in gold to the United States as damages. Anglo-American relations remained shaky despite this settlement. The sensitivity between the two countries, always more pronounced on the American side, ensured that it took very little to excite ill-feeling. Residual anti-British feelings, reinforced by the influx of Irish migrants meant that American politicians could always resort to a round of anti-British rhetoric if all else failed to bring them support. This situation was not to change significantly until the turn of the century.*

*

MEXICO

Mexico watched the American conflict with curiosity. This text offers a summary of events in which the place of slavery in the conflict is prominent. It is also worth noting that the text identifies the Ku Klux Klan as a "terrorist" group.

* Scott-Baumann, Michael (ed). *Years of Expansion: Britain 1815–1914*. London: Hodder and Stoughton, 1999, 192–95.

The North American Civil War (1861–65)

In the presidential elections of 1860, Abraham Lincoln, the Republican candidate from Kentucky [sic*], a slave state, had won by a healthy margin. A man of strong character and what many considered an unbending moral character, he showed moderate political convictions with respect to the slave issue. During the election campaign he proclaimed the necessity that it should not increase, neither in numbers nor area.

Lincoln's election put the southern landowners on the defensive, the same landowners who still hoped that the whole country would return to allowing the practice of slavery. In the North a powerful process of industrialization had been unleashed that resulted in the accelerated growth of the demand for available workers and the accumulation of enormous quantities of manufactured and industrial products for those wanting to see constant economic expansion. In the Southern states, meanwhile, the plantation owners continued to accumulate capital thanks to the exportation of agricultural products (cotton and tobacco) that relied fundamentally on the manual labor of slaves, an economy whose chief characteristic was the keeping of more than two million workers in virtual captivity.

In February 1861, South Carolina was the first state—ahead of Georgia, Alabama, Florida, Mississippi, Louisiana and Texas—to announce its withdrawal from the North American Union. Such was the make-up of the *confederate states* that sought to secede in order to form a new nation. In April the attempted seizure of Fort Sumter in Charleston Bay, South Carolina marked the first armed encounter and beginning of what came to be known as the Civil War. The conflict ultimately opposed the interests, opinions and resources of the industrial North with those of the slaveholding South. The states of Virginia, North Carolina, Arkansas and Tennessee eventually joined the secessionists, adding nine million inhabitants, half of whom were black.

The nineteen northern and western states had a population of close to 20 million people, resources of all types—agricultural, industrial, economic, and maritime—and an army that surpassed the Southerners by some 35,000 troops, although at a level of military preparedness inferior to that of its opponent.

---

* Lincoln was born in Kentucky but represented Illinois in the House of Representatives.

At the beginning of the war, the situation described above made it possible for the surprising advance of the confederates all the way to the doors of Washington, the Union capital (July, 1861) but economic and political developments dictated a subsequent turn of events. The most important were:

1) The tenacious decision by Lincoln to maintain the integrity of the Union.[...]

2) The industrial and naval superiority that allowed the Union army to blockade the principal southern forts and to prevent their reestablishment. In July 1863 the best of both sides met at Gettysburg, Pennsylvania. The casualties, dead and injured, surpassed 50,000; 28,000 for the South alone. Although the South could consider it a partial victory, it never recovered from the cost in lives of such a bloody battle.

3) The diplomatic and political skill of Lincoln: first, for negotiating the neutrality of the European powers (principally England and France), and secondly, for proclaiming the freedom of all slaves living in the confederate states (enforced beginning in 1863), whom he invited to "enter into United States military service." Although this last option had little effect, Lincoln was looking more than anything for international recognition and internal support for his reelection, which he won in 1864.

These fundamental circumstances and others of an economic and military nature worked decisively for the triumph of the Union forces (Yankees). In April 1865 their forces occupied Richmond, the confederate capital, and in the waiting room of the Appomattox courthouse the confederate surrender was signed. The Union had been saved, but the obstacles to reunification would prove difficult to overcome. The most immediate social effect of the Union's military triumph was the freedom of the five million blacks kept as slaves on the southern plantations.

On the fourteenth of that same month, Lincoln was assassinated in Washington by a Southern fanatic named John Booth. The period known as the *reconstruction* (1865–1870) was characterized by judicial, political and social confrontations between both sides including numerous isolated incidents of violence. Thousands of liberated slaves went on to suffer, from that period up to this day, the effects of *segregation*, understood as the refusal to admit them into society and the attempt to keep them separated from the material, political and cultural goods available therein. They also suffered the effects of *discrimination,* or the effort to deny them, for reasons of race, the legal civil rights guaranteed to every citizen in a democratic society.

In order to undermine the spirit of the newly amended Constitution of the United States that now considered the black population civilly and judicially equal, countless artificial barriers were erected, some legal, others illegal. Such was the beginning of terrorist groups like the Klu Klux Klan (1867) which resorted to all means of intimidation, including murder, in order to discourage the black and Latino minorities from fighting for their rights.*

---

* Palacios, Mario Alfonso Rodríguez, et al. *México en la historia.* Mexico: Trillas, 1992, 52–56.

14

Immigration

Immigration has played a vital role in the growth of the United States in the 19th and 20th century. U.S. textbooks typically see it from the receiving end, focusing on those who joined the "melting pot." Textbooks from other countries, understandably, focus to a much greater extent on the "push factors" leading to emigration to the United States.

★

JAPAN

This Japanese text deals not only with the reasons the Japanese decided to leave for the United States, but also with the positive and negative effects this immigration had on all nations involved.

There is a village in Wakayama Prefecture, the present Oaza Mio, Mihamacho, Hidaka-gun, which is popularly known as the "American village" because so many of its inhabitants migrated to the North American continent. The flow was touched off when a man who emigrated to

Canada from the village in 1888, having been successful there, encouraged his fellow villagers back home to come to Canada too.

The true beginning of emigration overseas is said to date from 1868, when settlers went to Hawaii. Emigration to Hawaii continued in the following years, and by 1895 the number of Japanese residents there had reached more than 22,000.

After Hawaii became part of the United States in 1898, the destination of Japanese emigrants shifted to mainland America and Canada. Many of them came originally from prefectures of western Japan such as Hiroshima, Yamaguchi, Fukuoka, Kumamoto and Okinawa. The emigrants to mainland America began working as laborers in railroad construction work, mines, and farms, replacing the Chinese who had hitherto been chiefly responsible for such work.

As the number of Japanese immigrants increased and Japanese laborers working long hours for low wages began to deprive white people of their jobs, ill-feelings among the latter, exacerbated by differences in culture and customs, increased. Following the Russo-Japanese War, antagonism grew between America and Japan, both of whom were in process of extending their influence in China; a campaign to expel Japanese immigrants spread, and in 1924 Japanese immigration was prohibited.

Nowadays, the descendants of the Japanese who emigrated in those days are active in places all over the world; it should not be forgotten, however, that behind the brilliant successes there lies the painful history of those who emigrated in the Meiji era and later.*

*

CANADA

This Canadian textbook presents a view of immigration into the U.S. that is virtually unknown to Americans.

In Canada West, most of the movement into the United States before 1870 was into rich agricultural districts of the American Midwest, and beyond. A constant stream of Canadians made their way across Ohio, Indi-

---

* *Japan in Modern History, Junior High School Textbooks.* Tokyo: International Society for Educational Information, 1994, 449.

ana, and Illinois onto the American prairies, contributing to the rapid settlement of states such as Minnesota and the Dakotas.*

★

NORWAY

This Norwegian text places immigration to the U.S. within the context of an entire worldwide movement. Here, one finds the emphasis on an economic interpretation.

"To live is to travel," wrote H.C. Andersen in 1855. One finds this point of view over and over again in a wealth of variations among the artists and intellectuals of the western world in the 1800s. They were excited, like Phileas Fogg, about the improvement of the transportation network which made it possible to travel independently over long distances in a reasonable time and to places which had previously seemed almost inaccessible. Yes, that gave perspective on one's life.

For a large part of the population, being able to travel was however not a question of living but of surviving. It was first of all necessity and to a lesser extent a sense of adventure which caused so many to move in the period 1850–1914. Shortage of resources, social poverty, and lack of work were the main causes of mass emigration. Even though emigration from Asian areas like India and China was great, too, it was the European emigration "the white explosion" that was most extensive.

The stream of emigration from Europe increased until the turn of the century and again up until World War I. USA was indisputably the preferred destination and took in a good 21 million immigrants from Europe in the time between 1860 and 1915. Many settled in other countries like Argentina, Brazil, Canada and Australia as well. As one can see . . . in the beginning, most people emigrated from northern Europe. Later most people came from southern Europe so that in the early decades of the 1900s Italy had the largest number of emigrants bound for overseas areas.

From 1850 to 1914 agricultural production in western countries increased tremendously. There were two reasons for that. First, the amount

* Bumsted, J.M. *A History of the Canadian Peoples.* Toronto: Oxford University Press, 1998, 169.

of cultivated land was greater, that was especially true for most European countries and not least for North America where settlers in the US and Canada almost tripled the amount of land under the plow. In North America the Indians were sacrificed for the colossal expansion of agriculture while the expansion in Europe to a great degree consisted of the seizure of former common areas that by and large was detrimental to tenant farmers and agricultural workers.

The other cause lay in the transition to capitalism farming with production for the market in mind. To produce with the intention of selling instead of only for one's own consumption—market economy instead of self-sufficiency economy—demanded a different organization of production. It was more goal-oriented and specialized with one of few crops. Gradually machines like the self-binder and thresher began to gain footing while more highly-developed agriculture and the use of artificial fertilizer were expanded at the approach of the turn of the century.

On the American prairies, the Russian steppes and the Argentine pampas the cultivation of grain, wheat above all else, increased dramatically and large quantities of grain were put up for sale on the world market. In the 1840s, Russia exported a good 10 million hectoliters of grain per year while export in the second half of the 1870s varied between 47 and 89 million hectoliters, and the US which perhaps had exported barely 5 million hectoliters, sold over 100 million hectoliters now. This growth in the supply of grain on the world market was so great that it surpassed demand by far. Prices began to fall and agriculture around the world was hit by a crisis in the 1870s and 1880s.*

★

IRELAND

This short Irish text paints a less than rosy outlook on the life of an immigrant. The Irish experience of immigrating to the U.S. was unusually bitter, as reflected in this excerpt.

---

* Eliassen, Jørgen, et al. *Spor i Tid: verden før 1850.* Oslo: H. Aschehoug and Co., 1997, 99–100.

Emigration

For many people during the Famine, there was the stark choice between death and emigration. As a result hundreds of thousands of people fled from the country in order to survive. Masses of people flocked into British ports such as Liverpool. Many arrived in a terrible condition, carrying diseases and needing immediate attention.

From Britain many emigrants set sail for Canada and the United States. The traffic in people became so great that direct sailings began from Ireland to North America.

Conditions on many of the emigrant ships were atrocious. Vast numbers of people were huddled together on old, overcrowded and unsafe vessels. Food and sanitation were appalling and disease, drunkenness and death were rampant. Some of the ships sank on the way. Because of this, these craft came to be called 'coffin ships'.*

★

ITALY

This excerpt from an Italian textbook alludes to the truly vast outpouring of Italian emigrants in the 19th and 20th centuries—not only to the U.S., but throughout the world.

Emigration

During the decades bridging the 19th and 20th centuries, the **population** of Italy **grew** considerably thanks to improved living conditions and the fight against deadly diseases.

The politics of the Italian government, known as **protectionism,** favored the development of industry, yet increased the **difficulties experienced by the agricultural sector.** The population explosion and the agricultural crisis were the main reasons for the enormous increase in emigration.

Emigration is not, for our country, a new phenomenon. For several de-

* Brockie, Gerard, and Raymond Walsh. *Focus on the Past.* Dublin: Gill and McMillan, 1994, 233.

cades many Italians—particularly poor laborers and farmers—abandoned their country, fleeing a life of hardship and poverty in the hopes of finding the means to earn a decent life elsewhere.

But at the end of the 19th and the beginning of the 20th century the rate of emigration increased to phenomenal proportions.

Emigration was not limited to the **south of Italy.** Many Italians left the poor areas of central and northern Italy, particularly the **Veneto and Friuli regions.**

The majority of Italian emigrants were drawn to regions where the demand for labor was extremely high, such as the **United States** and several South American countries, particularly **Venezuela** but above all **Argentina,** where today almost half of the population is of Italian origin. There was also high emigration to Australia, Canada, and several European countries—France, Belgium, Switzerland and, much later, Germany.

The emigration phenomenon attenuated during the First and Second World Wars, but resumed in the aftermath of World War II: from 1945 to 1956 another 1,600,000 Italian emigrants left our country. In spite of the numerous emigrants who returned to Italy, there are more than 50 million people living in the world who have Italian origins. This number is particularly revealing when one remembers that today there are roughly 56 million Italians living in Italy.

In general, emigration was a **painful and difficult experience** for those forced to live through it. The money and success earned by even the most capable and luckiest were often paid for at a very high price.

At that point in time, emigration was an advantage for the Italian economy: it reduced the amount of unemployment, thereby permitting those who remained behind to experience improved living conditions. Nonetheless many regions, especially the south, lost entire generations of workers to emigration. This resulting depletion of human resources would become an obstacle to their economic development.*

---

* Stumpo, E. Beniamino. *Il nuovo libro di storia: per i nuovo programmi.* Firenze: LeMonnier, 2001, 30.

PART III

A World Power

15

Opening of Japan

In 1853, American Commodore Matthew Perry entered Tokyo Harbor aboard the U.S. fleet nicknamed "The Black Ships" by the Japanese. A meeting between the Americans and Japanese leaders followed, which led to the negotiation of the Treaty of Kanagawa. Usually placed within the context of America's Manifest Destiny, the so-called "opening of Japan" is often seen in American textbooks as the event that forced the Japanese to open up their country and begin the process of Westernization. Here, we see a considerably more complicated version of events from the Japanese perspective.

★

JAPAN

In 1853 Perry, with his squadron of four U.S. warships, anchored off Uraga, near Edo. People were astonished by the big black ships giving off smoke from their funnels and called them the Black Ships.

Perry presented a letter from the President of the United States demanding that Japan should open its ports, then left for the time being. Until then, the shogunate had been dealing with diplomatic issues by itself.

Against all precedents, however, it now informed the chotei (imperial court) about the incident and sought opinions from the shogunate officials and daimyos. Many of them were of the opinion that Japan should avoid war at any cost, and quite a few were in favor of opening the ports of Japan.

The next year, Perry came back with a fleet of seven ships, landed on Kanagawa inside the Edo Bay, and urged the shogunate to give a reply to the president's letter. The shogunate feared that refusal might bring about a situation similar to the Opium War and thus agreed to conclude the 1854 U.S.-Japan Treaty of Amity (Kanagawa Treaty).*

Unequal Treaties

Under the international treaties inherited from the shogunate, the new government of Japan was forced to allow foreign settlements in Yokohama as well as the stationing of foreign troops in Japan. These unequal treaties also gave foreigners extraterritorial rights in Japan and robbed Japan of tariff autonomy, thus standing in the way of total Japanese independence and the expansion of Japan's industries and economy.

It happened to have been decided that revision of the U.S.-Japan Treaty of Amity and Commerce would be considered in 1872. That gave the Japanese government a chance to change the unfair contents of the treaty, which were working to Japan's disadvantage. Thus, as soon as the Meiji government had succeeded in replacing the feudal domains with prefectures, it sent a group of Japanese diplomats to the West. The main members of this diplomatic party were politically active men like Iwakura Tomomi, Okubo Toshimichi, Kido Takayoshi, and Ito Hirobumi. The large group became known as the Iwakura Mission.

Contrary to Japanese hopes, the western powers refused to negotiate with the Japanese on the grounds that they were not yet modernized. The Japanese diplomats were forced to give up their hopes of revising the treaties and returned to Japan in 1873 after studying the politics, economics, education, culture, and military of the West over the period of close to two years.†

* *Japan in Modern History, Junior High School Textbooks.* Tokyo: International Society for Educational Information, 1994, 33.

† *Japan in Modern History, Junior High School Textbooks.* Tokyo: International Society for Educational Information, 1994, 44.

16

The Spanish-American War

At the end of the 19th century, the United States encouraged Cuba in its struggle for freedom against its former colonial Spanish rulers. Anxious for the U.S. to be seen as a burgeoning world power and to expand their economic interests, many influential Americans were looking for a fight. The Spanish-American War provided them this opportunity. The Americans used Cuban freedom as a pretense to enter the fray, declaring war on Spain shortly after the U.S.S. *Maine* was sunk in Havana Harbor in February 1898. This particular moment is the subject of several different theories in the texts that follow.

★

SPAIN

The Liquidation of the Overseas Empire

Spain had lost the major portion of its American empire decades earlier (1824). The fractious domestic politics as well as the lack of resources and international support prevented the successful implantation of a vi-able political colony until after 1850. The first efforts came from [Spanish General] O'Donnel who in intervening in Morocco obtained some economic and territorial gains (1860); afterward, he annexed the future Spanish Sahara, which at that time was attractive for its rich fishing.

In 1868 Cuba experienced its first insurrection for independence (Grito de Yara) which would end more than ten years later with the agreement of autonomy for the island. Ultimately, their non-compliance set the stage for a new uprising supported by the North Americans who had vested economic interests on the island. Grito de Baire (The Proclamation of Baire) in 1895 was the beginning of a new *criollo** uprising: the war on the island spread. The government sent Martínez Campos, who had ended the previous rebellion through the Peace of Zanjón (Paz de Zanjón), as General Captain of Cuba. He tried to regain control of the political situation through military action but failed.

Facing the growing danger of intervention from the United States, Cánovas sent General Wyler in 1896 and mobilized more resources. However, this too proved insufficient. In 1897 a semi-autonomous government was organized in Havana. Those seeking independence were already too strong and demanded the total withdrawal of the Spanish. In February of 1898 the North American cruiser, Maine, anchored in the harbor of Havana exploded. The cause of the explosion was never clearly explained and the North American authorities attributed it to Spanish sabotage. The attempts at both a diplomatic solution and international mediation failed. April 23, 1898, the United States declared war on Spain.

The Defeat

The war was brief, despite the fact that the North Americans hardly had a professional army. They compensated for it with their powerful economy and with the proximity of their bases to the war zone, while Spain was far away and her coffers exhausted. The contest was decided at sea. The Americans first attacked the Philippines. In Cuba, the Spanish squadron was destroyed by the North American fleet. Without ships the Spanish could not send reinforcements and it no longer made sense to defend the island. The only logical solution was to ask for peace.

---

* *Criollo*, in this context, refers to those of European descent who were born in the West Indies.

The Paris Peace was signed in December 1898. Spain lost Cuba, Puerto Rico and the Philippines. The press and politicians had misled the public about the peace describing the Spanish victory over the United States as obvious, rapid and easy. The shock of '98 was one of the most tremendous suffered by Spain in its entire history and a heavy blow that undermined the tranquility of the Restoration.

The Impact of '98

In Spain, the debate in Congress about *The Disaster* only caused division; nobody was willing to assume responsibility. The republicans unleashed a lively debate against the liberal government, which it accused of not having been able to avoid war with the United States. In the end, it came down to accusations and attacks against the leaders of the army and navy.

The disaster of '98 gave birth to a feeling of profound frustration in the military community that grew into a deep mistrust of those parties involved in the whole affair. This only accentuated the crisis in Morocco. The military accused the government of not turning over the allocated funds for securing peace in the territory of Morocco; the politicians side-stepped responsibility by accusing the military of incompetence.*

★

PHILIPPINES

The Filipinos assumed the Americans were coming to assist them in overthrowing Spain. Unfortunately, they ended up on the losing end of their alliance with America, a turn of events that remains a sensitive issue in Filipino history.

While the Philippine Revolution was raging with fury, the Cubans halfway round the world were also fighting for their freedom against Spain. America's sympathy with the Cubans and her vast investments in Cuba's sugar industry dragged her into war with Spain. The Spanish-American War ended in the Treaty of Paris (1898), whereby Spain ceded the Philippines to the United States. The Filipinos, who expected the Americans to

---

* Diaz, Julio Montero. *Historia de España contemporánea.* Madrid: Luis Vives, 1996, 230, 231, 233.

champion their freedom, instead were betrayed and reluctantly fell into the hands of the American imperialists.

The Spanish-American War (1898)

The immediate cause of this was the blowing up of the U.S. battleship *Maine* at the harbor of Havana, Cuba, on the night of February 18, 1898. Although the *Maine* had been blown up by American spies in order to provoke the war, the public was not informed of the truth. Instead American newspapers stirred the war spirit of the Americans and blamed Spain. The cry "Remember the Maine!" swept the United States.

On April 19, the U.S. Congress passed several resolutions demanding that Spain evacuate Cuban soil. Spain did not want a war because at the time she was harassed by domestic trouble and two revolutions in her previous colonies—Cuba and the Philippines. To save her honor, however, she declared war against the United States on April 24. This is what the American government was waiting for. On the following day (April 25), the Congress declared war on Spain. Thus began the Spanish-American War.*

Filipino-American Collaboration

The outbreak of the Spanish-American War caught General Aguinaldo in Singapore. There he had several secret interviews with the American consul-general, Mr. E. Spencer Pratt, regarding Filipino-American collaboration against Spain. Mr. William Gray, a British businessman who had lived in Manila, acted as interpreter during the Aguinaldo-Pratt interviews.

Aguinaldo rushed to Hong Kong, but missed Dewey who had already sailed to Manila. He held several conferences with the American consul-general, Mr. Rounceville Wildman. He gave money to Consul Wildman for the purchase of arms for the Filipinos.

The Return of Aguinaldo

Upon the advice of the Hong Kong Junta, General Aguinaldo left on board the *McCulloch,* Dewey's dispatch vessel. He arrive[d] at Cavite on May 19, 1898.

---

* Zaide, Sonia M. *The Philippines: A Unique Nation.* Quezon City: All-Nations Publishing, 1999, 254.

Immediately after his arrival, Aguinaldo conferred with Dewey. Dewey was delighted to see him, because he needed Filipino assistance against the Spaniards. Aguinaldo was equally pleased, for he needed American help to win Philippine independence.

Secret Negotiation for Manila's Surrender

Meanwhile, as Aguinaldo was laying down the foundations of an independent government, troops were coming from the United States to reinforce Dewey. By the end of July 1898, the American troops had totaled nearly 11,000 men, under the overall command of Major General Wesley Merritt.

The city of Manila was doomed. It was cut off from the sea by Dewey's fleet and hemmed on land by Filipino and American forces. The Filipino troops numbered 12,000. They were entrenched beyond the city walls—at Malate, Paco, Sampaloc, San Juan, Caloocan, and La Loma.

On August 5, 1898, General Fermin Jaudenes succeeded General Basilio Augustin as governor general of the Philippines. Three days later Dewey and Merritt warned Jaudenes to evacuate the civilian population from Manila. This warning was followed by another message demanding the surrender of the city.

Jaudenes, through the Belgian consul, Edouard Andre, secretly told Dewey and Merritt that he would surrender after a little fight to save Spain's honor. The arrangement was agreeable to both American commanders. The rank and file of the Spanish, American, and Filipino troops, however, knew nothing of this secret arrangement.

The Capture of Manila

At 9:30 in the morning of August 18 [sic], 1898, the so-called "Battle of Manila" began. The day was cloudy and rainy. Dewey's naval gun shelled Fort San Antonio Abad near the Luneta. The Filipino and American troops, fighting side by side, rushed to the attack. General F.V. Greene's brigade captured Ermita and Malate, including Fort San Antonia Abad, General MacArthur's troops took Singalong. General Gregorio del Pilar's brigade captured Tondo. General Mariano Noriel's column defeated the Spaniards at Paco. General Pio del Pilar's troops advanced through Sampaloc. And General Artemio Ricarte's men captured Santa Ana.

At one o'clock in the afternoon, General Greene saw the Spanish white flag flying above the city walls, symbolic of Manila's surrender. Immediately all hostilities ceased. The American troops triumphantly entered the city gates, after which they closed the gates to prevent the Filipino forces who had helped them in the capture of the city from entering. Naturally the Filipino generals and their soldiers resented their exclusion in the joyous celebration of the taking of Manila.

End of Filipino-American Collaboration

The capture of Manila marked the end of Filipino-American collaboration. The Filipino troops deeply resented the American action of preventing their entry into the city. They had fought hard in the battle and had aided the Americans in capturing Manila. They naturally felt themselves entitled to some share in the victory celebration. Speaking of this unfortunate turn of events, Harry B. Hawes wrote: "The insurgents [Filipino patriots-Z.], who had fought long and bravely and who felt therefore that to their energies and sacrifices victory was mostly due were naturally indignant at the refusal to permit them to enter the city and participate in at least some of the pageantry. Then began the friction that begot first unfriendliness and ultimately open hostility.*

★

CUBA

One can legitimately ask if this text better represents the historical perspective of Cubans in 1898, or whether it more accurately comments on U.S.-Cuban relations in the latter half of the 20th century. What is certain is that no history book of this scope is published in Cuba without the government's explicit approval. Of particular interest is the conspiracy theory of the U.S.S. Maine's explosion.

Explosion of the 'Maine': U.S. Intervention—On February 15th, 1898 only weeks after the autonomous regime was installed and just before the island's parliamentary elections were held, an event occurred that

---

* Zaide, Sonia M. *The Philippines: A Unique Nation.* Quezon City: All-Nations Publishing, 1999, 260–61.

clearly announced the future: the explosion of the US battleship Maine in Havana Bay, with a toll of 266 crew members and two officers dead. The US government had sent the ship three weeks before with the pretext of serious unrest promoted in Havana by integration supporters against the autonomous regime. The "Maine" was an obvious sign that the United States was willing to directly intervene in the Spanish-Cuban war.

According to a US commission, the explosion had come from outside the ship; but a Spanish commission found that the blast had occurred inside. Actually Spain was doing everything possible to prevent a war with the United States and was careful not to commit any act of provocation. Hence, the Spaniards were not responsible for the blast. On the contrary, the US authorities were seeking a pretext to wage war against Spain. Besides meeting its old ambitions over Cuba [and] Puerto Rico, the Philippines and other militarily and economically important possessions could fall into US hands as a result of a war with the European country. And fearing that Cuba would obtain its independence and slip through its fingers, the US needed an incident like that of the "Maine". Consequently, everything points to a self-provocation. The theory concerning US responsibility was reinforced by the fact that almost all white officials escaped the catastrophe because they were not on deck at the time of the blast.

In a desperate attempt to prevent the US from getting involved in the conflict, the colonial government took two steps that had been demanded by that country's President, William McKinley, and which until that moment it had refused to accept: an end to the forced relocation and an end to hostilities with the island's independence fighters in order to reach a peaceful settlement. But both the Republic's Government Council and the Liberation Army's General in Chief immediately rejected the late truce offered by the Spaniards, claiming that they would only accept Cuba's absolute independence.

In the United States, the explosion of the "Maine" was blamed on Spain, sparking a wave of indignation. President McKinley sought authorization in Congress to put an end to the Spanish-Cuban war. On April 11th, 1898, congress granted the permission through a so called Joint Resolution, which also stipulated that "the island of Cuba is, and by right should be, free and independent". The road had been cleared for US intervention in Cuba.

On April 21st, the Joint Resolution was presented to the Spanish government as an ultimatum and Spain and the United States broke off diplomatic relations. Hours later, a US contingent led by Admiral William T. Sampson blockaded several Cuban ports, and President McKinley called on 150,000 volunteers to take arms, a figure which rapidly rose to 200,000. Artillery fire began falling on Cuban ports, paving the way for the arrival of the invasion army. Cannon shots were also heard over San Juan de Puerto Rico. At the same time, another US contingent entered Manila Bay in the Philippines, sinking the Spanish boats anchored there.

For its war in Cuba, the United States decided to begin the invasion in Oriente, the province where the Cubans had almost absolute control. With that objective, the US asked for and obtained the Liberation Army's cooperation. Cuban troops played a decisive role in establishing a "beachhead" and protecting the US landing in Daiquiri on June 20th, as well as the successful battles over El Caney and San Juan. Santiago de Cuba surrendered on July 16th. The Cubans completed the siege of the city and prevented the arrival of Spanish reinforcements. The Battle of Las Guásimas in which the Cuban troops did not participate was a disaster for the US Army. The Spanish contingent, led by Admiral Pascual Cervera, was destroyed in Santiago de Cuba's Bay on July 3rd. Cervera was captured by the Cubans, who supported the attack from the coast.

With Oriente under control and sure of its victory, the United States began to show its real intentions regarding Cuba. After the city of Santiago de Cuba was taken over by Cuban and US troops, General Nelson A. Miles would not allow the Cuban troops to enter in the city, claiming that they wanted to prevent clashes between Cubans and Spaniards. General Calixto García, head of the *mambi** forces in the Eastern department, ordered his troops to defend their respective areas, presented his resignation to the Government Council and wrote a memorable and dignified protest letter to general William R. Shafter, head of the US troops.

After having lost the Philippines and Puerto Rico and without hope of holding onto Cuba, Spain asked the United States to begin peace talks. On August 11th, the first agreements were reached and hostilities came to an end. On December 10th, the Paris Treaty was signed, putting an end to the war and leaving Spanish colonies in US hands.

---

* *Mambi* is an indigenous term that refers to the Cuban soldiers who fought against Spain in the Cuban War of Independence (1895–98).

With total disregard for the Cuban people, who had fought heroically for their independence for more than 30 years, the United States prevented Cuban representatives from taking part in the peace talks and in the signing of the Paris Treaty.

On January 1st, 1899 the government of Cuba was transferred to the United States.*

★

CARIBBEAN

The following Caribbean text offers another perspective on the events surrounding the Cuban rebellion and the Spanish-American War, with a notable emphasis on American imperialism.

The U.S.A. and the Spanish Colonies

BACKGROUND TO THE CUBAN REBELLION

José Martí and his supporters began rebellion against Spanish rule in 1895. By then few Cubans could see any value in remaining under Spanish rule. Now the slaves were emancipated, Spanish soldiers were no longer needed to deal with threats of revolt. Spain was the least important of Cuba's overseas customers and bought only 6 per cent of all the exports from the island. Yet all classes in Cuba suffered from the taxes demanded by the Spanish government.

The most important group of foreigners in Cuba were the American businessmen who had invested money in sugar, tobacco, railways and harbour works. The biggest part of Cuba's exports went to the USA, yet the gain was more America's than Cuba's. The United States placed high tariffs on cured tobacco and refined sugar so that American, and not Cuban, workers would have the jobs in curing and refining. In 1894 the USA also placed a high tariff on raw sugar. Cubans came to believe that America would lower these tariffs if their island was no longer a Spanish colony.

---

* Navarro, José Cantón. *History of Cuba: The Challenge of the Yoke and the Star.* Havana: SI-MAR, 2000, 69–72.

Many Americans were in sympathy with the Cuban Liberals and their struggle against Spain. Some were businessmen with interests in Cuba but others were ordinary people who had read the stirring articles on the Cuban liberation movement which José Martí wrote in their newspapers.

THE CUBAN STRUGGLE

José Martí was killed only a few weeks after the rebellion began, but his followers went on with all-out war. The struggle was a cruel one. Spain sent 200,000 troops but they found themselves faced by rebels from all classes and in every part of the island. The fighting was so widespread that the island's economy was almost completely ruined. In three years sugar production fell from 1,500,000 tonnes to 200,000 tonnes. Both sides tried to force the peasants and smallholders to join them. The rebels' leaders deliberately destroyed crops and buildings to make the island worthless to Spain. The Spanish commander-in-chief drove peasants into concentration camps to stop them from being recruited by force into the rebel armies. This move brought most American opinion firmly on to the side of the revolutionaries, who were shown in the American press as fighters for freedom and democracy against an Old World monarchy.

THE *MAINE*

The United States government began to see that intervention in the war would be popular. Americans who owned land or businesses which were being ruined in the fighting called on their government to send aid and bring about a quick rebel victory. Army and navy commanders pointed out that American defences would be stronger if Cuba was under United States influence. President McKinley hesitated and took time to think the question over. Meanwhile, he sent the warship Maine to Havana to protect American lives and property. On 15 February 1898 the Maine exploded in Havana harbour with the loss of 266 American lives. It had been blown up by an underwater bomb. Americans immediately blamed the Spanish. In fact the bomb was probably placed by Cuban patriots who saw the disaster as a way of bringing the United States into the war on their side.

THE TELLER AMENDMENT

Public opinion in the United States demanded war against Spain, although there were still some American politicians who feared that it would be used as an excuse for adding Cuba to the United States. Their fears were dealt with in an amendment to the Act of Congress which declared war on Spain. The amendment was put forward by Senator H. M. Teller and said that, once Cuba was free and peaceful, the United States would 'leave the government and control of the island to its people'. The amendment was passed. America was at war with Spain and prepared to fight her not just in Cuba but in the rest of the Caribbean and the Pacific.

THE SPANISH-AMERICAN WAR, 1898

The first fighting in the war took place in the Philippines, half way around the world from Cuba. An American naval squadron, led by Commodore George Dewey, seized the Spanish naval base at Manila. Immediately 11,000 American troops were sent to occupy the islands which Spain surrendered to the United States on 13 August 1898. Hardly an American life was lost. Shortly afterwards the Pacific island of Guam was also occupied.

In the Caribbean, American victories were just as complete. A small army landed in Cuba and entered Santiago a few weeks later. Another force marched through Puerto Rico as if it were on a holiday parade. The poorly organised Spanish simply gave up in the Caribbean. They agreed that Cuba should be left to the patriot forces and Puerto Rico was to be occupied by the Americans until a peace conference decided its future.

[. . .]

AMERICAN COLONIALISM

Now it had won the Spanish colonies, the American government had to work out a colonial policy. It had to please two sets of opinion, the expansionists and the isolationists.

American expansionists wanted to see outposts of the American way of life around the world. They looked on the new possessions as a chance for missionaries, teachers and charitable organisations to take a better way of life to less fortunate people. Many businessmen thought it would be safer to invest money in factories, plantations and public works in countries which were under American rule backed by American troops. Military leaders wanted naval and marine bases in the seas to the east and west of the United States.

There were not so many isolationists but they put their point of view forcefully. American liberals made the point that ruling colonies was against the spirit of their own political system. They reminded Americans that their own Declaration of Independence began by stating that all men are created equal. Labour leaders feared that immigrants from the new colonies would take jobs away from Americans. Some Southern politicians objected to the thought that there might be more black and coloured people in the country.

The ideas of expansionists and isolationists were brought together in the way that the American government managed the affairs of Cuba and Puerto Rico. Neither was turned into a full colony like those owned by Britain or France, and yet the United States kept control of their affairs. This pleased both expansionists and isolationists. The United States gained the greatest share of the wealth created by the people of these islands without allowing immigration into America. This satisfied both businessmen and labour leaders. *

---

* Claypole, William, and John Robottom. *Caribbean Story, Bk. 2: The Inheritors.* Kingston: Carlong, 1994, 173–75.

17

Philippine-American War

Viewed as a pivotal historical event in most Filipino textbooks, this war is hardly mentioned in U.S. history textbooks. According to U.S. texts, the "Philippine Insurrection," as it was previously known, lasted from 1899 to 1902, when President Theodore Roosevelt declared an end to the fighting. Filipino texts, in contrast, argue that the war actually endured for months, if not years, after the formal declaration from Roosevelt, owing to Filipino resistance in the southern islands.

★

PHILIPPINES

Outbreak of the War of Philippine Independence

The rise of the Republic worsened relations with America. The Filipinos resented the American treachery in depriving them of entering Manila after its capture. For their part, the Americans used another incident to hasten their annexation of the Philippines.

On Saturday night, February 4, 1899, an American soldier named Private Robert W. Grayson shot and killed a Filipino soldier who was crossing San Juan bridge. By firing the first, unprovoked shot, the Americans ignited the War of Philippine Independence. To add insult to injury, the Americans called the war a Filipino "insurrection".

News of the outbreak of hostilities was telegraphed to President Aguinaldo in Malolos. Immediately he declared war on America, whose forces had drawn the first blood.*

Filipino Victories

The war was not a record of continuous American victories, for there were cases in which the Filipinos registered military triumphs. On April 23, 1899, in Quinqua (now Plaridel), Bulacan, the Filipino troops of the youthful General Gregorio del Pilar repulsed the cavalry charge of Major J. Franklin Bell and killed Colonel John M. Stotsenburg.

American prestige suffered a serious blow on December 19, 1899 when General Lawton, splendid soldier and veteran of the American Civil War, was killed by General Licerio Geronimo's men in the Battle of San Mateo.

In the year 1900, the Americans suffered several defeats at the hands of the Filipino guerrillas. On January 17, 1900, the Filipinos captured an American pack train in Alaminos, Laguna, killing some guards and chasing the survivors. On September 13, Colonel Maximo Abad and his guerrillas routed the American troops in the Battle of Puland Lupa near the town of Santa Cruz, Marinduque, and captured their commander, Captain James Shields. Four days later (September 17, 1900), General Cailles and his Lagunense forces decisively defeated Colonel Cheatam's troops in Mabitac, Laguna.

The worst military disaster of the U.S. Military forces in the Visayas was the annihilation of the American garrison in Balangiga, Samar, on September 28, 1901, by General Vicente Lukban's bolomen. Of the 74 American officers and soldiers composing the garrison, 50 were slaughtered (including the commander Captain Thomas O'Connell) and only 24

---

* Zaide, Sonia M. *The Philippines: A Unique Nation.* Quezon City: All-Nations Publishing, 1999, 268.

survived the Filipino bolos by running away during the bloody fight. The victorious patriots captured a rich booty of war—100 Krag rifles and 25,000 rounds of ammunitions. American writers called this U.S. military debacle the "Massacre of Balangiga."*

End of the War

The capture of Aguinaldo marked the end of the First Philippine Republic, but not of the war. The fiery and fearless General Miguel Malvar continued the hopeless fight. In a stirring manifesto to the Filipino people, dated July 31, 1901, he urged the continuation of resistance to American invasion. "Forward, without ever turning back!" he said. "All wars for independence have been obliged to suffer terrible tests!"

But further resistance to the much stronger foe was futile. The American military commanders in the provinces took ruthless measures, such as concentrating civilians within military zones, burning the hostile villages, and destroying the crops and work animals with the primary objective of starving out the guerrillas.†

Results of the War

The superior arms of Uncle Sam crushed the short-lived First Philippine Republic, the same arms which, strangely enough, helped to establish the Cuban Republic. In forcing her sovereignty upon the Filipino people, the United States crossed 7,000 miles of ocean, using 126,468 men, of whom 4,234 died; she spent the vast sum of $600,000,000 and engaged in 2,811 recorded fights. On the other hand, the Filipinos, in the defense of their independence, suffered greater losses—16,000 died in action, 200,000 civilians perished from famine and pestilence, and untold millions of pesos worth of property were destroyed.

Although beaten in war, the Filipinos did not give up their independ-

---

* Zaide, Sonia M. *The Philippines: A Unique Nation.* Quezon City: All-Nations Publishing, 1999, 272.

† Zaide, Sonia M. *The Philippines: A Unique Nation.* Quezon City: All-Nations Publishing, 1999, 275.

ence ideal. They lost the war but continued the good fight with their wits and their hearts set on liberty.*

In their desperation, the American soldiers turned arsonists burning whole towns in order to force the guerrillas to the open. One such infamous case of extreme barbarity occurred in the town of Balangiga, Samar, in 1901–1902. Balangiga was a peaceful little port off the southern tip of Samar, but it was garrisoned by Americans who could not pinpoint the nerve-center of guerilla activities in the town. Many American soldiers who garrisoned the town were veterans of the Boxer Rebellion and had participated in the capture of Peking. The American soldiers were busy one morning taking their breakfast when suddenly they were attacked by Filipinos in their employ. The church bells rang, and soon about 180 Filipinos fell upon the Americans, many of whom were killed instantly. The other Americans who tried to escape were boloed to death, while others were hacked from the nose to the throat. The news of the guerrilla attack gave rise to pained cries throughout the United States and so President Roosevelt gave orders to pacify Samar. Assigned to the task was General "Jake" Smith. "I want no prisoners," he said firmly. "I wish you to kill and burn; the more you burn and kill the better it will please me." Forthwith he ordered that Samar by transformed into "a howling wilderness." Orders were also issued to shoot down anybody capable of carrying arms. By "capable of carrying arms," General Smith meant to include even boys ten years old, for the latter could carry rifles and swing bolos. In six months, Balangiga became "a howling wilderness." The barbarity with which General Smith subdued the people of Samar touched the conscience of the American people. After the end of the bloody campaign, Smith was court-martialed and retired from the service.†

* Zaide, Sonia M. *The Philippines: A Unique Nation.* Quezon City: All-Nations Publishing, 1999, 276–77.

† Agoncillo, Teodoro A. *History of the Filipino People.* Quezon City, Manila: Garotech Publishing, 1990, 229.

18

The Boxer Rebellion

With the United States becoming a colonial power in the Pacific after its victory in the Spanish–American War, many American imperialists desired to extend U.S. economic expansion to China. America textbooks point out that the United States was recovering from one of its worst depressions when the opportunity to go after the elusive "China Trade" became a reality. U.S. economic imperialism was nearly thwarted, the texts add, by the "great powers" (i.e., Western Europe and Japan) who had already carved China into their own "spheres of influence." Coveting the China trade, the American Secretary of State circulated his "Open Door Notes" to the great powers.

Here, U.S. textbooks explain that economic imperialism met with Chinese opposition, in the form of a group nicknamed the Boxers. The Boxers themselves appear as a footnote to a larger history of imperialism; the history of the rebellion itself receives scant mention.

★

CHINA (HONG KONG)

This textbook from Hong Kong emphasizes the unique origins of the revolt and the aggressive intentions of the foreign powers. *

Rise of the Society for Righteous Harmony

The "Society for Righteous Harmony," originally named the "Fists of Righteous Harmony," was a secret society among the lower classes which practiced martial arts and magical charms, and which at first aimed to overthrow the Qing dynasty and restore the Ming dynasty. They said of themselves that they had divine protection for their bodies, so that neither knives nor guns could hurt them. After China's defeat in the Sino-Japanese war, however, they changed into an anti-foreign movement, and grew rapidly after gaining support from Li Bingheng, prefect of Shandong province, where the Society for Righteous Harmony was based. [. . .] With official support, the Society for Righteous Harmony grew more active, and began to tear up railroads, burn churches, and kill and maim ministers; foreign countries expressed their protests to the Qing court. Therefore, in 1899 the Qing court sent Yuan Shikai to take over as prefect of Shandong, and he began to implement repressive policies toward the Society.

Yuan Shikai's repressive measures did not cause the surrender of the Society, nor did they gain the universal support of provincial gentry. At the beginning of 1900, local units of the Society for Righteous Harmony in the northwestern part of Shandong began to spread out into neighboring Hebei province, and there it quickly organized and incorporated pre-existing martial arts societies is southeastern Hebei. Within four months, central Hebei came under the control of the Society, and Beijing gradually came under threat from them.

---

* This selection comes from a textbook published in Hong Kong in 1997, the same year that control of Hong Kong was passed from Great Britain back to China. Chinese educators suggest that it is not as nationalistic as other texts from mainland China.

Campaign of the Eight-Nation United Army

The Qing government, with the Empress Dowager Ci Xi at its head, did not have a settled policy toward the Society for Righteous Harmony. On the one hand, because there was no support among the foreign great powers for her conservative policies [. . .], she planned to use the Society to oppose the great powers. On the other hand, the rapid growth of the Society for Righteous Harmony thoroughly frightened her. Thus, from 1898 to 1899, government policy toward the Society alternated between repression and support. Moreover, some officials told their superiors in the government that the Society for Righteous Harmony were brave and noble, did apparently have divine assistance, and could be relied upon to smash foreign powers. Under the influence of conservative ministers of state, Ci Xi decided to support the Society and made a proclamation officially recognizing it.

Because the Qing court was more supportive than restrictive toward the Society, the organization was able to develop even more quickly, so that the group soon entered Beijing. Ci Xi decided to take from the Society for Righteous Harmony "their young and vigorous, to be enlisted into an army"; and thereupon the Society's numbers in Beijing quickly swelled to 100,000.

At the same time, Ci Xi also ordered that a division of the Qing army advance into the capital to assist the Society for Righteous Harmony. Thus, Society members and regular troops went burning churches and homes of Christians, and even came into conflict with foreign troops stationed in the embassy district.

From the winter of 1899, the great powers met repeatedly with the Qing government, urging action against the Society. In 1900, they threatened that they might have to take "necessary measures" to deal with the problem. Before long, naval ships of the great powers began to gather on the shore at the town of Dagukou, and demanded that the Qing government pacify the Society for Righteous Harmony within two months. After that, a combined force of 2,000 troops from Britain, Russia, Germany, France, America, Italy, Japan, and Australia invaded and captured the port city of Tianjin under the command of the British general Seymour. When they got to the area of Yangcun, they ran into combined forces of the Society for Righteous Harmony and the Qing army; and without any means to advance, retreated to Tianjin.

Under pressure of invasion from this Eight-Nation United Army, Ci Xi and her conservative ministers declared war upon the foreign nations.

After receiving reinforcements, the foreign forces totaled 20,000, and again pushed forward from Tianjin to Beijing, and occupied the city for thirteen months. Slightly later, the foreign powers heavily reinforced their troops in the capital, with the total rising to 100,000 at its peak, and command of the forces was turned over to general commander of the German contingent, Waldersee. The united army carried out violent reprisals in Beijing, widely looting the city, massacring residents, and burning royal palaces; corpses piled up in the city, and the Imperial Summer Palace was particularly heavily looted and despoiled.*

★

JAPAN

The elite club of imperialist nations that existed at the end of the 19th century had two new additions at that time: the United States and Japan. By joining the expedition into China, Japan was establishing itself as the dominant Eastern power and selling itself up for future political advantage. This Japanese text highlights Japan's role in the region as a major power.

In China popular agitation to exclude foreigners intensified, and in 1899 the Righteous Fists (Boxers) rose in revolt mainly in Shandong Province (the Boxer Rebellion). The Qing dynasty Chinese government helped them secretly, and thus the riots spread to Huabei and then into Manchuria. In 1900, the foreign powers jointly sent troops and, with Japan and Russia providing the main force, defeated the Boxers.

After the Boxer Rebellion, Russia continued to occupy Manchuria. In Korea, the Japanese influence was reined in, and a government was established in cooperation with Russia.

Great Britain, with India, its colony, threatened by Russia, came to fear for the rights of China as well. Thus, Japan and Britain, which had similar interests with respect to Russia, signed the treaty for the Anglo-Japanese

* Huiyi Liang, Shu Longde, and Gu Cuixia (ed). *Chinese History, vol. 3, 2nd edition.* Hong Kong: Wenda Publishing, 1997, 88–92.

Alliance in 1902. The United States, which did not welcome a Russian invasion of China, took the position of supporting the moves of both Japan and Britain.*

★

GREAT BRITAIN

This British text places the Boxer Rebellion within the context of international relations at the turn of the century. Also notable is this text's concern over French and Russian expansion, America's "open-door" policy, as well as British "diplomatic goals" during this entire period.

The growing realisation that China was in a weak condition encouraged other European powers to seek rich pickings in Asia. In the 1880s France arrived in Indo-China, capturing Tonking, Cambodia and Saigon. The British responded to the French threat by taking formal control of Burma, Malaya and Borneo. Germany and the USA also arrived to take control of several Pacific Islands. Japan and Russia were also interested in expansion.

This wave of 'new imperialism' in Asia nearly led to the European powers partitioning China. The naval attacks aimed at enforcing the 'open-door' policy were followed by military attacks. In 1860 Russia attacked China and annexed a large amount of territory near the Amur River. This allowed Russia to build the ice-free naval base of Vladivostock. In 1894 Japan, the most rapidly advancing independent Asian power, attacked and defeated China. As the price of victory Japan demanded large amounts of territory. This alarmed Britain, Russia, Germany and France, who intervened diplomatically. In the end Japan accepted a £30 million war indemnity. But China could not pay. This opened the way for European banks to lend money to China in return for mineral rights, railway contracts, and land.

The European powers began to view China as a 'dying' power in a world where only the fittest were destined to survive. In 1898 Germany captured the port of Kiao-Chow, Britain took Wei-hai-wei, and the Rus-

* *Japan in Modern History*. Tokyo: International Society for Educational Information, 1994, 70–71.

sians grabbed Port Arthur. In 1900 China, historically the most powerful
and influential state in Asia, was perilously close to partition; so close that
Germany, France, Britain, and Russia had already drawn up plans to ensure that the division of the spoils would be carried out peacefully. The
Times, which was known as 'the voice of the British Government', summed
up the prevailing view of China's sorry plight in 1898 when it suggested
that any attempt to prevent a partition of China would be like 'trying to
keep the ocean out with a mop'.

However, the Chinese were not prepared to give up their independence without a struggle. In 1900, with partition imminent, large numbers
of Chinese nationalists rose up and attacked Europeans wherever they
were to be found. This was 'The Boxer Rebellion'. Many Europeans and
many more Chinese rebels were killed before Germany, France, Russia
and Britain intervened, suppressed the rebellion, and restored order.

In the end China was only saved from partition because the European
powers feared the ambitions of each other more than they wanted to rule
China. They finally agreed to accept a partition of trading concessions in
China. Russia took control of trade in the north (including Peking),
France gained exclusive trading rights in the South, and Germany gained
concessions in Shantung. This left Britain with the Yangtse valley—the
most important trading region of all. But as Britain had previously controlled over 70 per cent of all Chinese foreign trade this was hardly a completely satisfactory outcome. What did satisfy Britain was the survival of
an independent China. This was what British diplomacy had been aiming
at all along.*

* McDonough, Frank. *The British Empire 1815–1914.* London: Hodder and Stoughton, 1994,
64–68.

19

U.S. Interventions in Latin America and the Caribbean

It is difficult to read a Latin American textbook without finding references to two main themes in national histories: the Monroe Doctrine and U.S. interests in Latin America. The reality of U.S. power in the region has indelibly influenced historical perceptions of the U.S.

★

BRAZIL

An Emerging World Power

The victory of the industrialized North against the agrarian South accelerated the US industrial progress. Gradually, the US economy bypassed that of France, Germany and even England in productivity and economic development, eventually emerging as the first World superpower at the end of the 19th century. The prosperity enjoyed by the United States became an additional incentive for immigration, pushing demographic growth from little more than 30 million habitants in 1865 to 90 million in 1914.

The consolidation of the capitalist regime after the civil war also favored the US imperialist expansionism throughout the American continent and Asia. The Monroe Doctrine and the theory of Manifest Destiny formed the ideological basis for the US to assume the guardianship of the entire American continent, especially Central America. President Theodore Roosevelt (1901–1909) adopted the fundamentals of the Monroe Doctrine, which became known as "Roosevelt's Corollary." The US aimed to serve its own political and economic interests and as such guaranteed itself the right to use military force to intervene in the countries of the continent, claiming for itself the title of "America". Among the many US interventions, we have highlighted here the ones in Cuba, Panama and Nicaragua since the end of the 19th century until the last decades of the 20th century.

Cuba, in 1898, was a Spanish colony and it was fighting for its independence under the leadership of José Martí. Under the pretext of protecting North American properties and lives, the US intervened in the region, combating the Spanish army and winning Cuba's independence. In this war, the US obtained for itself the annexation of Puerto Rico in the Caribbean and the Philippines in the Pacific Ocean.

The Cuban Constitution of 1901 included, by US imposition, the Platt Amendment, which gave the right to the US to intervene in the country, in addition to the concession of an area of 117 Km, Guantánamo Base (still today, an American military base on Cuban territory). The intervention in Cuba lasted until 1959, when Fidel Castro assumed the government of the island and installed a socialist regime.

In 1903, the US encouraged the Panamanian separatists' movement in Colombia. In exchange, the US received from the newly formed Panamanian government the right to finish the construction of a canal, linking the Atlantic to the Pacific Ocean. That work started in 1881 by France. Later, the US also obtained from the Panamanian government the right to control the Canal Zone indefinitely. But during the 70's, a nationalist campaign promoted by the Panamanian government denounced that agreement and the US agreed to turn the canal back to Panama at the end of the 20th century.

The US also intervened in Nicaragua in 1909, and occupied its territory until 1933 aiming to stabilize the region which was in a near constant state of rebellion. During the period of occupation there were insurrections against the American military presence in the country. Augusto Cesar Sandino, a guerrilla countryman, was considered a national hero. Decades later, his name inspired another nationalist movement, the aim of which was to defeat the dictatorship of Anastacio Somaza in 1979, an American ally.

Through its many military interventions, the US ended up exerting complete economic guardianship in the region.*

★

COSTA RICA

Costa Rica has long been considered a reliable U.S. ally. These excerpts, however, reveal a perspective that is hardly uncritical of U.S. dominance in the region.

Latin America in the 20th Century

The political and economic situation of Latin America at the beginning of the 20th century coincided with the expansion of the United States and the weakening of the principal European powers who were absorbed in a battle of interests that would lead them into the First World War.

The United States displaced England in the area of economic domination in Latin America and France in the area of cultural domination.

Large US companies set up subsidiaries in Latin American territories. Their presence influenced not only the economy of our country, but legislation as well.

Each time that a nationalist movement placed in danger the presence of one of these companies in our country, there was an intervention of North American soldiers. This was justified by citing the "defense of US interests in the region."

Thus, Latin American countries were built on a legislative and economic base that depended on the economic necessities of a foreign power.†

* Vicento, Cláudio, *História geral*. São Paulo: Scipione, 2002, 334
† Alvaro, Ana Lorena Orozco, and Efren Molina Vega. *Estudios Sociales 10*. San José: Santillana, 1999, 66.

SOCIO-ECONOMIC SITUATION

[. . .]

At the beginning of the 20th century, the Latin American economy, at that time bound to the US economy, remained restrained by a strict financial dependence. Moreover, US enclaves began to form in the Latin American countries, or more specifically, in regions controlled by companies like the United Fruit Company (UFCo) and Standard Oil that influenced not only production, but politics in the country as well.

The foreign companies were developing in those territories that controlled an economy in parallel with that of the host country, where, in general, US laws governed both contracts and workers and dollars were used as currency. Moreover, these companies imported European, Asian, and African workers who were establishing cultural and ethnic customs different from those of the country in which these enclaves were located.

The necessities of US consumers determined the type of Latin American production. For example, the expansion of the automotive industry in the United States favored the exploitation of rubber in the Amazon basin and to the growing boom of petroleum in Venezuela, Colombia, Peru and Mexico.

While the Caribbean specialized in the cultivation of sugar cane, the United Fruit Company dominated vast plantations of bananas in all of Central America, Venezuela and Colombia. The economics of Brazil and Costa Rica also depended to a high degree on their coffee production and the demand for their product in Europe and in the United States. In the south, Argentina and Uruguay specialized in the exportation of wool, meat and grain; Chile in copper and Bolivia in tin.*

MOVEMENTS IN CENTRAL AMERICA AND THE CARIBBEAN

The political activity from 1930 to 1980 was marked by numerous *coups d'etat,* generally carried out by members of the army. In Central America and the Caribbean this situation was frequently due to the proximity of the United States, a country that "looked after" the interests of companies like the United Fruit Company.

* Alvaro, Ana Lorena Orozco, and Efren Molina Vega. *Estudios Sociales 10.* San José: Santillana, 1999, 69.

For this reason, the United States supported certain governments that favored North American interests in the region, although they were led by dictators like Somoza in Nicaragua, Jorge Ubico in Guatemala, Rafael Leonida Trujillo in the Dominican Republic and Fulgencio Batista in Cuba. [...]

In Guatemala the dictator, Jorge Ubico, was overthrown in 1944. The new president, the writer Juan Jose Averato Martinez, wrote a work code and instituted a series of reforms that benefited Guatemalan workers. His successor, Jacobo Arbenz, began agricultural reforms that benefited some 100,000 peasant families.

The reforms hurt the interests of the Guatemalan oligarchy and of the United Fruit Company now that it held the title to the banana fields. The government of Guatemala tried to pay the US company, as an indemnity, the value of the lands it (the UFCo) had claimed they were worth to avoid taxes.

The government of the United States was not disposed to accept that a US company be expropriated and accused Arbenz of communist conspiracy. From the plantations of the United Fruit Company, the United States prepared an invasion headed by the Guatemalan, Carlos Castillo Armas. The movement overthrew Arbenz in 1954 and halted his reforms.*

INDUSTRIALIZATION AND URBANIZATION

The consolidation of the Cuban Revolution caused a change in relations between the United States and Latin America. The government of the United States realized that the Cuban example could spread throughout the entire region.

President John F. Kennedy pushed for a political approach of economic aid to the region called Alliance for Progress, which intended to improve the situation of the neediest groups. The US government tried, as well, to give more support to pluralistic governments rather than dictatorships. The goal of the program was to give larger economic and political participation to the needy classes, with the objective that they not follow the path of insurrection.

* Alvaro, Ana Lorena Orozco, and Efren Molina Vega. *Estudios Sociales 10.* San José: Santillana, 1999, 76, 77.

The achievements of the Alliance for Progress were few. After the death of Kennedy in 1963, the following North American officials abandoned the idea of multilateral aid for Latin America and opted instead for commerce and investment in countries considered strategic, like Brazil.*

THE MEXICAN REVOLUTION

[. . .]

Intending to punish the United States for this intervention and for the assassinations of Mexican workers along the border between the two countries, Pancho Villa, along with 300 men, attacked the North American town of Columbus in March of 1916.

The US army crossed into Mexico hoping to capture Villa, but could not accomplish its goal and had to withdraw for three reasons: the entry of the United States in the First World War, the resistance of the Mexican people that repelled the invaders, and the solidarity of the US laborers who rose up against the action.

OTHER U.S. INTERVENTIONS

The interventions of the US army were common in Latin America during those years. The United States had dominated Cuba and Puerto Rico since 1898 and hoped to extend its economic power in the Caribbean area.

They incited dictatorial movements in Central America and promoted the separation of Panama, which was a Colombian territory in 1903, with the goal of constructing the inter-ocean canal in the new republic. To consolidate its presence in the zone, it intervened militarily in the Dominican Republic in 1916 and maintained a presence there until 1930 when Rafael Leonidas Trujillo, an unconditional ally of the North American government, ascended to power.

Nicaragua was invaded by US troops in 1912 and again later in 1926. This second invasion encountered the resistance of a guerilla group headed by Augusto Cesar Sandino. When they departed from Nicaragua,

---

* Alvaro, Ana Lorena Orozco, and Efren Molina Vega. *Estudios Sociales 10*. San José: Santillana, 1999, 78.

the US forces left in power, Anastasio Somoza Garcia, who had Sandino killed in 1934.

They also invaded Haiti in 1915 and backed the dictatorial government of Jorge Ubico in Guatemala. The interventions by the North Americans caused strong sentiments of anti-imperialism in Latin America and sympathies for the revolutionary process that was underway in Russia.*

★

CUBA

Following the U.S. victory over Spain in the Spanish-American War, the United States occupied Cuba, considering it a protectorate. This text is unsparing in its criticism of U.S. interests.

The First U.S. Occupation

When the first US governor, General John R. Brooke officially took over the administration of Cuba, the United States realized one of its oldest and dearest ambitions. It considered Cuba a vital enclave in its economic, political and military strategy, as well as a testing ground where it could try out all forms of domination that it would then implement in other countries of the Americas. At that moment, however, the US hadn't yet decided on the form in which it would exert that control. Though it intended to annex the island, its plans found serious obstacles both in Cuba and in the United States.

There were those who advocated annexation, but the steps taken by the US in that direction clashed with the fierce resistance of the patriotic forces. The Cuban people had fought fierce battles for their independence for 30 years; they had been the main protagonist of Spain's defeat; they had an experienced and well organized army with a deep-rooted independence ideal, and though their most enlightened leaders had been killed, their ideas were still firmly rooted in a group of *mambi* officers, in outstanding revolutionary professionals and intellectuals, as well as in the

---

* Alvaro, Ana Lorena Orozco, and Efren Molina Vega. *Estudios Sociales 10*. San José: Santillana, 1999, 72.

people, who wouldn't passively accept the nation's collapse. On September 29th, 1898, the Liberation Army's General in Chief, Máximo Gómez who had camped with his troops in Yaguajay, Las Villas province, issued a document in which he warned that the island was "neither free nor independent yet", and stated his decision not to lay down his arms until the conclusion of the work to which he had devoted his life: the independence of Cuba.

On the other hand, there was harsh opposition to pro-annexation projects inside the United States. The Cuban people's heroic struggle had garnered the sympathy of large sectors of US society, which demanded compliance with the Joint Resolution's statement that Cuba must be free and independent. In addition, an influential portion of the US ruling classes, including the beat sugar growers from the south and the tobacco producers, saw a serious danger in Cuba's annexation. Their interests might be affected by the competition which Cuba could offer with its cane sugar and tobacco potential, products which, in case of annexation, would enter freely into the United States.

The struggle between those issues caused hesitation in the interventionist government, which couldn't determine Cuba's future status beforehand or how long the occupation would last. But, besides the form of domination that it would adopt (annexation or protectorate), the United States had big obstacles to overcome, and immediately started to clear the way.

The United States against the Cuban nation. Elimination of Cuba's representative bodies—Governor Brooke quickly strengthened his ties with both Cuban and Spanish classes as well as sectors who could be his allies: the big sugar bourgeoisie, import traders, land owners, the clergy, intellectuals with ties to those classes and sectors, as well as with a group of Cubans coming from the pro-annexation, Reformist and even pro-independence, right-wing ranks, who favored US rule.

Without consulting the Cuban people or their institutions, Brooke set up a civilian government; divided the island into seven departments ruled by US governors; named civilian governors in the provinces as well as mayors and representatives in the municipalities, and kept many Spanish colonial government officials in their posts. In addition, he ordered people to turn in their weapons and, completely ignoring the *Mambi* Army, he created a repressive force, the Rural Guard, and a municipal police corps, both at the service of the occupation forces. The Rural Guard was, from that moment on, the most loyal defender of the interests of large landowners and the big sugar bourgeoisie. The US administration created the judicial power with its courts legally based on the same civil and criminal codes of the Spanish government.

On the other hand, even before taking over the country's government, the occupation forces began maneuvering to get rid of the Cuban nation's three representative bodies: the Cuban Revolutionary Party, the Liberation Army and the Assembly of Representatives of the Cuban People in Arms (usually called Santa Cruz or Cerro Assembly, depending on where it gathered). The interventionist government ignored them completely; but they existed and were faithful forces. That's why the US used all possible means to get rid of them, something which was achieved in the first six months of 1899.

The first one to be eliminated was the Cuban Revolutionary Party. The United States relied on Tomás Estrada Palma for that. Estrada Palma had taken over as Delegate of the Cuban Revolutionary Party following Martí's death and had reduced the organization's activities to raising funds and preparing expeditions, depriving it of all political functions. After the war was over, Estrada Palma thought that those activities were no longer necessary and dissolved the party in December 1898, just a few days after the signing of the Paris Treaty. There was neither an independent country nor a democratic republic yet, the party's two main objectives, but Estrada Palma, who admired the American way of life and refused to believe that the Cuban people were able to govern themselves, explained the dissolution claiming that the objectives for which the party had been set up had already been met. Thus, one of the Cuban people's main tools to confront [the] US role disappeared.

By means of maneuvers and skillfully taking advantage of the lack of future vision and contradictions among the Cuban patriots, the occupation government managed to destroy the Liberation Army and the Cerro Assembly. Previously it had managed to bring Máximo Gómez at odds with the Assembly, which dismissed "the Great Dominican" as General in Chief.

Consequences of the war and U.S. interference—The elimination of the national liberation movement's three representative institutions allowed the United States to reach its objectives of economic and political domination. The disastrous situation of Cuba after the war also helped.

A census conducted in 1899 revealed the great human loses and destruction of the island's wealth, as well as the backwardness to which education, health and other important sectors of the country's life had been subjected by the colonial regime.

Cuba's population amounted to 1,572,000 inhabitants, a considerable reduction from four years before. It is estimated that 400 thousand people, including 100 thousand children, died from 1895 to 1898. The western part of the island was the most affected, since the war was harshest there and forced relocation more rigorous.

Seventy-five per cent of cattle were lost during those three years; 81 percent of the sugar mills were completely or partially destroyed, causing the sugar harvest to be cut by one third; tobacco production didn't even reach 20 percent of that which was achieved in 1895.

The neglect of public health and education was worse than during the years of the war. Yellow fever and other epidemics decimated the population, and there were only 904 public schools across the island.

Thousands of people who had lost their homes and other properties due to the forced relocation wandered about on the streets without shelter or employment. Most Liberation Army members were also without a job or a salary.

With this situation, many thought the help of a powerful and prosperous nation like the United States was needed to rebuild the country. And the occupation government also took advantage of that. Using the island's economic reconstruction as a pretext, the US laid the groundwork for US capital's absolute control over the Cuban economy by direct investments in that area, the restructuring of a local oligarchy which would historically be its ally, and the annulment of an incipient and weak national bourgeoisie which was never able to play an important role in the country's destiny.

★

NICARAGUA

As this text points out, long before the Sandinista-Contra conflict of the 1980s, the U.S. had a history of intervention in Nicaragua.

The Estrada Revolution and the
First North American Intervention

General Estrada managed to militarily dominate the Atlantic region. During the military operations, the government ordered the execution of two North Americans fighting alongside Estrada's troops. The North American government sent a message of protest to the Nicaraguan Chancellery via the North American diplomat, Philander Knox. In the message they made it clear that Zelaya should abandon power. He did so and the presidency fell to Doctor José Madriz. The North American government, which had broken off relations with the Nicaraguan government, refused to recognize Dr. Madriz.

On May 19, 1910 North American troops aboard the "Dubuque" and "Paduco" disembarked at Bluefields in order to protect American properties and to establish a **"neutral zone."** Estrada was permitted to take possession of the supplies at Bluefields. The regime of Dr. Madriz collapsed and Estrada entered triumphantly into Managua.

The European creditors called the debt owed them by Zelaya. Estrada gave all the guarantees to North American banks so they could lend at whatever rate to the new government. The customs became mortgages. With the goal of guaranteeing monetary stability, the Banco Nacional de Nicaraqua was created in 1912; it established the **córdoba** as monetary unit.

The conservatives made claims for the damages caused them by the Zelaya government and although they had helped Estrada they were not happy with him for being liberal. At the head of the discontented parties was the General Emiliano Chamorro.

Estrada was dismissed from the presidency. The National Assembly, presided over by the conservative Luis Mena, named Adolfo Díaz as the new president. Díaz dismissed Mena and replaced him with Emiliano Chamorro.

On August 4 of 1912 the Marines arrived in Managua with the goal of establishing order in favor of Adolfo Díaz. Bluefields was occupied militarily.

Between Managua and Granada, the liberals still held the "El Coyotepe" fortress across from Masaya that controlled the railway. When the Marines headed for Granada to convince Mena to recognize Díaz, they decided to attack it. The fortress was defended by General Benjamin

Zeledón who refused to surrender. On October 3, 1912 the fortress was bombarded and attacked with the Marines' artillery and with the aid of the government's troops. At 6:00 am on October 14 Zeledón died. His combatants were defeated. Adolfo Díaz retained his power.*

★

CARIBBEAN

This Caribbean excerpt explicitly treats the United States as an imperial power, vying with other powers for its slice of the pie: in this case, Latin America and the Caribbean.

American Business in the Caribbean

In Chapter 10 we saw how Baker and Keith discovered the profits to be made by importing bananas and other foods from the Caribbean and Central America. Other Americans were making fortunes from railways, mines and public works in Central America, often with the help of West Indian immigrant labour. But the biggest interest in expanding American business came from industrialists and bankers. They made huge profits in the United States and looked for new places where they could invest their surplus funds.

They found many opportunities in the Spanish-speaking Caribbean. During the 1880s, American bankers took over the foreign debt of the Dominican Republic. Within a few years they actually controlled the country's customs service. At the same time, millions of dollars were invested in the Cuban sugar industry. By the 1890s, American trade with the island was valued at $100 million each year. Americans had gained the most important share of the trade of Puerto Rico, Haiti, the Dominican Republic, San Salvador, Honduras and Guatemala. All together, the markets in the circum-Caribbean and the Caribbean itself made up over 40 per cent of all the American overseas investment.

---

* Romero Vargas, Dr. Germán, *Nuestra Historia,* Managua, Nicaragua: Editorial Hispamer, 1995, 97–98.

American Imperialism

This change in American opinion came at the time of a new surge of imperialism by European powers. France, Britain and Germany were active in areas which had not before been colonised. Between 1880 and 1900 they carved up the whole of the interior of Africa between them. In roughly the same period, China was forced to allow Europeans to control her ports and rivers, railway building and her customs service. Islands and coastal strips throughout the world were seized to provide coaling stations for the new steamships which linked the world-wide trading networks.

American leaders began to feel that this race to colonise the remaining free parts of the world would create a threat to American interests. Military and naval experts, such as Captain Alfred Mahan, thought that these interests should be protected by the United States becoming imperialistic herself. Mahan studied the way Britain defended her empire and overseas trade. He believed that America, too, needed a chain of overseas bases and a strong navy, backed up especially by a large force of marines who could be carried to wherever there was a threat to her interests.

So, from the late 1880s, America herself became an imperialist nation. Some of the first moves were made into the Pacific where she gained several island possessions. But most Americans thought that Latin America and the Caribbean were more important. They believed, as James Blaine stated in 1884, that 'It is the special province of this country to improve and expand its trade with the nations of America.' In 1888 Blaine, who was now Secretary of State, called a Pan-American Conference which met in Washington the following year. Blaine hoped that the USA and each of the Latin American states would sign a treaty to help each other in trade and defence. He failed because the Latin American countries would not agree to long-term arrangements binding them closely to the United States.

In the end, the only lasting result was an organisation, later called the Pan-American Union, for encouraging trade and cultural exchanges between the American nations. From Blaine's point of view the conference was a disappointment, but it was a way of announcing to the world that the United States was ready to take up the leadership of the Americas which she had claimed in the Monroe Doctrine. It was a step on the road to a full military imperialism which came about when the United States was drawn into a colonial war with Spain in 1898. The main cause of this was the state of affairs in Cuba.*

Dollar Diplomacy and War

It would have been difficult for Roosevelt to be more insulting to America's neighbours, but his language made his intentions clear. The other states in the Americas had to accept that the United States had taken over leadership in the region. In any case it had become increasingly difficult to shake off United States' pressure because of the rapid spread of American trading and business interests.

This expansion of American activity was given strong support by the government of Howard Taft who became president in 1908. Subsidies were given to shipping, public works and mining and construction companies which wished to invest in the Caribbean or Latin America. American-owned plantations were helped by placing high customs duties on sugar, bananas, coffee and other crops which did not come from areas where Americans had investments in agriculture.

Taft spoke of this policy as 'dollar diplomacy'. By helping the economic development of poorer neighbours, the United States could gain influence and cut down the interference of European powers without having to use force. Dollar diplomacy, he believed, was a better way of carrying out America's foreign policy than the threatening attitude of Roosevelt's Corollary.

However, Latin American and Caribbean states still fell in debt to European bankers and many still suffered from political upheavals and disorders. So direct interference by the American government continued. Then, in 1914, war broke out in Europe. The United States entered the war in 1917 but, before that, she was concerned that European powers would seize positions in the Americas as naval bases or for supplies of raw materials and food. To prevent this, and to check any threat to her own defences, the United States herself sent troops to several neighbouring countries to ensure that their governments remained friendly.

---

* Claypole, William, and John Robottom. *Caribbean Story, Bk. 2: The Inheritors.* Kingston: Carlong, 1994, 171–72.

PART IV

World War I

20

Causes of World War I

Although the murder of the Archduke Franz Ferdinand is often cited as the beginning of the Great War, the actual causes were far more numerous. These European texts outline some of these. Nearly a century after the fact—and despite the integration of Europe—it is remarkable how different these explanations are in their approaches and points of emphasis.

★

FRANCE

This French textbook describes the nationalistic developments at the turn of the century and up to the eve of the war, and how blind patriotic nationalism and fear had spread across the European continent.

Patriotism: A State Religion

A patriotic education was guaranteed by the schools and the army. All over Europe elementary education came under the state's supervision. School books and those for youth taught a love of country and taught an ethic of sacrifice. In France republican values were exalted; in the monarchical regimes it was fidelity to the sovereign and to the reigning dynasty that were glorified. At school, the regional dialects were suppressed in favor of a unifying national language. The same held true for the army.

The government encouraged a veritable state religion, worshipping the flag and multiplying the national holidays and commemorative monuments. In France, July 14th became the national holiday in 1882; the centennial of the French Revolution was celebrated in 1889. In Italy, the secular state multiplied the celebrations: State holidays, King and Queen's birthdays, pilgrimage of 1884 to the tomb of Victor-Emmanuel II. A patriotic ideology was created.*

International Relations Were Disrupted by the Explosion of Nationalism

The active nationalism deeply modified the traditional activities of European diplomacy. The ambitions of the old countries (Great Britain, France, Austria, Russia) as well as those of the new (Germany, Italy), big and small alike (Greece, Serbia, Romania, Bulgaria), became a web of conflicting interests which multiplied the opportunities for conflict. The great powers sought to use or eliminate the smaller nations.

A general sense of disquiet spread everywhere. Aggressive public declarations and demonstrations in one country alarmed the neighboring countries. Germany was alarmed by French jingoism and, conversely, France by its neighbor's Pan-Germanism. Russian expansion caused fear in Germany and Austria. Each country felt threatened by the other. The sentiment of fear and the impression of aggression were only augmented by the national presses. The exasperation with the perceived hostilities explains the arms race, the build up of troops and the multiplication, in each country, of military laws. Each country was prepared to defend its own national territory.†

---

* Baylac, M.-H., et al. *Histoire—1ʳᵉ*. Paris: Bordas, 1997, 134.
† Baylac, M.-H., et al. *Histoire—1ʳᵉ*. Paris: Bordas, 1997, 140.

★

GERMANY

In contrast to the French selection, this German excerpt focuses on the details of the alliances and agreements that helped precipitate the war.

"July Crisis 1914 and Declarations of War"

[. . .]

Austria-Hungary wanted to take the murder of its heir to the throne as an opportunity to use armed means to eliminate Serbia, which had tolerated the secret organization held responsible. Because the protective power Russia stood behind Serbia, it [Austria-Hungary] had to attempt to prevent a Russian intervention. That only appeared possible by common action with Germany. The German Empire answered an inquiry corresponding to this on the 5th of July with the so-called **blank check,** a promise of common action also in the case of attack, which was not covered by the Dual Alliance: the defensive union was unnecessarily expanded to an offensive union. Encouraged by the German promise, Austria-Hungary gave Serbia an **ultimatum** on the punishment of the assassin of Franz Ferdinand. Under the impression of a French guarantee of loyalty to the alliance (France's blank check), Russia now decided to support Serbia. Although Serbia agreed to the ultimatum except on a minor point, Austria-Hungary declared war against it on the 28th of July. The following day Russia ordered mobilization against Austria-Hungary. Because Kaiser Wilhelm perceived the Russian mobilization as a threat to Germany, he gave Russia the ultimatum to reverse course and France the ultimatum to remain neutral in a German-Russian conflict. As neither achieved its objective, **Germany declared war against Russia on August 1st and against France on August 3rd.** *

"War Aims"

After the Imperial government under Bethmann Hollweg decided, in light of the shaken Dual Alliance, to engage in war in order to secure Germany's

* Jager, Dr. Wolfgang, et al. *Kursbuch Geschichte.* Berlin: Cornelsen, 2000, 352–53.

great power status, the Empire made a move from the calculated risk of intensifying the conflict to a preventive war, in order to gain the military advantage primarily over Russia in the two front situation. Begun without intentions of territorial gain, the initial successes soon led to an expansion of war aims. According to the ideas of the military in the September program, the partial German hegemony in the middle of Europe was to be forever secured and the colonies multiplied by a vassal status of Belgium and Poland.

All war-waging powers saw the conditions for a lasting peace in their war aims, so that the intentions that connected the individual states to the war, proved themselves to be actual obstacles in the way of a cease-fire and peace.*

★

ITALY

This Italian text places Italy's historical experiences and role at the center of an explanation of the war's origins.

Two Crises in the Balkans: Simple Local Conflicts

The Balkan Peninsula had been the theatre for a number of indirect clashes amongst the European powers. Austria, Russia and Turkey—all of whom were anxious to extend their influence into the region—faced off against the new nations born out of the dismemberment of the Turkish empire, nations that, unlike Italy and Germany, had not yet completed the process of independence and national unity. The first major crisis arose in 1909 when Austria annexed Bosnia-Herzegovina, a territory it had administered for some 30 years. Serbia protested bitterly, for it would have liked to claim the territory as part of its plan to create a Great Serbia. Russia also protested, but did not intervene: as a natural ally of Serbia, with which it shared the Christian-orthodox faith and Slavic blood, Russia feared that on this occasion Germany would side with its Austro-Hungarian allies.

The second serious crisis emerged when Italy claimed Libya from the

---

* Jager, Dr. Wolfgang, et al. *Kursbuch Geschichte*. Berlin: Cornelsen, 2000, 354.

Turks. The Balkan countries, taking advantage of the Turco-Ottoman Empire's state of weakness, seized a number of its other territories and then turned against one another in a fight to divide the booty (First and Second Balkan Wars, 1912–1913). These two crises, as dramatic as they were, both resolved themselves without a major war breaking out between the larger European powers.

A Third Slavic Pole in the Austro-Hungarian Empire and the Assassination in Sarajevo

During these same years the Archduke Francisco Ferdinand, heir to the Imperial Hapsburg throne, was seeking to foster new stability within the Empire. To the Austrian and Hungarian power centers, he wanted to add a third: the Slavs, freshly liberated from Hungarian domination. The Archduke's project was met with stern resistance by Hungary, who saw its power dwindling, and by Serbia, who saw its dreams of Balkan hegemony dashed. It was in these tense times, during the course of a visit to Bosnia, that Francisco Ferdinand and his wife were assassinated in Sarajevo by the Serbian student Gavrilo Princip (June 28, 1914).

The War Fosters a New and Virtuous Form of Humanitarianism

The new world that the war promised to create was an enticing one. Indeed, each man aspired to participate first-hand in world history and to live that unique moment in which his heroic acts would allow him to experience life as a free man, a protagonist of his own destiny. The war, then, was a sort of burning furnace into which men could throw themselves, without the aim of victory or power—for on the battlefield he might lose his life. It was for this reason that the war could generate a new form of humanitarianism that would be both virtuous and moral. Ultimately the war appeared to create a sense of fraternal brotherhood. Men and women, rich and poor, intellectuals and uneducated all clasped hands warmly. No one could be considered a foreigner anymore, for they all belonged to a single nation.

In truth, however, the war did not eradicate differences between people: the rich remained rich and the poor remained poor, nevertheless they banded together to face the same destiny of suffering and death. And in the end, little by little, the enthusiastic days of August was replaced by periods of struggle and desperation.*

★

GREAT BRITAIN

In this selection, Great Britain focuses far more attention on the diplomacy surrounding the beginning of the conflict, diminishing the impact of Archduke Ferdinand's assassination. This text also raises the additional factor of a potential "Irish civil war" at home, which the British had to consider.

As war broke out in 1914, Edward Grey was deemed to have failed in maintaining the 'concert of Europe'. Any assessment of this needs to start with the European events which led to the outbreak of war. The Balkans had been fomenting since 1912, when the Balkan League of Serbia, Bulgaria, Greece and Montenegro had attacked Turkey in the first war, rapidly followed by a second which broke out because Bulgaria was dissatisfied with the spoils they received. The results were an angry Bulgaria and a much enlarged Serbia whose vigorous nationalism would prove a threat to the Austrian Empire. In hindsight, the dangers were clear; Austria-Hungary felt Serbia should be silenced as nationalism would destroy Franz Josef's Empire, and Vienna was getting assurances of support from the Kaiser. If Austria-Hungary crushed Serbia, Russia would certainly become involved as the defender of Slav nationalism and Germany would seize the moment to attack Russia which it saw as a growing threat. There was still no feeling of panic even when Franz Ferdinand (the heir to the Austrian throne) was assassinated in Sarajevo on 28 June. There was an attitude of 'why should a shooting halfway across Europe cause concern to the British when there was the possibility of an Irish civil war on the doorstep?'

Perhaps the mood changed in the Foreign Office when, on 23 July, Austria sent an ultimatum to Serbia, although no one would have thought so on the floor of the House of Commons when Lloyd George claimed

---

* Drago, Marco and Andrea Boroli (dir.), *Storia,* Novara: Instituto de Geographico de Agostini, 1998, 68–75.

that relations with Germany were so very good. Grey was trying to encourage the powers to attend a conference in London, to no avail.

28 July   Austria declares war on Serbia
30 July   Russia mobilises its armies
31 July   German ultimatum to Russia demanding a stop to
             mobilisation
 1 August Germany declares war on Russia.

What was Grey to do? As a public policy, Grey repeated that the government had made no commitment to France's defence. However, Grey's secretive approach to the Entente's military conversations must have been perceived by the French as some sort of commitment. The *Times* debated what might happen if France's coast was attacked and wondered 'if the word honour should be erased from the English language'. On 1 August the Cabinet was still wavering, repeating its 'no commitment position'. But the tide was turning towards involvement. What sealed it was the German request that troops should be given passage through Belgium. Belgium refused and Grey under some strain, told the House of Commons on 3 August that not only Belgian independence was at stake, but also the future of Europe which might be under the domination of one power. That would be an intolerable position for Britain. On 4 August, an ultimatum was sent to Germany and in the end only two members of the Cabinet resigned. Both Morley and Burns argued that Britain would have a free hand if no military conversations with France and Russia had taken place.

Others said that Grey should have been more resolute and decisive—a firm alliance would have deterred Germany. However, Germany was undeterred from invading Belgium and Grey would have found it difficult to swing the Cabinet and public behind him if he had attempted an Anglo-French alliance. As it was, the decision was taken out of his hands by the attack on Belgian neutrality. It enabled Grey as he said 'to bring the country into it [the war] unitedly'. Had there ever been a real alternative to the way Grey had conducted Britain's foreign policy?*

Even today, over 70 years later, it is far from clear exactly what was the real cause of the war or who was to blame. In 1919 the Allies made Germany

* Murphy, Derrick, et al. *Britain: 1815–1918*. London: Collins, 1998, 353–54.

take all the blame for starting the war. Modern experts agree that the German military were, indeed, 'thirsting for war and no longer to be restrained'. But, as you have seen, the celebrations at the outbreak of war were not confined to Berlin or Munich. Nor were the Serbians, Russians, French and British entirely free from blame either. The general atmosphere in 1914 was tense. The reasons why are not hard to find.

1 **The Alliance System.** France and Germany hated each other. The French bitterly resented the fact that Alsace and Lorraine had been taken by Germany after her defeat in the Franco-Prussian War in 1871. This is why both countries sought alliances with friendly nations. Germany was particularly concerned about the threat from her colossal eastern neighbour, Russia. As a consequence, Europe separated into two armed camps. On the one hand, Germany, Austria-Hungary and Italy—the Central or Triple Alliance powers. On the other hand, France, Russia and Britain—the Triple *Entente* powers.

2 **Balkan Nationalism.** Russian and Austrian rivalry in the Balkans was another potential cause of war. The Austro-Hungarian empire was already in decline. It was further weakened when Russia encouraged the Slav nationalists who wanted to create a Pan-Slav union of all the Slav peoples under the protection of Russia. Since many Slavs lived in Austria-Hungary, the Austrians saw Slav nationalism, especially in Serbia, as a serious threat to their empire and a potential cause of war.

3 **The Arms Race.** Every major continental power had a huge conscript army which could be mobilised at a moment's notice. Guns, shells and bullets had been stockpiled in case of war. This arms race made the prospect of war more rather than less likely, since commanders on both sides were keen to use their new weapons and to try out their new armies. British and German rivalry in building dreadnought battleships also contributed to the arms race. Although Britain had only a small professional army, she did have the most powerful navy in the world to defend her islands and empire overseas. By 1909, Britain had eight dreadnoughts and Germany had seven. Influential voices in Britain urged the Government to build more. By 1914, Britain had 29 and Germany had 17.

4 **Colonial Rivalry.** Germany wanted a colonial empire to rival the British and French empires. Since most of the world's surface had already been claimed by the colonial powers, any growth in the size of the German Empire could only be made at the expense of existing empires, such as those of France or Britain.

5 The Schlieffen Plan. Germany feared an attack on two fronts—from France in the west and from Russia in the east. The Kaiser regarded it as essential to find a way of meeting this threat without splitting the German forces in two. However, General von Schlieffen had calculated that it would take Russia, with her primitive railway system, at least six weeks to mobilise her armies and prepare for war. This would give Germany enough time to knock France quickly out of the war, if the German army made a surprise attack through neutral Belgium where the French least expected it.

The acceptance of the Schlieffen Plan meant that Germany would always have to start a war with France and Russia, since it would defeat the object of the plan to wait until they had mobilised their armies and were ready to fight. The main snag was that Britain guaranteed Belgium's neutrality. Would Britain enter a war if Belgium was attacked?

6 German Militarism. Many high-ranking German commanders believed that fighting a major war now, sooner than later, was essential. Russia was already modernising and expanding her armies and her railway system. She would soon be a formidable enemy. At a secret meeting on 8 December 1912, the Kaiser, "predicted that if the Austrians did not now face up to the Serbian menace, they would have considerable trouble from the Slav minorities within the Austro-Hungarian monarchy: the fleet must henceforth look on England as an enemy. Moltke [the Army chief] regarded war as unavoidable, 'the sooner the better': Tirpitz [the Navy chief] still wanted another eighteen months before the navy was ready." *†

Britain did not want to go to war in 1914. The war she had to fight turned out to be far more destructive and lasted much longer than anyone had dared imagine before it started. Though Britain emerged on the winning side, the war had many damaging consequences and the post-war period of adjustment was extremely difficult.‡

* Sauvain, Philip. *The Modern World: 1914–1980.* Cheltenham: Stanley Thornes, 1989, 2–15.

† Palmer, Alan, *The Kaiser,* Weidenfeld and Nicolson, 1978.

‡ Roberts, Martin. *Britain 1846–1964: The Challenge of Change.* London: Oxford University Press, 2001, 161.

21

The Great War

Most U.S. textbooks focus on the brutality of the war. And despite the late entrance of U.S. soldiers into the conflict, U.S. textbooks are unanimous that U.S. intervention decided the outcome of the war. But there remains disagreement over who actually "won" the "war to end all wars."

★

FRANCE

As elsewhere, this French excerpt is notable for the degree to which it subjects the French experience to criticism.

From a War of Movement to a War of Position

In four months the illusion of a short war evaporated. The German strategy, based on the Schlieffen plan of speed and rapidity, was designed to pass through Belgium in order to encircle the French Army before turning toward Russia. The better equipped Germans outflanked the French defenses and threatened Paris by September 2. After their failure in Lorraine (plan XVII), the French, under the command of Joffre, led a victorious counter-offensive in the Marne in which they were facilitated by the Russian attack in Eastern Prussia which forced the Germans to fight on two fronts. In the West, the French and Germans tried unsuccessfully to outflank one another all the way through Flanders; it was the "race to the sea." In December, the front stabilized and dug in from the North Sea to Switzerland. [...]

Attempts at wearing down the enemy had failed by 1916. The strategy shifted to totally exhausting the enemy, to inflicting the most horrific losses possible in order to drive them to seek negotiations. From February to July the Germans tried to bleed the French Army white at Verdun, a key to the French defenses. Pétain resisted. From July to September the Franco-British fought the Battle of the Somme. The German lines were hardly affected. All armies taken together, losses on the Western Front for 1916 totaled more than 1.7 million victims.*

New Forms of War

On the ground the front followed the lines of trenches. Tied together by passageways and protected by a network of barbed wire and mine fields, they faced each other for more than 700 km. The "poilu"† lived there in deplorable sanitary conditions victims of the mud, rats and lice. Heavy artillery became capital in the effort to bombard the enemy's trenches or to prepare the way for an assault. The weaponry grew more brutal with the addition of grenades, machine guns, mortars and eventually tanks (1916). Asphyxiating gasses were used as well as flame throwers. In order to protect the soldiers, the metal helmet made its first appearance.‡

National unity lasted into 1916. In an epoch of exalted national sentiment it was a sense of resolve that dominated the two camps. Each side

---

* Baylac, M.-H., et al. *Histoire—1ʳᵉ*. Paris: Bordas, 1997, 200.

† *Poilu* (literally *hairy*) was a nickname given to the French soldiers on the front during WWI. Body hair was considered a sign of virility at the time, thus the name was meant as a compliment meaning "brave."

‡ Baylac, M.-H., et al. *Histoire—1ʳᵉ*. Paris: Bordas, 1997, 202.

felt itself attacked and showed itself ready to defend the threatened home-land. Everywhere the socialists stood resolutely behind their governments. In France, it was the Sacred Union. To sustain morale, opinion was cen-sored in the mail, press and books as well as subjected to propaganda through film and song: it was nothing short of "brain washing." The mili-tary leaders became cult figures while the pacifist movements, begun in Switzerland, had only a small impact. [. . .]

The mutinies increased on the front in 1917. This increase was due to several factors including the breakdown of the Allied offensives on the Western Front [. . .] and the failure of German submarine warfare.

These mutineers revealed the weariness of the combatants and their re-fusal to be sacrificed in some vain offensive meant to wear down the enemy. In France, the repression was relatively moderate (49 executions). Pétain improved conditions for the soldiers and banned the useless as-saults. In Russia, numerous regiments fraternized with the enemy while desertions multiplied.*

★

CANADA

This Canadian text gives credit to the bravery of the Canadian soldiers who fought and suffered far from home. Its celebratory tone contrasts sharply with other ex-cerpts in this section.

The Great War

The entrance of Canada into the First World War marked a triumph of sorts for Canadian imperialism. Canada did not make its own declaration of war, but simply joined the British war effort. Before it ended, the war had inflicted extremely heavy Canadian casualties: 60,661 killed in action and 172,000 wounded out of some 620,000 Canadians in uniform drawn from a population of only 8 million.

[. . .]

---

* Baylac, M.-H., et al. *Histoire—1ʳᵉ*. Paris: Bordas, 1997, 204.

Canadians entered the war with no idea of its ultimate length, intensity, or futile savagery. The initial enthusiasm of English-speaking Canadians assumed a short and swift defeat of Germany and its allies. By 1917 support for the war effort emphasized the extent of the sacrifices already made. Canada's military contribution was substantial. Nevertheless, Canadians who fought in Europe were almost exclusively volunteers. Serving as the shock troops of the British empire, Canadians achieved an enviable reputation for bravery and fierceness. Their commanders continually placed them in the most difficult situations, and they performed well. The list of battles at which they fought heroically (and at heavy cost) was a long one, beginning at Ypres in 1915 and continuing through to the Belgian town of Mons, where fighting ended for the Canadians at 11 a.m. on 11 November 1918.*

It was at the second battle Ypres, Belgium, in 1915, that Canadian soldiers received a brutal introduction to the nature of modern war. In defiance of international agreement, the Germans had decided to use a lethal weapon—chlorine gas. A British general had been informed of this possibility, but refused to pay attention to such reports. On the afternoon of April 22, thick, yellowish clouds of chlorine began to drift toward the Allied forces. French colonial troops were the first to breathe in the asphyxiating gas. They broke ranks and fled, leaving a 6-km gap in the Allied ranks. The Canadians moved in, and, with handkerchiefs soaked in urine held to their faces, tried to plug the gap until reinforcements arrived. Though they too fell back, their stand was crucial in slowing the German advance. Fighting continued for three more weeks with mounting casualties. Yet in the end the German and Allied lines remained exactly where they had been at the start of the battle. All the deaths—German, British, French, Canadian—had been for nothing.

[. . .]

The successful capture of Vimy Ridge in France in 1917 shines brightest in the battle honours won by Canada's soldiers. At Vimy German soldiers had occupied a ridge overlooking British army units below. As in other

---

* Bumsted, J.M. *A History of the Canadian Peoples.* Toronto: Oxford University Press, 1998, 260–61.

points along the Front, they had fortified it very thoroughly and had even dug an underground railway to supply their bigger guns. Two previous Allied attempts to take the ridge, one of the most important in the Front, had failed. Overall command of the operation was the responsibility of British General Julian Byng, together with his Canadian subordinate, Arthur Currie. In preparing the assault, they made meticulous plans. Surveillance flights by aircraft yielded information about German positions that made possible detailed maps. Nightly raiding parties, often with high casualties, into no-man's land also provided information about German positions. [. . .] The raid began with a heavy one-week bombardment, which made it impossible to supply German trenches. These preparations paid off with the capture of the ridge after two hours of intense fighting, even though casualties were high. Other battles were yet to come but the taking of Vimy eclipsed them all. At Vimy Canadians gained the reputation for being excellent shock troops; in subsequent engagements, when Germans learned Canadians were coming they realized that a major assault was planned.*

★

GREAT BRITAIN

Like many of the other texts on WWI, this British textbook covers the war of attrition and the war at sea. It naturally focuses on the British role, but focuses far more on strategy and tactics than on the experience of the war itself.

The Germans expected their carefully planned advance on Paris through Belgium to win them a quick and decisive victory. However, as agreed during the pre-war Anglo-French military conversations, the small British Expeditionary Force (BEF), 100,000 strong, entered Belgium to fight alongside the French. It first met the enemy in Belgium near Mons but was swept back with the French by the surging German advance. The instinct of the British commander, Sir John French, was to desert his French colleagues and head for the safety of the Channel ports. However, General Kitchener, ordered him to keep in contact with his French allies.

* Francis, Daniel, and Sonia Riddoch. *Our Canada: A Social and Political History.* Scarboroug: Pippin, 1995, 452–54.

Consequently, the BEF marched furiously south to take part in the Battle of the Marne.

The part it actually played was decidedly odd. The main German armies were wide apart and struggling to hold off the counter-attack of the French. The BEF found itself advancing into the gap between the German forces and experienced few casualties. The Germans then decided that their strategic position was fragile and retreated. As they reached the River Aisne, they discovered that by digging trenches they could, with their machine guns, hold off their pursuers fairly easy. The British and French then tried without success to prevent them from extending their defensive line to the Channel.

Note: Gallipoli and the Easterners

The 'easterner' strategy was an imaginative one. This was the plan. Compared to Germany, the Turkish Empire and Austria-Hungary were weak, so:

- Seize the Gallipoli peninsula to the south of Constantinople.
- Take Constantinople.
- Link with Russian forces and, by a co-ordinated attack defeat Austria-Hungary.
- Germany would then have to make peace.

Unfortunately, the attack on Gallipoli was an appalling bungle. Allied troops had to be withdrawn having failed to get off the beaches. Winston Churchill, whose plan it was, resigned from the government and the 'westerners' led by generals like Haig kept a grip on strategy. Victory would be won, they insisted, by a breakthrough on the Western Front.*

★

ITALY

A perspective rarely discussed in American textbooks, this Italian text discusses what life was like for the Italians and their soldiers who fought against the Central

* Roberts, Martin. *Britain 1846–1964: The Challenge of Change.* London: Oxford University Press, 2001, 161–62.

Powers. It offers a stark contrast to the jaunty tone of the Canadian and British excerpts.

Heroism for Few; Hunger, Death, and Rebellion for Many

The war had by this time lost the fascination that had spurred the young bourgeoisie to enlist voluntarily. It remained the theatre of heroic action for very few parties: the Sturmtruppen (the German assault force), the Italian Arditi,* and the warplane pilots. Millions of farmers and workers accepted the war grudgingly as one accepts a natural disaster that cannot be avoided and whose weight must be borne.

Otherwise, in two and a half years the war had consumed all provisions and revolt had insinuated itself almost everywhere. At home, food and fuel were rationed; hunger and cold killed their first victims, and the people began to protest against the high cost of living and the war. On the front lines the troops protested the useless massacres: the number of draft-dodgers and deserters rose dramatically. The situation was such that in France, after the Battle of the Somme, entire platoons of soldiers were shot as punishment for the army's failure.

Arrival at the Front

In order to understand the mindset of the soldiers, it is enough to know about their lives in the trenches—structures that, although intended to be temporary, became permanent. The soldiers arrived at the front either by train or bus. As soon as they jumped off the transport, they were divided into platoons and sent to the trenches. They could hear the far-away thunder of the cannons while an airplane flies overhead. With their rifles on their backs, they stepped quickly. The luckiest soldiers were sent to the third line, but even those who end up in the second line wouldn't have such a bad time of it. The others, those soldiers who are sent to the front lines, weren't sure that they would see the dawn of the next day.

---

* The *Arditi* were elite Italian assault troops used during WWI. *Arditi* means brave or bold in Italian.

Life and Death

The corporals give the order to run and then shout "hit the ground!": a hissing sound is followed by a crash and suddenly the earth is torn open by grenades. A bit further away you can see the communication trenches.

In the sky above floats a balloon: on board there are two observers with binoculars whose gaze is fixed on the far-off enemy. BOOM!—the aerostat is hit and transformed into a ball of flames as it falls to earth. This is how the newly-arrived soldiers learn to recognize the death that is announced in the sky.

There are no longer any women at the front: the ones remaining were in the back lines, the auxiliaries or the Red Cross. In and around the trenches, all that is left of the women's presence is a memory or perhaps a photograph tucked securely away in a pocket over the heart.

Life in the Trenches: The Futile Assault

Very little food and weeks on end wearing the same clothes, without showering: in the winter mud, snow and frost; in the summer scorching heat and the stink of the latrines. From the trenches now, you can even see the enemy; he's not so far away. If it weren't for the continual thundering of the artillery that eats at your nerves, you could even talk to him. But it isn't good to linger on, staring: a sniper might pop up—and they shoot to kill. The assault usually begins at dawn. Intensive artillery fire hits enemy positions in order to open up a passage. But the enemy knows what is about to happen and prepares to face the assault. The soldiers head into battle armed with special scissors designed to cut barbed wire. They try to avoid mines; they fire haphazardly at the slightest noise . . . they see the enemy: he is there, he is a man, and yet they attack him, beating him with their bayonets. But, as it always happens, if they get through the first line, they are pushed back at the second. Unless they are dead or wounded, they return to the trenches. Night falls: crusted with blood and mud, the soldiers certainly don't feel like singing—perhaps just a smoke before drifting off to sleep.*

*Drago, Marco, and Andrea Boroli (dir). *Storia*. Novara: Instituto de Geografico de Agostini, 1998, 76–77.

★

GERMANY

Every country recognizes the horrors of WWI. But the especially jaded perspective of this excerpt must be read in light of Germany's 20th-century history of militarism and defeat.

Artillery and machine guns, battle cruisers and submarines, as well as the first tanks and bombers led to an extermination of people and materials, which exceeded anything previously imagined. Poison gas, first employed in 1915, was one of the especially dreadful battle means employed. It signified the great downfall of the values of civilization in the consciousness of contemporaries. The First World War bore the traits of a **total war** from the beginning. The war-waging nations mobilized every member of their societies for the war at the front and on the "homefront," which led to a shaky separation between the military and the civil sphere. In the course of the war almost the entire civilian population, male and female, was involved in the war, both in the armaments factories and in the "normal" work positions, where women replaced men who were drafted into the military. "The present war," noted the French ambassador in St. Petersburg on August 20, 1914, "does not belong to those that can be ended by a political treaty [. . .]; it is a war of life and death, in which every fighting nation puts its national existence at stake." The First World War meant the **breakdown of the system of states,** but not simply because all great powers were part of it, as a hundred years before in the Napoleonic Wars. Rather all the states and peoples involved felt and experienced it as an **existential struggle for survival.** As varied as they were in the details, the war goals on both sides aimed at a destruction of the former international order: to the German Empire it was not only about territorial gain, but about an unchallenged hegemony in Europe as a starting point for the achievement of a position as a world power; the opposing coalition wanted the great power status of the German Empire in Europe destroyed forever, because, in their eyes, it had shown itself to be a notorious disrupter of peace. Therefore, the only war aim that mattered was the complete subjugation of the enemy nation.

At the beginning there was great enthusiasm for war in every country.

As the anticipated short war turned into a long war with an unforeseeable end, all war-waging parties began using directed **war propaganda.** This propaganda attempted to drum into the population that it was not only political interests at stake, but collective, national value systems as well: about the "essence" of one's own nation against the foreign power (perceived as threatening), about civilization against barbarity, about Germans against Slavs. In this manner they hoped to strengthen the "will to hold out" in their own people and to cripple the will to fight among the enemy's troops and civilian population. Actually this war patriotism developed a tremendous power of integration, which concealed the tensions within populations and consequently deepened the chasms between the nations. Not since the wars of religion in the 16th and 17th centuries had the population been drawn in such measure into the occurrences of war as both fighters and sufferers—and that meant **mobilization, nationalization, fanaticism,** in completely new dimensions.*

---

* Jager, Dr. Wolfgang, et al. *Kursbuch Geschichte*. Berlin: Cornelsen, 2000, 359–60.

22

Aftermath of the War

★

GERMANY

When Germany first sued for peace, it did so according to President Wilson's 14-point peace plan. The inability to accommodate this peace plan at Versailles has been the source of much speculation. What if President Wilson's 14 points had been strictly applied and respected? In the end, this German text, like others elsewhere, draws a straight line between Versailles and two new developments: decolonization and World War II.

"The Endangered Peace"

"Like everything good, war is difficult to bring to an end at first. When it flourishes, it's tenacious; then the people recoil from peace like the dice player from stopping, because then it must be tallied, what they have lost." The playwright Bertolt Brecht (1898–1956) wrote these words for the character of a farm hand from the Thirty Years War in one of his theatre pieces. But they also appropriately describe the First World

War and the subsequent efforts at reaching a stable peace among the peoples.

At first there were great hopes for a more peaceful and better world, which was nourished by two events during the still ongoing war actions. In 1917 the United States entered the war on the side of the Entente, which had unified France and Great Britain (among others) against the central powers of Germany, Austria-Hungary, and Bulgaria. Thus did the USA decide the war in favor of the French and British. In this context the American President **Woodrow T. Wilson** (1856–1924, President 1913–1921) formulated his goals for international politics in a **14 Point Program for World Peace.** Seen from today, the program was pioneering as it meant a radical departure from the old principles of European great power politics. It called namely for the general enforcement of liberal democracy, the respect of peoples' right of self determination, the creation of a League of Nations as a tribunal among the nations, as well as justice for the colonial peoples. The second event of the year 1917 that was significant for international politics was the **Revolution in Russia,** from which the Communists emerged as victors. For the first time there was a socialist state in the world. The new Soviet power under **Vladimir I. Lenin** (1870–1924) proclaimed immediate withdraw from the war and stood up for a peace on all sides without territorial alterations and war reparations, as well as for the emancipation of all colonial peoples.

The lofty goals of President Wilson quickly moved to the background in the peace negotiations begun by the victorious powers, without the participation of Russia, in **1919** at the **Versailles** palace. This dampened hopes. The victorious European states held to their national and power politics ideas from the pre-war era and wanted to protect themselves militarily from Germany, pressing for reparation payments. The conquered powers did not take part in the negotiations; the decisions of the peace conference were pronounced to them. Proceeding in this manner, and the great size of the reparations, precipitated great outrage, especially in Germany, which could always be mobilized for political purposes in the domestic realm. The call for revision of the Versailles "humiliation and dictate peace" developed into a battle cry with great popular appeal and became a heavy burden for the young democracy of Weimar.

The **League of Nations,** established on the suggestion of President Wilson, could hardly influence the practice of international politics. The conquered powers as well as communist Russia were denied admittance. Out of disappointment in a peace treaty that it considered false, the USA remained distant to the League—against the wishes of Wilson. And the constraint of unanimity rendered the League practically helpless, making it nothing more than a forum of international discussion.

The **struggle over nationality** [as it related to state borders] had been one of the causes of the outbreak of the First World War. But long beforehand European peoples like the Poles, Czechs, Slovaks, Serbs and Croats, as well as the Arabic people in the Ottoman Empire had strove for **national self determination.** In order to promote the general acceptance of nation-state principles in this part of the world as well, the victorious powers dissolved Austria-Hungary and the Ottoman Empire, took parts from the old Russian Empire, and created totally new states. Nevertheless the principle of self determination of the peoples, which was promulgated as a fundamental principle in the formation of new states and guarantor of peace, quickly found its limits. In reality there were mixed areas of nations everywhere. Moreover, many people in the new and old states did not identify with the socio-political states and border delineations. For example, many Germans did not come to terms with the new borders of Poland, Czechoslovakia, and Austria. The Arabic peoples, on the other hand, did not receive the proposed right of self determination and were placed under British and French administration. In the eastern Mediterranean this led to points of contention, which are to the present day the cause of armed conflicts.

From an economic standpoint, all European states had lost the First World War, entirely in contrast to the USA. And the **political supremacy of the Europeans in the World was broken.** The European great powers had used the people in the colonies for their war and in return had given them the promise of greater independence. As this failed to materialize, resistance began to stir in the colonies, which set in motion the long process of **Decolonization.**

After the First World War, the **leading role in world politics** was taken over by the so-called **Wing powers** [meaning geographically peripheral to central Europe] **of the USA and the Soviet Union,** which were to determine international politics till the political upheavals of the years 1989/91.*

---

* Jager, Dr. Wolfgang, et al. *Kursbuch Geschichte.* Berlin: Cornelsen, 2000, 360–61.

★

FRANCE

There is a graph included in most French history textbooks covering this war that represents a population chart of the French citizenry. A normal population graph looks like a gently rounded mountain; the elderly population at the top is smaller than the younger populations toward the bottom. In France, this population graph has shown a severe hourglass figure that slowly creeps up as the WWI generation ages. So many French were killed during the war that demographic trends were altered for most of the 20th century.

The Cost of the War and the Decline of Europe

A HUMAN, MATERIAL, AND FINANCIAL DISASTER

The war cost Europe more than 8 million dead and 6 million injured. It also led to a deficit in births since most men old enough to be fathers had been at the front. 1918 Europe included 4 million widows and 8 million orphans.

Material losses were considerable. They affected all areas of combat. In certain regions everything needed to be rebuilt. France and the United Kingdom lost a significant portion of their merchant navies that they had to rebuild. Used to the point of being worn out, industrial and transport material would have to be replaced.

The financial and monetary situation of Europe was dire. To finance their supplies and war materials, the belligerent nations had to revert to domestic and foreign loans leading to a considerable public debt whose interest would have to be paid. They practiced inflation, which provoked depreciation in European currencies against the dollar. Furthermore, after the conflict the public financial outlay remained high due to the pensions of war victims and the cost of rebuilding the devastated areas, which led in turn to the European states seeking loans.

The world ended up completely reversed after the war. Having once been the world's bankers, the Europeans were now the principal debtors to the Americans who owned half the world's gold.

EUROPE'S DECLINE

Europe lost its economic dominance. Formerly an exporter, it became an importer of agricultural and industrial products during the war. The conflict caused it to lose its supremacy in maritime transportation and on the world market in general.

The obliteration of Europe benefited Japan and, even more, the United States. Japan became Europe's chief competitor in the Pacific, Southeast Asia and China. Its trade surplus increased its gold reserves. But it was the United States above everyone that benefited from the war. American businessmen organized a program to corner the world markets, consolidating industry, trade, and banks. The American fleet, now second in the world, facilitated this expansion especially in South America, a market formerly reserved for the Europeans. The United States rivaled Great Britain in its role as depot and hub of trade. New York replaced London as the capital of world finance just as the dollar now rivaled the sterling.

The decline of European influence was also felt in its colonies. The colonies had participated, voluntarily or not, in the military effort of their metropole. They sent men to the front or into their vacated positions and increased their agricultural production in order to supply Europe. The colonized people expected an improvement in their lot at the end of the conflict. The hopes for independence were only encouraged by the Wilsonian principles of a people's self-determination and by the communist doctrine. Nationalist demonstrations occurred in 1919 in India, Egypt and North Africa. Even if they didn't succeed, they nevertheless marked a fundamental turning point in the relationship between colonizers and colonized.*

★

NIGERIA

Europe's colonies in Africa supplied a number of troops for the European war. For most African soldiers, it was the first trip they had ever taken to Europe; for many, it was also the last. Perhaps the first casualty among the African troops was the myth of European "civilization." This shattered aura, and the newly-asserted principles of

---

* Berstein, Serge, and Pierre Milza. *Histoire—1ʳᵉ*. Paris: Hatier, 1997, 204.

the Versailles Treaty, inspired many European colonies to achieve their own self-determination.

After the First World War many people throughout the world began to challenge colonial rule and racial prejudice. Many Nigerians, for example, had fought and died in the European war. When the soldiers returned to Nigeria they asked themselves 'If the white man thinks we are good enough to fight and die in a white man's war, then why do they deny that we are good enough to rule our own country?'

It was under these conditions of racial prejudice that the Lagos branch of Marcus Garvey's Universal Negro Improvement Association was formed in 1920 by Rev. W.B. Euba and Rev. S. M. Abiodun. The Association shared the views of the black American leader, Marcus Garvey, that the black man should not just fold his hands but must revolt against the idea that 'the African was destined to take the back seat forever', and that he should work tirelessly to reject the 'alleged inferiority' of the African.

Reasons for the Failure of the Early Nationalists Movements

The Colonial Office was worried in 1920 when it learned of the establishment of a branch of the Universal Negro Improvement Association. For the Colonial Office knew of the work of Marcus Garvey who had started the Association in America. Garvey's paper *Negro World* with its message of the need for solidarity of black people was considered subversive. When Garvey sent a message of solidarity to the Irish nationalist leader, de Valera, in 1920, the suspicions of the British government, which was at war with the Irish nationalists against Garvey, increased still further. The Association was painted as hostile to the interest of the Empire. Nigerian nationalists were therefore scared away by the propaganda, for they were proud citizens of the Empire. Only a few determined fighters, such as Euba, remained but with such few supporters the fight could not be sustained.*

---

* Omolewa, Michael. *Certificate History of Nigeria*. Lagos, Nigeria: Longman Group, Ltd., 1991, 185–87.

★

GREAT BRITAIN

This British excerpt comes from a section discussing the economic, social, and political consequences of the war. Aside from counting the toll of lost lives, this text argues that the national psyche suffered irreparable damage as well.

The Social and Economic Consequences of the War

These were widespread and far-reaching.

On the negative side, 750,000 men were dead, another 1,500,000 were permanently affected by the effects of wounds or gas. A generation of parents and loved-ones had to bear a burden of grief without precedent in British history.

The economic effects on Britain were also very damaging. U-boats had sunk 40 per cent of British merchant shipping. To keep the war going, Britain had lent around £1,800,000,000 to her allies and borrowed about £850,000 from the USA. In the chaos of the inter-war years, she got few of her loans back, while remaining indebted to the USA. Consequently, Britain never regained her pre-war international financial predominance. Some of her overseas markets, which had been closed to her during the war, were lost to the neutral competitors who had taken them over.

[. . .] What cannot be ignored is the death, destruction and sheer horror of the war and its impact on the national mood. During the nineteenth century most Britons had looked forward to the future with confidence. They had, for the most part, a real if simple belief in progress. That confidence was shattered as a consequence of the 1914–1918 war. The attempts by national leaders to solve the acute problems of the 1920s and 1930s were characterized by a caution, a nostalgia for pre-1914 certainties and a determination to maintain peace at any price which were an important, direct and harmful consequence of the four ghastly years of the Great War.*

---

* Roberts, Martin. *Britain 1846–1964: The Challenge of Change.* London: Oxford University Press, 2001, 167.

23

Invasion of Russia

After signing their treaty with Germany and exiting World War I the Bolsheviks found themselves in a bitter civil war with the opposition forces (the Whites). Using the civil war as a pretense, many Allied nations sent troops (the U.S. sent 8,000) to Russia's arctic ports on August 2, 1918. Two weeks later, more troops landed in eastern Siberia. Most U.S. textbooks cite April 1920 as the final date in this episode, when the Allies pulled out of Russia.

★

JAPAN

Dispatch of Troops to Siberia

After the Soviet government had made separate peace with Germany, the imperialist nations sent troops to Russia to try and hold back the spread of the revolution. Japan sent a force of over 70,000 to Siberia. However, faced with severe cold and strong resistance from the Soviet forces, the powers withdrew from Siberia, and only Japan remained. Eventually, in 1922, under the pressure of mounting criticism from home and abroad, Japan finally withdrew, having spent a huge amount of money and suffered huge casualties.*

★

GREAT BRITAIN

In 1918 small expeditions composed of British, French and American troops seized Murmansk and occupied Archangel, in order to aid the White Russian forces against the Bolsheviks. Sporadic operations were conducted for over a year until the final evacuation of allied troops in Sept. 1919.†

* *Japan in Modern History.* Tokyo: International Society for Educational Information, 1994, 280–81.
† Cook, Chris, and John Stevenson. *The Longman Handbook of Modern British History: 1714–2001.* London: Longman, 2001, 279.

24

The Treaty of Versailles

The victorious nations met in the Palace of Versailles, just outside of Paris, to draw the war to a close and to lay the groundwork for a society or system capable of preventing another similar war. Unfortunately for the victor and the vanquished, this treaty would not accomplish its loftiest goal, a stable peace. The Treaty of Versailles is a key political moment in many history textbooks, not only for its own significance, but also as a catalyst for the events that would follow. Some countries are quick to assign blame to various leaders for unforgiving positions, or to isolationist legislators; others blame the idealists for not being firm enough with the defeated countries.

★

GERMANY

Instead of focusing on the politics of the treaty and the central characters, Germany focuses on the consequences for its already decimated infrastructure, and the reaction to it from the German populace are virtually unique in German textbooks pointing out the "disregard for Wilsonian principles" that caused public indignation in Germany.

Effects of the Treaty of Versailles on Germany

PARIS PEACE CONFERENCE

While in Germany the national assembly began work on a constitution of a parliamentary-democratic state order, the peace conference of the victorious powers met in Paris to create an international post-war order. Unlike earlier peace conferences such as the Congress of Vienna 1814/15, the conquered states were excluded from the negotiations in Paris and could only state a position on the treaty drafts in writing. The plenary meeting of 32 represented states at the conference had little importance. The decisions fell to the **Upper Council of the great powers,** consisting of the government heads and foreign ministers from the USA, Great Britain, France, Italy and Japan. Japan left soon after the beginning of the conference and Italy participated only intermittently out of protest against the regulations that it judged as insufficient. Therefore the determinations of the post-war order were shaped by the interests of the three main powers: USA, Great Britain, and France.

INTEREST POSITIONS OF THE MAIN VICTORIOUS POWERS

Although Wilson's "14 points" had led to a cease-fire, the American perspective of a global peace order could not avail itself in Paris or, if at all, only partially. Under **President Clemenceau,** France pursued a policy that aimed at the greatest possible security against Germany, which involved ceding territory, economic sanctions, and a weakening of the military. The British **Prime Minister Lloyd George** supported the French security policy, but tended not to favor French continental hegemony. It was in agreement with the USA in wishing to shield the continent against the Russian Revolution. For this Germany was indispensable as a central power bulwark. Therefore, Lloyd George warned against a peace unacceptable to Germany. In the British perspective, the question of security was in relation to Russia first and Germany second. In the end, the French interest in a significant weakening of Germany took precedence over German integration in a new European order.

MAIN POINTS OF THE TREATY OF VERSAILLES

The territorial determinations of the Treaty of Versailles on June 28th, 1919 were partially tied to plebiscites in the affected areas, which could only be carried out after the signing of the Treaty of Versailles. Including in the territorial balance sheet the decisions of the Allies according to the plebiscites, Germany lost 13 percent of its state territory. In addition to Alsace-Lorraine, which had to be returned to France, the cession of territory to Poland composed the main portion. The loss of industrial areas and raw material stocks meant a considerable impairment of economic strength: 15 percent of the arable land, 17 percent of the potato and wheat harvest, 75 percent of the iron ore, 68 percent of the zinc deposits, 26 percent of the hard coal output, and the potash monopoly were lost.

In **Article 231,** the so-called war guilt article, Germany was made responsible as the instigator for all war losses and damages of the Allies. Article 231 therefore formed the basis for the economic compensation payments (**Reparations**), whose final extent—in addition to sums immediately payable—was to be determined by a reparations commission.

Germany had to cede its heavy armaments, air force, submarines and battle cruisers, and 90 percent of its merchant fleet as well. The Army was limited to a voluntary force of 100,000 men and the western side of the Rhine in Germany was demilitarized and occupied.

German Criticism of the Treaty of Versailles

The creation of a lasting order that would have established internal and external stability for Germany was not achieved in the Treaty of Versailles. The circumstances of the treaty negotiations, from which Germany was excluded, and the signing under pressure of a threat of the continuation of war led **to unanimous rejection of the Treaty** as a "dictated peace" or—in the language of the right—as a "disgrace dictate" of Versailles.

The content of the treaty itself provoked a discussion that would not end. It was not actually compensation payments and territorial losses that excited the public; Germany had already committed itself to that at the cease-fire. Especially scandalous was the **disregard of the right of self determination** of the Germans in Memelland, in upper Silesia, in the Sudetenland, and in German-Austria despite the fact that all new national states created by the Paris treaty were supposedly formed in the name of the right of self determination of peoples.

Question of War Guilt

"Which hand would not have to wither, which would put itself and us in such chains?" This formulation in the Speech of Imperial Chancellor Scheidemann in the national assembly on May 12th, 1919 reflected the mood in the Empire at the announcement of the Treaty of Versailles draft. There was a coalition among practically all parties against the Treaty of Versailles, though the commitment to actively work for revision of the Treaty was variable in the party ranks. Critical voices in the SPD [Social Democratic Party of Germany] could not gain general acceptance. Even the Communists, for whom capitalism and imperialism respectively bore the responsibility for the World War, spoke of a "rapacious peace treaty" when it came to reparations. The enmity against "Versailles" became the most effective means of negative integration of the Weimar Republic.

Reparations

For the material damage payments the Treaty of Versailles had only created a framework, which was to be filled in by later agreements. At the determination of the reparations, inter-Allied interest conflicts came to the fore again, but without putting the reparations in general in question. A thorough consideration of the economic consequences, as it was critically discussed by the American academic Keynes, did not materialize.

To France the reparations appeared as an effective instrument to prevent a long-term reinvigoration of Germany. In addition the reparations payments were a welcome source for **repayment of the war loans to the USA** by the Allies. For Germany's economic problems, however, each enactment of higher mandatory payments intensified the domestic crisis. As the amount of reparations was made dependent on the productivity of the German economy only with the Dawes-Plan 1924, the economic and social problems of the Weimar period could easily be blamed solely on the reparations obligations.*

* Jager, Dr. Wolfgang, et al. *Kursbuch Geschichte.* Berlin: Cornelsen, 2000, 380–82.

★

JAPAN

Usually a forgotten member of the Allies in World War I, Japan did gain some of the German-held territories in the Pacific as a result of the Treaty of Versailles. What seemed in 1919 to be a relatively minor decision would have a significant impact on how World War II would be fought in the 1940s.

Troops were still being dispatched to the war in Siberia when, in 1919, the victorious powers held a peace conference with Germany in Paris. U.S. President Wilson advocated for the sake of world peace that there should be no annexation, no compensation claims, and that the right to national self-determination should be given to all peoples. But the victorious powers, demanding that their own interests be honored, refused to concede. In the resulting **Treaty of Versailles,** Germany lost all of its colonies and part of its own national territory and was ordered to pay heavy indemnities.

The world after the war—At the peace conference, independence was recognized for the Eastern European peoples that had been under the control of Russia, Austria, and Turkey. This was also for the purpose of preventing the spread of socialism from Russia to other parts of Europe.

However, the Arab people who had been under Turkey's control and the colonies of Germany in Asia and Africa were either placed under the mandatory rule of the victorious nations or made colonies and were not given their independence. Japan was given the rights Germany had held in Shandong Province in China, and the League of Nations appointed Japan to rule Germany's former South Sea Islands territory.*

★

GREAT BRITAIN

This British perspective on Versailles lays out the direct, causal relationship between the treaty and the resulting instability in Europe.

* *Japan in Modern History, Junior High School Textbooks.* Tokyo: International Society for Educational Information, 1994, 281.

A Dictated Peace

The peace conferences which ended the War were held in and around Paris in 1919–20. A separate peace treaty was drawn up for each of the five Central powers. The peace settlement with Germany, which followed the Armistice, was signed six months later, on 28 June 1919, at Versailles. It was drawn up by the great powers, chiefly Britain, France, Italy, and the United States. But many other countries were also represented at Versailles, notably Japan, China, and the Commonwealth countries.

Germany was not consulted, so it was not a negotiated treaty. It was forced on the Germans, as were the other treaties on Austria, Hungary, Bulgaria and Turkey. This imposition of the Treaty by threat of force, infuriated many Germans, such as Adolf Hitler. It lit a fuse which later led to the crises which exploded in the years immediately before the outbreak of the Second World War in 1939. A final straw was the Allied insistence that the Germans acknowledge that they alone were guilty of starting the War. They did not even let Germany keep the gains she took from Russia at Brest Litovsk. On the other hand, the Allies did not invite Russia, either, to take part in the peace talks.

A Revengeful Peace

For much of the time, the conference delegates argued among themselves. Much of the fighting during the War had been on the Western Front in northern France. By contrast British and American soldiers fought on foreign soil, as did the Italians for most of the War. Many French towns and villages had been reduced to rubble during four years of heavy fighting. Fields and woods were pitted with craters and shell-holes. Hundreds of thousands of French people were homeless. One and a half million French soldiers had been killed in action. Clemenceau spoke for the French people as a whole when he demanded peace terms which would use German money to help restore and rebuild France. The French wanted revenge. They wanted to punish Germany and weaken the country so much, that the German people would never again be strong enough to wage war against France. They even argued strongly that the River Rhine should be made the new frontier between the two countries. This would have given France a large portion of Germany.

A Just and Lasting Peace

The Americans were more concerned about getting a just and lasting peace. President Wilson did not want the European powers enlarging their own frontiers and empires at the expense of the Central powers. On the other hand, he had no intention of letting the Germans escape without paying some form of penalty. Lloyd George also sought a satisfactory peace settlement which would hold. He wanted a peace treaty that would exact fair compensation from the Central powers without reducing them to poverty and anarchy. The British had no desire to see Germany, or the countries of the former Austro-Hungarian empire, succumb to a new Bolshevik Revolution. By then danger signals were already being sounded in different parts of Europe. They threatened the fragile peace. There had been left-wing uprisings in several countries following the earlier Bolshevik Revolution in Russia in November 1917. The Spartacist uprising had taken place in Berlin in January 1919. Communists led by Bela Kun had already taken over in Hungary in March 1919.

In the end the peace settlement was something of a compromise. It was neither as tough as that demanded by the French, nor as fair as that for which the British and Americans had argued. Only one Allied delegate, from China, refused to sign. Some delegates, such as Orlando from Italy, walked out of the Conference in disgust. Others, like Japan, expressed dissatisfaction with the terms of the agreement. To Wilson's disappointment, the US Senate later refused to ratify the Treaty because it would have meant joining the League of Nations.*

★

FRANCE

In only a few paragraphs this French text sets the stage for the conflicts in Europe and the Middle East that would dominate the 20th century.

---

* Sauvain, Philip. *The Modern World: 1914–1980*. Cheltenham: Stanley Thornes, 1989, 37–38.

A Difficult Peace

THE TREATIES OPEN A PERIOD OF INCERTITUDE

1. Victors, all-powerful but divided

The Peace Conference brought together only the victors. It reunited 32 countries in Paris beginning on January 18, 1919. The principle negotiations, however, were conducted by the representatives of the five main powers (United States, France, Great Britain, Japan, Italy), and later amongst the "Council of Four" between Wilson, Clemenceau, Lloyd George and Orlando.

The victors' interests diverge. Sticking to his message from January 8, 1918, Wilson wanted to impose a peace founded on rights and justice: respect among nations, free trade and navigation, disarmament, and creation of a League of Nations employing a transparent diplomacy. The Europeans were more concerned about their particular interests. In order to guarantee the security of France, Clemenceau wanted to take from Germany the Rhineland. In order to maintain balance in Europe and to contain the Bolshevik threat, Lloyd George preferred not to weaken Germany. Italy, Romania and Greece wanted to increase their territories according to the promises made to them upon their entry into war.

2. Deep rumblings

The Treaty of Versailles, signed on June 28, 1919 weakened Germany. Held responsible for the war, Germany suffered harsh punishment territorially, militarily and economically. It lost its colonies and 15% of its territory, most notably Alsace-Lorraine (given back to France) and Posnania (handed over to Poland). Eastern Prussia was thereafter cut off from the rest of Germany by the Dantzig corridor. Its military might was destroyed: mandatory armed service was abolished and the army reduced to 100,000 men. The left bank of the Rhine was to be occupied by the Allies for 15 years and then demilitarized. Germany lost its foreign assets, foreign rights, part of its merchant marine and the coal mines of the Sarre, conceded to France. Finally, it was forced to pay war reparations for the damages suffered by the Allies.

The Map of Europe and the Middle East was profoundly modified by the treaties of Saint-Germain, Neuilly and Trianon (1919–1920). The dismemberment of Austro-Hungary and the territorial redistribution gave birth to several new States: Austria, Hungary, Czechoslovakia, and the Kingdom of Serbia, Croats and Slovaks (future Yugoslavia). Poland was reconstituted and obtained access to the sea. The Treaty of Sèvres stripped the Ottoman Empire of her Arab territories, declared Armenia independent and gave autonomy to Kurdistan. The new Turkey was reduced to Constantinople and upper Anatolia.

The League of Nations, created in 1920 had to oversee the fragile peace: resolving problems by mediation, working for disarmament, managing the international territories, organizing plebiscites in order to determine the outcome of disputed regions, and overseeing the mandates of the former German and Ottoman colonies whose administration had fallen to the victors.

3. Discontent and delayed problems

The treaties carried the germ of deep dissatisfaction and left several questions unanswered. Imposed on the defeated, they were rapidly rejected: the Germans talked of a "Diktat". In the victors' camp, Italy protested its "mutilated victory" which was not worth the territories gained. The United States, returning to their traditional isolationism, did not ratify the treaties and chose not to enter into the League of Nations. Their absence, along with that of the defeated and Russia, transformed the organization into a group of European victors without any real means.

The right of a people to decide for themselves was only partially recognized, even though plebiscites were organized in the disputed territories. Significant minorities were swallowed up within certain States. Czechoslovakia, for example, included six million Czechs, three million Germans, three million Slovakians and groups of Ruthenians, Magyars and Polish. Fearing the reconstitution of a powerful Germany, the victors forbade the eventual reunion of Austria with Germany (*Anschluss*). In the Middle East, the British failed to keep their promises made during the war to create an Arab kingdom and to establish a Jewish haven in Palestine.*

---

* Baylac, M.-H., et al. *Histoire—1ʳᵉ*. Paris: Bordas, 1997, 220.

★

RUSSIA

This excerpt comes from a Russian text about world history. Russia had pulled out of WWI intending to take care of its own business, namely the Bolshevik Revolution. The outcome of the Treaty of Versailles was affected in no small way by the events transpiring in Russia at the time.

The conference of World War I victors opened in Paris on January 18, 1919. The choice of date had historical significance: on that very day in 1871, the existence of the German Empire was declared in the Palace at Versailles. Opening the Peace Conference, French President A. Poincare said: "Born in illegitimacy, Germany ended its existence in dishonor."

Representatives from twenty-seven nations that had declared war against Germany arrived in the capital of France for the negotiations. Among the countries not invited were Germany and her allies, as well as Soviet Russia. The "Russian question" worried the leaders of the conference primarily as part of their plans to continue military intervention in Russia and to divide its territory. An uprising of French sailors on military ships in Odessa, however, cooled off the warlike spirits of European leaders.

The peace conference was led by the Big Three: French Prime Minster Georges Clemenceau, British Premier David Lloyd George, and Woodrow Wilson, the President of the United States. Among them, the most vocal was Clemenceau, who became known as the Tiger for his temperamental attacks against his opponents.

Decisions arose out of heated discussions, as the participants' goals were varied and often opposite to one another. The French delegation called for the greatest weakening of its traditional enemy—Germany, which would have allowed France to dominate continental Europe. British Premier Lloyd George, on the other hand, wanted to preserve a strong Germany, hoping to use it to balance a potential French hegemony on the continent, as well as the "Bolshevik threat." Wilson held a more moderate position towards Germany, as he wanted to avoid British and French dominance in post-war Europe. A lot was decided at the conference behind closed doors.

At Woodrow Wilson's insistence, a decision was made at the Paris Peace Conference to create the League of Nations—an international organization, whose goals included the preservation of international peace. Wilson also insisted on the inclusion of the League's by-laws in the preamble to the peace treaty. The League's highest body was the Assembly, where each member nation was represented. The League Council was a smaller body, which was endowed with great powers. The five Superpowers became the Council's permanent members: USA, Great Britain, France, Italy, and Japan. By-laws of the League of Nations recommended political and economic sanctions against aggressor nations as a measure of preserving international security. In addition, the by-laws established a new system of international rule—the mandate system—which gave the League the power to give a nation a "mandate" over a certain colony, allowing it to rule that colony and prepare it for independence. In reality, this cleverly conceived formula only served as a cover for the redistribution of colonies. Nonetheless, the creation of the League of Nations gave birth to a period of pacifism following the conclusion of World War I.

The Versailles Peace Treaty turned out to be a far cry from the "fair and democratic peace", promised by the leaders of the conference. According to the Treaty, named after the Great Palace at Versailles where the document was signed, Germany was named responsible for initiating the war and was thus required to be punished. Germany was deprived of all its colonies, was forced to cede some of its territory to neighboring nations, and to pay enormous reparations for the damages done against the victorious countries.

[the provisions of the Treaty of Versailles]

The question of war reparations was postponed until further agreements, but a total sum of 132 billion gold marks was determined. In addition, a part of Germany on the left bank of the Rhine was to be occupied by an international army for 15 years, with Germany footing the bill for its maintenance.

The Versailles Peace Treaty was very harsh on the German people and deeply wounded the country's national pride. In the subsequent decades, these feelings among the Germans fed nationalistic ideas and the promises for revenge, which were used successfully in the 1930s by the Nazis in their rise to power.*

---

* *The World in the XXth Century.* Moscow: Prosveshchenie, 1999, 67–71.

★

ITALY

This collection of brief selections represents an Italian account of the treaty.

This text describes the views of three of the four deciding powers:

... while France's right wing, with President Poincaré and Marshal Foch, pushed for a total annihilation [of any German power], England's prime minister Lloyd George, fearing an excessive growth of French power, was against the full attainment of this objective. Clemenceau's wish to maintain England and the United States' support of France moved the Treaty to a resolution, a compromise between the two inclinations.*

Italy left the Treaty discussions without having gained the promises made to it prior to its engagement in war, for that was, as this text notes, what the chief powers were seeking.

Each one of the winning powers, who during the war had born immeasurable sacrifices and run severe risks, had no intention of turning down the profits of their victory, in terms of a conquest of territory, economic benefits, and political positions.†

Wilson's demand that Germany return the territories it had invaded . . .

... was understood as the Allies' right to obtain reparations for the damages caused to their people by the German troops, and the colonial question was resolved with the legal pretense of 'mandates.'‡

The text makes it clear that these "mandates" did not in any way benefit postwar Italy:

The German colonies were divided, under the form of 'mandates' (in other words as protectorates that in practice were the same as colonies),

* Villari, Rosario. *Storia Contemporanea*. Bari: Laterza, 1990, 412.

† Villari, Rosario. *Storia Contemporanea*. Bari: Laterza, 1990, 413.

‡ Villari, Rosario. *Storia Contemporanea*. Bari: Laterza, 1990, 413.

among England, France, Belgium, Japan, and Australia. Italy, who had been vaguely promised a part of the colonial booty, was excluded from the distribution.*

Another reason for Italy's dissatisfaction with the outcome of Versailles was the Treaty's reassessment of European borders. The divisions of Poland, Czechoslovakia, and Romania are described by the text as acceptable. Ample space, however, is devoted to the problems that arose from the division of bordering Yugoslavia, again citing disillusionment with the outcome of the London Pact:

The creation of the new Yugoslav state, which Italian diplomacy had not foreseen when it signed the London Pact, caused objections and complications when it came time to work it out with Italy.†

Italy promptly invaded Fiume in protest.

. . . it was unavoidable that such a vast political and territorial reordering would provoke protests and negative reactions that were felt not only short-term but also, more gravely, more long-term. Right away there were attempts to modify the treaties' decisions by putting force up against what had already been decided.‡

---

* Villari, Rosario. *Storia Contemporanea.* Bari: Laterza, 1990, 414.

† Villari, Rosario. *Storia Contemporanea.* Bari: Laterza, 1990, 415.

‡ Villari, Rosario. *Storia Contemporanea.* Bari: Laterza, 1990, 416.

PART V

---

*The Great Depression
and World War II*

25

The Great Depression

The Great Depression showed the world how intertwined its economies were. Especially after the crash of 1929, many U.S. banks and investors grew wary of lending money to other nations. This drying up of investment hit Europe especially hard, since it was still rebuilding and repaying costly debt from the First World War.

★

RUSSIA

Within four months of President Hoover's inauguration, the seemingly blooming American economy stood on the threshold of a never-before-seen crash. Immense panic began on the morning of October 24, 1929 on Wall Street, the heart of American business. The victorious slogans about crisis-free economic development and optimistic predictions of an upcoming time of prosperity turned out to be no more than an empty bluff. The stock market crash in New York signaled the start of the global cataclysm that would become known in literature as the Great Economic Crisis of the 1930's.

The crisis deeply affected the economy of the United States throughout the decade. The crisis of overproduction in many sectors of the economy started a chain reaction of dropping stock prices and bankruptcies among even the largest of companies. By 1932, over 10,000 banks and 135,000 companies were out of business, and industrial output dropped to 53.8% of the pre-crisis levels. The crisis touched virtually all segments of population and society: workers, civil servants, scientists, lawyers, businessmen. At one point, 17 million people were unemployed. The crisis became a complete disaster for American farmers, who, unable to find buyers for their products, resorted to slaughtering massive herds of cattle and to pouring milk out into rivers.

The Republican government, led by President Hoover, stuck to the traditional ideas of free market economy and unrestricted competition and demonstrated its helplessness and inability to deal with the growing social and economic problems. In 1930, so-called "hunger marches" on Washington and other cities began, organized by unemployed workers demanding that the government take action to improve the situation. The 1932 march on Washington organized by war veterans was dispatched of by the government with the use of mounted troops and tear gas.

As a result of its inability to improve America's economic situation, the Hoover administration suffered a crushing defeat at the hands of the Democratic Party, led by Franklin Delano Roosevelt, in the 1932 Presidential elections. Roosevelt was born in a rich family (he was related to Theodore Roosevelt) and received an aristocratic upbringing. His youth and childhood were spent in luxury. Nonetheless, from the very beginning of his political career, Roosevelt displayed an uncanny understanding of socio-political reality. Both his allies and opponents noted his decisiveness, as well as his ability to comprehend and state specific needs and desires of large masses of population. It is also worth noting that, in 1921, at the age of 39, he became paralyzed after swimming in cold water and was confined to a wheelchair for the rest of his life. Roosevelt frequently spoke out against outdated government initiatives and programs and, as governor of New York, showed that he could not accept the idea that government did not play a role in the economic and social life of the nation.

After coming to power and leading the Democratic Party to a victory in Congressional elections, Roosevelt claimed that the nation needed political experiments and proposed his massive program of reforms, known as the "New Deal." The government took a central role in most of these reform programs and took it upon itself to regulate a lot of economic activity and social processes in the country. To further this goal, many new agencies and committees were created to regulate and control these aspects of life in society.

As part of the New Deal, many laws were passed that marked a significant change to the political course of the nation. The first order of business was to deal with the bank catastrophe that broke out with full force as Roosevelt was just beginning his term in office. A presidential decree of March 6, 1933 closed all banks in America. They were reopened gradually as widespread panic subsided and only after careful examinations of each bank's financial state. Other laws passed in 1933 further increased the government's control and monitoring of the whole banking system in the United States.

Another law created the National Administration for the Restoration of Industry (NRA), which gave government the right to interfere directly with the actions of individual corporations, setting quantities of goods to be produced, their price levels, and things such as the length of a work day. An important part of this law required corporations and manufacturers to acknowledge workers' unions on their premises and to sign collective bargaining agreements, guaranteeing the rights of workers and employees. For the purpose of reducing unemployment, this law also created thousands of public jobs, using the unemployed to beautify neighborhoods, pave roads, build power plants, and plant trees. All these initiatives were paid for entirely by the government.

Roosevelt also passed a law dealing with agriculture, which aimed to put an end to overproduction of agricultural goods by way of cutting down on lands used for farming and regulating the sizes of meat-producing herds. The government also bought up large amounts of cotton, grain, and meat to be held at government warehouses until the overproduction subsided. The Wagner Law, named after the senator who proposed it, was passed to not only mandate employers to acknowledge unions, but also to punish entrepreneurs for "unfair labor practices", which involved threatening union leaders and hiring strike-breakers. One of the other central measures taken by Roosevelt's administration was the creation of a system of social security, which created government pensions and welfare for the first time in American history.

The goal of all of these laws and initiatives was to overcome the most urgent and socially volatile problems. While making considerable changes to the existing system, Roosevelt's reforms acted to preserve capitalism and the system of free enterprise. Nonetheless, the critics of the New Deal attacked the Democrats and argued that many of the new laws and measures were unconstitutional. As a result, many laws, including those dealing with industry, were repealed.

Despite these setbacks, the success of Roosevelt's reforms could not be stopped. This was evidenced, in part, by the fact that Roosevelt was victorious in his bid for re-election in 1936. The New Deal became one of the crucial turning points in the history of the United States. From that point on, the concept of government intervention in the economy and society became a very important element of America's socio-political system. As a result, the reforms of the New Deal put down a firm foundation for widespread prosperity in the United States.*

★

FRANCE

This is a good example of how French textbooks use world events to spur discussion about the ideas that underlie or influence them. Here, a summary of the Great Depression leads to a discussion about the effects on democratic governments in Europe and North America.

The Worldwide Depression

THE CRISIS OF 1929 IN THE UNITED STATES

• **The American prosperity of the 20s was fragile.** Industrial production in America increased rapidly, 26% between 1923 and 1929. The buying power of salaried employees increased significantly as well but at a lower rate, 12% during the same period. The production capabilities risked

---

* *The Newest History of Foreign Nations: XXth Century.* Moscow: Vlados, 1998, 106–10.

outpacing the capacity for domestic consumption while demographic growth was not strong enough to make up the difference. The increase in American exports could not off-set the potential saturation of the domestic market. Meanwhile, American agricultural products found it harder and harder to sell on the European market once Europe had returned to pre-1914 production levels.

• Warning signs of the crisis began to show themselves: in 1927, a drop in agricultural sales; in March 1929, automobile production began to decline. These signs were not recognized at the time. The massive reliance on consumer credit, which permitted the American households to buy durable goods, successfully masked the situation. This new practice caused higher demand and maintained growth. At the stock market in New York, speculators bought massive quantities of shares, also on credit. The explosion of shares did not reflect the real state of the economy.

• **The crash on Wall Street occurred in October 1929** when some began to realize that the share prices for certain companies were neither gaining nor declining. They understood the time had come to get rid of their shares. Thursday, October 24, 1929, **Black Thursday,** 13 million shares were sold, then another 16.5 million the following Tuesday, the 29th. At this point, the market collapsed. The **stock market panic** led to massive amounts of cash being withdrawn from bank counters. Many of them failed, others refused new loans. The **lack of new credit** for consummation caused the "house of cards", on which the American prosperity had been based during the twenties, to come crashing down. **Overproduction** was exposed. There was a drop in sales, prices dropped (an average of 32% between 1929 and 1932), companies produced less and let go of their workers. Unemployment grew (more than 13 million unemployed in the United States in 1932), which only drove the consumer capacity lower. A **downward spiral** ensued, crisis feeding crisis.

THE SPREAD OF THE AMERICAN CRISIS WORLDWIDE

• **The American crisis pushed the rest of the world into depression as well.** The collapse of their foreign orders lowered the activity in the supplying countries, and from near to far, the crisis spread from continent to continent. **The contraction of the world economy** was spectacular; it was reduced by two-thirds between 1929 and 1932. The decline in prices didn't limit itself to the United States but spread across the globe. Furthermore, in need of capital back in the US, American bankers divested themselves of their holdings in Europe and Latin America. There followed a **European banking crisis** which peaked in 1931: the *Kredit Anstalt* of Vienna failed in May; in June, two German banks, the *Danat Bank* and the *Dresdner Bank* stopped making payments and were barely saved thanks to the government; in July, it was the British banks' turn to feel the crisis deeply.*

The Depression in Democracy

THE CRISIS TEARS APART SOCIETY

• **Democracy suffered the most** because it had taken root in the wealthy countries, those most affected by the depression. In North America and Europe, poverty returned like the plague in industrialized societies.

• **It was complete social chaos.** Unemployment, the lack of buying power for workers and employees, the failure of industries, the **uneasiness of the middle classes,** all these ills increased the bitterness felt in society. Demonstrations and **hunger marches** increased. The situation was difficult for the democracies to handle, resulting in political problems, more or less severe according to the country.

The Impotence of the Governments

The crisis was severe in the United States and in Great Britain, but it didn't threaten the established order, quite differently from the other democracies in question.

• **In the United States** President Hoover, a republican, didn't doubt that a recovery would take place of its own accord: "Recovery is just around the corner," he said. His action was timid, totally insufficient for staying the rising unemployment in the city and the impoverishment of the farmers, many of whom were saddled with debt and on the verge of foreclosure from their banks and creditors.

On the European continent, the social crisis led to a radicalization

* Frank, Robert and Zanghellini, Valéry. *Histoire—1re*. Paris: Bélin, 1997.

of the extremes. On the left, the **audience of the communist party grew** in the worker milieu, at the expense of the socialists, especially in Germany. This rise of communism struck fear into a large part of the middle class, or the *haves*, and encouraged the reaction of growth in the far right. The latter supported a strong state, authoritarian, capable of maintaining the threatened "status quo". It went as far as blaming the "foreigners". One saw in France, as well as in Central Europe and Germany, a **renaissance of racism and anti-Semitism.**

• **Everywhere unemployment rose to alarming rates:** more than 6 million unemployed in Germany, 3.5 million in Great Britain.*

★

CARIBBEAN

The inability of U.S. consumers to buy products from suppliers that counted on U.S. markets ensured that the economic crisis would spread. This excerpt reflects the central importance of staple agricultural products to the historical experience of the region.

Crisis in the 1920s

The wartime sugar boom was followed by a slump in world sugar prices which began in 1920. The slump had a harsh effect in Cuba where sugar was the leading business and the biggest provider of jobs. Many estates went bankrupt and there was a new wave of selling to American private businessmen and banks. The government of Cuba was also heavily in debt.

The economic troubles led to political chaos. It came to a head in the elections of 1921 which were won by Alfredo Zayas, a close supporter of Menocal. Opposition groups immediately said the election had been rigged. The country was about to break into anarchy and the United States sent an unofficial adviser, General Crowder, to help restore order. Crowder got his way by using the fact that Cuba needed large American loans to avoid bankruptcy. He arranged for Zayas to stay as president, but insisted that he run the country along guidelines that Crowder laid down.

* Frank, Robert and Zanghellini, Valéry. *Histoire—1re*. Paris: Bélin, 1997, 230.

Many Cubans objected to Crowder's position in the government and the Americans called him home in 1923. In 1925 new elections brought another pro-American, Gerado Machado, to power as president. He built up a personal dictatorship based on heavy bribes and the thuggery of his force of private gunmen, the 'Porristes'. Machado's rule began a new stage of American business involvement. Even more sugar factories, estates and public works passed into American hands. These were also years when hundreds of thousands of pleasure-seeking Americans turned to Cuba. The boom for hotels, nightclubs and casinos was helped by the fact that alcohol could not be sold in the USA in the years of prohibition from 1919 to 1933.*

PUERTO RICO AND THE DEPRESSION

The great depression of the 1930s hit Puerto Rico hard. As America went into economic slump her people stopped buying, and imports from Puerto Rico were cut savagely. Cigar and cigarette factories were forced to close. Thousands of sugar workers lost their jobs in 1934 when the industry had to cut its production by half, as ordered by an act of the United States Congress. The landowners received compensation; the workers were given nothing. The needlework industry dwindled away as exports valued at $20 million in 1937 fell to less than $5 million in 1940.

Franklin Roosevelt was elected United States President in 1932 during the depression. In his first term of office he began his promised 'New Deal' programme to get Americans back to work. Billions of dollars of government money were spent on forestry schemes, dams, roads and social insurance schemes. The programme was extended to the overseas protectorates of the United States. In Puerto Rico it became known as the 'Little New Deal'.

The first step was to set up an Emergency Relief Administration in Puerto Rico to provide immediate help for the most distressed workers. Like the ERA in the United States, the Puerto Rican Emergency Relief Administration offered work on public works programmes. As much as one-third of Puerto Rico's workforce earned some wages from ERA

* Claypole, William, and John Robottom. *Caribbean Story, Bk. 2: The Inheritors.* Kingston: Carlong, 1994, 186.

schemes. Then responsibility for social and economic programmes was taken away from the Department of War and given to the Department of the Interior. This department helped set up the Puerto Rican Reconstruction Finance Corporation and the Puerto Rican Reconstruction Administration. By 1938 these two bodies had spent over $57 million on relief schemes.

The Little New Deal saw Puerto Rico through the worst depression years but did little to correct the deep-rooted problems of the island. Too much money had been spent purely on relief and too little on starting schemes which would provide long-term employment. With good reason Governor Beverley criticised the whole programme and charged that too much of the relief money had ended in the pockets of local politicians as well as doctors, lawyers and officials hired to run the schemes. Both American administrators and local politicians were discredited by the charges. This helped to win support for a new political movement begun by Puerto Ricans who believed that the time had come to solve their own economic problems.*

---

* Claypole, William, and John Robottom. *Caribbean Story, Bk. 2: The Inheritors.* Kingston: Carlong, 1994, 201.

26

World War II: Europe

World War II is among the most popular topics in history courses taught in the United States. U.S. textbooks typically offer a linear history, focusing on the military conflict: D-Day, the liberation of Paris, the Battle of the Bulge, and the collapse of Germany. These textbooks, moreover, generally offer a polarized, binary vision of history, in which the good guys are good and the bad guys are bad. European textbooks, on the other hand, are full of nuances and shades of gray: from discussions on Europe's appeasement policy and eventual Resistance (including in Germany) to the debate over the loss of art and architecture in the Allied bombing campaigns. The experience of the war itself has influenced the European psyche, forming a general attitude of distrust toward strongly held convictions.

★

GREAT BRITAIN

Because of its appeasement policy, Great Britain is often blamed for allowing Hitler's armies to spread across the European continent. This British selection explains this policy and, like many British textbooks, looks at the corresponding historical debate.

Britain did very well, in the short-term, out of the Versailles Treaty. She removed the German navy and added to her Empire. Apart from the USA, she had no rivals remotely as strong as she was, so her international position was apparently both impressive and secure. However, the weaknesses of the Versailles settlement and the international tensions which stemmed from those weaknesses undermined that position. Britain did not have the resources to defend the British Empire, act as the League's policeman and restrain aggressive dictators in Europe; hence the readiness of her government to pursue appeasement policies in the 1930s.

Since Britain made major gains from the Versailles settlement, her aims to keep the peace and avoid change meant that British governments often took an unsystematic appeasing approach in the 1920s. However, during that decade, they made frequent use of 'collective security', most obviously at Locarno in 1925. The Labour Party committed itself firmly to collective security and disarmament into the late 1930s.

The international situation deteriorated sharply after 1929. The aggression of Japan, Italy and Germany created an international climate where collective security had less and less chance of working. The League of Nations could only have been more effective if Britain and France had been ready to allow it more teeth in the settlement of international disputes and provided most of the teeth themselves from their military resources.

The National governments of the early thirties pursued collective security and appeasement simultaneously. MacDonald played a leading role at the international disarmament conference in Geneva in 1932–1923 [*sic*], while appeasing Japan over Manchuria. Increasingly Britain moved more completely to appeasement. Chamberlain merely brought to the policy a sharper focus and greater vigour. Churchill and 'Cato' quickly condemned the appeasers as 'Guilty men'. Revisionist historians have defended the appeasers and in turn have provoked some counter-revisionism which argues that the first criticisms, though fierce, were essentially just.*

World War II wrought many changes in Great Britain, from its position as a world power to the general perception of the poor within England. This selection recounts these changes and what it meant for the British.

* Roberts, Martin. *Britain 1846–1964: The Challenge of Change.* London: Oxford University Press, 2001, 249.

From a world perspective, if the First World War turned out to be quite unlike any other and much worse than anyone had predicted, the same was true only more so for the Second World War. The battles between Germany and Russia on the Eastern Front between 1941 and 1945 far surpassed those of the trenches in casualties and in savagery. The Nazi treatment of the Jews and of other peoples they considered inferior was so appalling that when the truth first began to emerge, the reaction of the world opinion was disbelief.

For Britain, it was a strange war with contradictory characteristics. Britain started fighting alongside France, then fought alone and ended up playing third fiddle to the USA and USSR. Whereas Lloyd George came to power in 1916 and galvanized the country to *win* the first war, Churchill came to power in 1940 to galvanize the country *not to lose* the second one, and to hang on until 1941 when both the USSR and the USA became allies.

Britain's war effort was a triumph by which the nation contributed more to the freedom of the world than at any time in her history. In a genuine sense 1940 was, as Churchill had hoped, Britain's 'finest hour'. But it was also a disaster in terms of Britain's position as a Great Power. If Britain won the war, she also lost the peace. The economy was gravely weakened, and her standing as one of the world's leading nations with a huge and united empire was fatally undermined.

Simultaneously, the war caused a social revolution. The British people become more united and more equal. Most ended the war more prosperous and healthy. Again in marked contrast to the First World War, people looked forward to creating a better world once the war was over, not returning to the pre-war days.

[. . .] the six years of war marked [. . .] the decline of Britain as a Great Power, and in the progress of British society towards becoming wealthier, fairer and more caring than it was before.

The Main Phases of the War

PHASE I: 1939–1941 GERMANY TRIUMPHS IN EUROPE

Though Britain and France went to war to defend Poland, they could not have chosen a more difficult European ally to defend. France had only prepared for a defensive war against Germany. Britain's army was still small and totally unprepared for continental warfare. The only way that Britain and France would defeat Nazi Germany would be slowly, by economic blockade and bombing, and by building up a massive joint army to attack should blockade and bombing not be enough.

Consequently, unfortunate Poland was rapidly crushed and divided by the Germans invading from the west and the Russians from the east. No one then knew what to do. Hitler had thought Britain and France were bluffing when they warned him that they would go to war over Poland, so he had no plans to fight them. For their part, Britain and France needed all the time they could get to strengthen their forces. The autumn and winter of 1939–40 was a war of curious inactivity. The British christened it the 'bore war' but the American phrase the 'phoney war' is the name that has stuck.

The phoney war came to a sudden end in April 1940 when the German army shocked Europe by some of the most brilliant victories in the history of warfare. By co-ordinating their air, armoured and infantry forces in a new and devastatingly effective way, and by attacking with speed, flair and confidence, they conquered Western Europe in two months, April/May 1940. First to fall was Norway which Germany had to secure to safeguard her supplies of iron. Then the combined British and French armies, which were as large and well-armed as their German opponents, were taken apart by the surprise armoured attack through the Ardennes. While the main French armies tried and failed to prevent the Germans advancing deep into France, the British retreated hastily to Dunkirk. From there 300,000 British troops, plus another 100,000 French, were evacuated from the beaches by whatever ships small and large could get across the Channel from England. France surrendered.

In May Churchill had replaced Chamberlain as Prime Minister. What was the point of Britain fighting on alone? She had no chance of defeating Germany by herself. Where were her allies? The USA showed no sign of wishing to get involved in a war against Hitler.

Hitler and the rest of the world expected Britain to approach Germany for peace terms. Extraordinarily, the question never seems to have been formally discussed once by the British War Cabinet. Chamberlain and Halifax were in favour of at least exploring what Hitler had to offer. Churchill, however, made it clear that as long as he was Prime Minister he had no goal but total victory and that was that. The British people seem to have shared their Premier's bloody-minded obstinacy. They did not know how they would win, but win they would.

[...]

THE BATTLE OF BRITAIN

Britain came close to defeat in August/September 1940 in the air battle, which Churchill called the Battle of Britain. Hitler prepared an invasion force. It had no chance of success unless the Luftwaffe, the German air force, gained control of the skies above the Channel and southern England. If that air supremacy was won, the invasion had abandoned most of its weapons in France. The Luftwaffe mounted wave after wave of attacks on the RAF.

For a few days in August, when it concentrated on the destroying the radar defences and airfields and the RAF was running out of pilots, defeat seemed imminent. However, at a crucial moment the Luftwaffe switched to bombing London. The RAF regained the upper hand and caused Hitler to call off his invasion plans.

The Battle of Britain was a much greater setback for Hitler than it seemed at the time. Britain was clearly going to go on fighting and would not be easy to defeat. As long as she continued fighting she proved to be the rallying point of anti-Nazi resistance throughout Europe. When the USA eventually came into the war, the British Isles acted as a vast aircraft carrier from which the military might of the USA, with British support, launched itself decisively across the Channel against Nazism.

PHASE 2: 1941–1942 WORLD WAR: JAPAN USA AND USSR

The nature of the war changed decisively in 1941. In the summer, Hitler turned his armies on the USSR. Then, in December, with characteristic recklessness, he declared war on the USA in support of his Japanese allies who had attacked the American fleet at Pearl Harbour. If the unlikely alliance of the USSR, the USA, and the British Empire could avoid military defeat in 1941–1942 and then hold together long enough, their combined resources were so much greater than those of Germany and Japan, they must win. Such was the common hatred of German

Nazism and Japanese militarism that the Grand Alliance held together, despite considerable tensions, until victory was won in 1945.

1941 and 1942 were very bad years for the Allies. The German armies reached the suburbs of Moscow and then drove deeply south and east towards the oilfields of the Caucasus. In the Far East, the Japanese control of both sea and sky brought them another series of striking victories, the most notable of which was the capture of Singapore, Britain's most important naval base in Asia. Simultaneously in North Africa, where Britain's war effort was concentrated, the German Afrika Korps commanded by Rommel drove the armies of the British Empire back to the Egyptian border. And the U-boats seemed to be winning the Battle of the Atlantic.

PHASE 3: 1942–1943 THE TURNING OF THE TIDE

By the summer of 1943, the war was effectively won. The most decisive battle was on the Eastern Front, where Russian armies outfought the Germans at Stalingrad. After Stalingrad, the Germans began the long retreat back to Germany. In the Pacific, the Battle of Midway ended the advance of the previously all-conquering fleet of Japanese aircraft carriers. After Midway, the Japanese were retreating too, bitterly contesting every island. In North Africa British Empire troops played their part. Skilfully generalled by Montgomery and now superior to Rommel's army both in numbers and weaponry, they first won the battle of El Alamein and then met up with the Americans to drive the Germans and Italians out of Africa. In Atlantic waters, better methods of detection helped the Allies get the upper hand over the U-boats.*

★

GERMANY

This short selection provides a quick summary of German strategy in declaring war on the United States in 1941. It also alludes to the "merciless" bombing carried out by

* Roberts, Martin. *Britain 1846–1964: The Challenge of Change*, London: Oxford University Press, 2001, 251–252.

Allied warplanes on German cities, which is still a topic of political significance in contemporary Germany.

The Declaration of War against the United States

At the turn of the year from 1942 to 1943 the war was no longer limited to Europe. The confrontation between Japan and the United States of America had intensified after Japan occupied the northern part of French Indochina and was about to reverse the opening of east Asia to the world market, which the United States, in large part, had forced in the nineteenth century. When the United States imposed an oil embargo on Japan and demanded the withdrawal from China, Japanese planes launched a surprise attack on the American base in Hawaii, **Pearl Harbor,** on December 7, 1941. The Japanese military command apparently believed it possible to drive the USA out of east Asia with a concept similar to the German "blitzkrieg" without having to risk a larger war.

In the USA and in Germany, however, one understood the Japanese-American conflict as part of the power struggle for a new world order, which was being fought in Europe since 1939. The American and British declaration of war against Japan followed the German declaration of war against the USA on 11 December 1941, in the expectation that it could make the USA [fatally] split up its forces between Europe and Asia—to no avail. England and the USA agreed that first a decision would have to be made about war in the European field first.

After the defeat of the German-Italian units in Africa, the Allies crossed over into Italy in the summer of 1943; that brought with it the downfall of Mussolini, who had to draw back to the area in northern Italy held by German troops. The almost defenseless German cities were at the mercy of **aerial warfare,** begun by England and the USA in 1943. In the East, German troops had to gradually retreat under great losses. In **June 1944** the reconquest of the European continent began with the **invasion of the western Allies at Normandy.** *

---

*Jager, Dr. Wolfgang, et al. *Kursbuch Geschichte.* Berlin: Cornelsen, 2000, 469.

★

RUSSIA

The Second World War represented two distinct conflicts for the Soviet Union: World War II (1939–1941) and The Great Patriotic War (lasting from the German invasion of Russia in 1941 until Germany's surrender). This division still holds true for Russian text- books in the post–Cold War period. What was once seen as the inevitable victory of communist socialism has given way to an historical reading of the heroic destiny of Mother Russia. The central plot now involves Russian heroism and exceptionalism; the main motivation has become love of the motherland instead of inevitable class struggle of the Soviet proletariat against imperialist forces. In Russian textbooks, the suffering no longer belongs to all Soviet peoples but specifically to the Russians themselves.

Early morning on the 1st of September, 1939, German troops entered Poland without a declaration of war. From three different directions: West, North, and South, five German armies attacked Poland. Contrary to Hitler's expectations, two of Poland's allies, Great Britain and France, declared war on Germany on September 3. Shortly thereafter Britain and France's colonies and protectorates entered the war. World War II had begun.

Polish troops fought back heroically, but the small and poorly armed Polish army could not resist German tank and motorized divisions, sup- ported by a powerful air force. Two weeks after the start of the war the Pol- ish army was crushed.

At the same time the Soviet Union, in accordance with the secret pact with Germany signed on August 23, 1939, also attacked Poland. On Sep- tember 17 Soviet troops entered Poland and did not encounter much re- sistance. Over 200 thousand Polish soldiers and officers were captured by the Soviets. In the spring of 1940 over 20,000 of them were executed by the NKVD near Katun, several hundred miles West of Moscow, and in other places.

On September 28, 1939 a German-Soviet cooperation treaty was signed in Moscow, coordinating German and Soviet actions in Eastern Europe.

The Polish state ceased to exist. Western Ukraine and Belorussia be- came Soviet territory, while Polish lands bordering Germany were made into a German protectorate ruled directly from Berlin. In addition, the Soviet government forced Estonia, Latvia, and Lithuania to sign treaties promising mutual assistance and allowing the USSR to place troops on those nations' territory.

Simultaneously the Soviet Union demanded that the Finnish border be moved further away from Leningrad, offering Finland a larger, but scarcely populated, area in Soviet Karelia as compensation. After prolonged negotiations Finland refused.

On November 30, 1939 Soviet troops began war against Finland. What followed was a relatively short, but extremely bloody, Soviet-Finnish war. The League of Nations condemned the USSR's actions and expelled the Soviet Union from its membership.

At the same time, all was quiet on the Western front. The Anglo-French troops situated there were taking no action against Germany, even though they had a large advantage in numbers, since the bulk of German army was in Poland. The stand-off on the Western front, lasting until the spring of 1940, became known as the 'strange' or 'sitting' war.

The governments of Britain and France stuck to a defensive-minded strategy during the 'strange' war. They expected that the superiority of their joined navies would allow them to maintain a blockade of Germany while the mighty fortified Maginot Line, built by the French on the German border, would make a German invasion of France impossible.

By the spring of 1940 Soviet troops managed to break the defensive Mannerheim Line built by the Finnish to protect against invasion. Finland was defeated and signed a peace treaty on March 12, 1940, giving the part of Karelia North of Leningrad over to the Soviet Union.*

Russia's view of the War as the "Great Patriotic War" gives the reader an idea of the place it occupies in Russian history. The remaining Russian excerpt deals with the aggressive enemies that Russia had to overcome. One is struck by the inclusion of France.

The Great Patriotic War of the Soviet Union.

In the summer of 1941 Germany completed its preparations for the invasion of the Soviet Union. According to the Barbarossa Plan, German

* *The World in the XXth Century.* Moscow: Prosveshchenie, 1999, 165–66.

armed forces planned to "crush Soviet Russia after a quick campaign even before the conclusion of the war against Great Britain." Hitler planned to use the European part of the USSR as "living space" for German colonists. The Slavic population was to be turned into slaves or destroyed. Germans built specialized death camps in Poland, which were meant for the extermination of "undesirable" ethnic groups, which primarily included Jews and Slavs. Over the course of the war, over eleven million people were murdered in camps, such as Auschwitz, Maidanek, and Treblinka.

On June 22, 1941, at 3:30 in the morning Nazi troops entered Soviet territory without a declaration of war. The Great Patriotic War of the Soviet Union had begun. Germany was joined in its war effort by Romania, Hungary, Finland, Italy, Slovakia, and Croatia. General Francisco Franco's Spanish government and the Vichy government in France both sent volunteers to assist the German army. The total forces invading the USSR were made up of 190 divisions, 153 of which were German, accounting for almost 80% of the entire German military. The Soviet-German front became the most important front of World War II.

The fascist invasion put the Soviet Union in a very difficult situation. There were close to 170 divisions located in the Western part of the USSR, close to the border. The total number of Soviet tanks and airplanes surpassed that possessed by the German army, but most of the Soviet tanks and airplanes were outdated. The fighting capacity of the Soviet army was weakened by massive repressions of the late 1930s, during which the army lost over forty thousand officers and military staff. Their replacements were frequently underprepared and inexperienced. Relying on Hitler's promises and believing that Germany, already involved in a war with Great Britain, would not start a two-front war, Stalin disregarded the continuing flow of information suggesting that Germany was preparing for a massive invasion of the USSR. He dismissed that information as anti-Soviet propaganda. As a result, the general staff and leadership of the Soviet military were caught entirely by surprise when Hitler attacked. Sudden air assaults by the Luftwaffe on Soviet airfields on the morning of June 22 put a significant portion of Soviet aviation out of commission. German tank and motorized divisions, supported by the air force, advanced rapidly through Soviet territory. The Germans were met by furious resistance from the Soviet troops, which suffered extremely heavy casualties and could not stop the enemy. By winter of 1941 German forces took control of the Baltic states, Moldavia, Ukraine, and Belorussia, surrounded and created a blockade of Leningrad, and got as far as the sub-urbs of Moscow.

In December 1941, during the battle of Moscow, Soviet troops carried out a massive counter-attack, the first attacking operation of the Great Patriotic War. The enemy was forced back 100–250 km away from the capital.

In the summer of 1942 the German army resumed attacks on the Eastern front. The Germans managed to break through Soviet defenses near Kursk and Kharkov. By the fall of 1942 they approached Stalingrad (now Volgograd) and the Caucasus mountains. This would be the furthest advance of the invading forces into Soviet territory.

At the same time as Germany was leading an assault on the USSR, the government of Japan was considering where to direct Japanese expansion: to the North, against the Soviet Union, or to South Pacific, against the United States and Great Britain. Originally plans were made for assaults on both fronts, but at a meeting on July 2, 1941, the leaders of Japan, with input from the emperor, decided to make their primary goal "expansion to the South."

Japan's first target was the Pacific Fleet of the United States, the majority of which was based at Pearl Harbor in Hawaii. On December 7, 1941, a large flotilla of Japanese warships, including six aircraft carriers, approached Hawaii in complete secrecy. An air attack launched from the ships that day delivered a crushing blow to the American fleet. The majority of the ships based at Pearl Harbor were either sunk or seriously damaged.

Simultaneously with the attack on Pearl Harbor, Japanese fleet and air force suddenly attacked American and British naval bases in the Philippines and Malaysia, a British colony. After winning the advantage at sea and in the air through these attacks, the Japanese sent troops into the Philippines, Malaysia, and the Dutch colony of Indonesia. Japanese forces entered Thailand and occupied it without resistance and immediately used it as a base for an invasion of the bordering British colony of Burma.

The Japanese army was well-prepared for military action. In addition, Japan fought under the premise of freeing Asia from "white imperialism", which won support from parts of local populations of invaded countries.

By the summer of 1942 Japan controlled Indochina (Vietnam), the Philippines, Thailand, Burma, Malaysia, and Indonesia, in addition to parts of China and Korea conquered before the start of the war. Japanese troops got as far West as the Indian border and almost reached Australian territory to the South. Only then, in the summer of 1942, the United

States and Great Britain managed to stop Japan's rapid advance at the naval battles of the Coral Sea and at the island of Midway in the Pacific.

The attack of Germany and its allies on the Soviet Union, as well as Japan's aggression against the United States and Great Britain, led to a unification of all the nations fighting against fascist aggressors into one anti-fascist coalition. The coalition's most important document was the Atlantic Charter, signed by Churchill and Roosevelt in August 1941 during their meeting off the Eastern coast of Canada. The Charter said, among other things that USA and Great Britain "do not desire territorial or any other gains and respect every people's right to select its own form of government.". The two nations claimed that "after the final extermination of Nazi tyranny" they hope to create a lasting peace that will allow every person to "live his life without knowing fear or need". The USSR joined the Atlantic Charter.

On July 12, 1941, an Anglo-Soviet agreement was signed guaranteeing mutual cooperation between the two countries in the war against Germany. President Roosevelt extended the Lend Lease Act to apply to the Soviet Union, and the USSR started receiving American weapons and supplies. The Soviet Union signed long-term mutual cooperation agreements with both Great Britain and the United States in 1942. This formed a military and political union of the three superpowers: USSR, Great Britain, and the United States of America.

The main factor that united these three nations was their common struggle against fascist aggression. Roosevelt and Churchill both believed that cooperation with the Soviet Union was absolutely necessary if victory over Germany and its allies was to be achieved, but at the same time denounced the Soviet political regime and feared its spread to other nations. As a result, there were many difference and contradictions in the coalition, particularly connected with the allies' postwar plans.

A major source of disagreement between the allies became the question of the second front. The Soviet Union, which had to face the bulk of German invading forces, demanded that the United States and Britain open a second front against Germany in Western Europe as quickly as possible. However, the governments of the USA and Great Britain, claiming a lack of military power, insisted that the creating of a second front in Europe was, for the time being, impossible.*

The World in the XXth Century. Moscow: Prosveshchenie, 1999, 170–75.

27

D-Day and the Liberation of Europe

Most U.S. history textbooks describe D-Day as the turning point of the war in Europe. For the other countries that participated directly in the invasion, the landing also merits a long and detailed explanation, usually focusing on the heroics of their forces. Yet for most others, D-Day does not occupy such a pivotal position in the history of the war; it is simply the title applied to the return of Allied forces to France.

★

GREAT BRITAIN

Stalin had urged Churchill and Roosevelt to open a second front in Europe in order to take the pressure off the Soviet Union. But the Allies knew the risk involved if such an invasion failed. This is why they made detailed and comprehensive plans in advance. The decision to go ahead was agreed at the Teheran Conference at the end of 1943.

General Dwight Eisenhower was appointed Supreme Allied Commander of 'Operation Overlord', as it was called. He assembled a team of high-ranking officers from Britain and the United States to train the forces, make preparations and ensure that supplies could be quickly sent to the armies once they had secured a bridgehead in France. Floating harbours (codenamed Mulberry) and an underwater oil pipeline (PLUTO) were constructed to speed up supplies to the invasion force in France.

Bad weather nearly postponed the invasion of France but a favourable forecast persuaded Eisenhower that Operation Overlord could go ahead as planned. 'O.K. Let's go,' he said. On Tuesday 6 June the great armada sailed, the greatest naval invasion in history.*

Phase 4: 1944–1945 Allied Victory

The USA gave priority to victory in Europe. By the D-Day invasion of France in June 1944, American and British armies at last opened up the second front. However, remorseless bombing by both the British and American air forces failed to disrupt seriously the German economy. Nor did it break civilian morale. The Germans kept fighting until the American and British troops had crossed the Rhine and the Russians were shelling Berlin. Then Hitler committed suicide and the German resistance ceased.

[. . .]

As the war progressed, it became clear that the post-war world would be dominated by the USA and by Russia. At the Big Three conferences of Teheran (1943) and Yalta (1945), Churchill's aim was to gain the best deal for Britain. This meant sustaining his special relationship with the USA and as friendly a one as possible with Russia, while restricting Russia's gains in Eastern Europe as far as he could.†

[. . .]

The Costs of the War

About 360,000 Britons lost their lives, about half of the number killed in the First World War, though the Second World War lasted two years

---

* Sauvain, Philip. *The Modern World: 1914–1980.* Cheltenham: Stanley Thornes, 1989, 267–68.

† Roberts, Martin. *Britain 1846–1964: The Challenge of Change.* London: Oxford University Press, 2001, 255.

longer. A higher proportion were civilians, mainly as a result of bombing. Two out of every seven houses suffered some form of bomb damage and some cities, like London, Southampton, and Coventry were hit particularly hard. Bombing also led to the mass evacuation of children from the threatened cities into the safer countryside. There is some controversy among historians about the social effects of evacuation. However many middle-class Britons seem to have been genuinely shocked by the effects of deprivation on working-class children which they observed for the first time, and they became more supportive of social reform.*

★

CANADA

D-Day and the Normandy Invasion

Two days after capturing Rome, the Allied forces invaded France. The lessons of Dieppe were taken to heart in planning the invasion. Massive air and naval firepower and better communications from ship to shore were put in place. New versions of the Sherman tank, called "Funnies," were built. They could wade through water, bulldoze obstacles, explode mines, and throw bursts of flame. Allied soldiers worked hard to prepare for action. By early June, more than thirty thousand Canadians were ready to do their part on "D-Day," the day scheduled for the Allied invasion of Europe. The invasion plan called for five divisions to land along an eighty-kilometre front. American forces were to attack at the western end of Normandy Beach, and British and Canadian troops were to land farther to the east. The 3rd Canadian Division was to land with the first wave of attackers in an area called Juno Beach. The sky above Juno Beach was to be protected by RAF bombers, many of which were flown by Canadian bomber crews. The invasion force also included 171 air squadrons to knock out the German Luftwaffe and destroy enemy tanks. More than seven thousand Allied ships of all descriptions—navy landing craft, destroyers, cruisers, corvettes, frigates, torpedo boats, and minesweepers—were also scheduled for the invasion.

* Roberts, Martin. *Britain 1846–1964: The Challenge of Change*. London: Oxford University Press, 2001, 255.

D-DAY BEGINS

It took enormous care and good luck to keep the massive invasion plans secret, but the Allies had done it. As dawn broke on June 6, 1944, surprised German defenders looked out to see a huge flotilla of ships sweeping toward the French coast. "As far as your eye could see, there were ships," said one sailor aboard the Canadian minesweeper *Canso.* "I always said that if you could jump a hundred yards at a clip you could get back to England without even wetting your feet. That's how many ships were involved."

The invasion did not go perfectly because some of the German positions had not been knocked out by the massive Allied air and sea bombardments. Many soldiers had to scramble for cover across exposed beaches raked with artillery fire. The landing of the 3rd Canadian Division was delayed by reefs and choppy seas for an hour and a half. By the time the Canadian forces touched down on Juno Beach, the enemy was ready for them. The worst trouble, however, occurred in the American sector at Omaha Beach. American forces were at the mercy of German defenders who fired down at them from high ground. Casualties were heavy, and the Americans lost 7500 soldiers.

Despite the heavy setbacks, the invasion was considered a success. By the end of D-Day more than 155,000 soldiers, 6000 vehicles, and 3600 tonnes of supplies had been landed in France. The fighting on the beaches had destroyed the defending German division, and Allied forces moved inland. The Canadians had pushed to within five kilometres of the city of Caen, farther inland than any other Allied troops. Canadian losses were also lower than had been feared. Still, almost a thousand Canadian soldiers were killed, wounded, or captured that day.

Germany was now fighting the land war on three fronts: the Soviet Union, Italy and France. On the Eastern Front, the Soviet Union continued to drive Germany back. In Italy, the Allies were pressing north. A new invasion through France would almost certainly mean the defeat of Germany.*

---

* Newman, Garfield. *Canada: A Nation Unfolding.* Toronto: McGraw-Hill, 2000, 236–37.

D-DAY AND THE LIBERATION OF WESTERN EUROPE

On June 6, 1944, the long-awaited Allied invasion of Western Europe was finally launched. At several key points along the 90-km coast of Normandy, France, massive land, sea and air attacks gave the Allies the footholds they needed to challenge Germany's four-year control. Offshore, battleships hammered away at the German defences, and in the air, British, American and Canadian bombers dropped hundreds of tons of bombs. Then the troops, both airborne and carried ashore in a flotilla of landing craft, poured onto the beaches. In spite of the power of technology hurled at the Germans' "Atlantic Wall", the Allies suffered losses in the thousands as the Germans answered back with their shore batteries, smashing landing craft and tanks, and trapping soldiers in deadly crossfire. Yet the Allies captured every beach.

Canadian and British troops fought their way through to Caen, then battled German panzer divisions for several weeks on the way to Falaise. Meanwhile, the Americans had broken through on the peninsula from Cherbourg, trapping several German divisions. As the British headed toward Brussels and the Americans struck for the Seine liberating Paris on August 25, the Canadians pushed toward the coastal ports. At Dieppe, the scene of the tragedy two years earlier, they were greeted by a celebrating populace. By the end of September, the channel ports had been virtually cleared of enemy resistance and the flying-bomb sites destroyed.

The Canadians were then given the task of clearing the Scheldt estuary so that the Belgian port of Antwerp would be available to the Allies as a supply base. Only then would they be able to obtain the arms, ammunition, reinforcements and other support necessary for an advance on the "Siegfried Line" of German defences and the Rhine River. In some of the most savage fighting of the war, the Canadians slogged across the flooded countryside of Holland, routing Germans from dikes and canals. By November, Allied convoys were delivering supplies to Antwerp.

While Canadian forces were clearing the Germans out of Holland, the First Canadian Army joined the Allied offensive, the final campaign to conquer Germany and impose unconditional surrender.

WAR'S END

By April, 1945, the retreating German forces were engaged in a hopeless fight to the death, their depleted ranks filled with untrained young boys and old men. As the British, Americans, Canadians and other Allies converged on German cities from the West, millions of Soviet troops were driving the German armies out of Poland and other countries on the East. In the race for Berlin, the Soviets arrived first and occupied the ruined German capital. Hitler had committed suicide in his underground bunker. The final German surrender, a total acceptance of Allied victory, came on May 7, 1945.

The war in the Pacific, where Canada had played a limited role, raged on, but the Americans had decided to use a weapon that would end the war suddenly. The dropping of atomic bombs on the cities of Hiroshima (August 6) and Nagasaki (August 9) knocked Japan out of the war, and brought an end to the "hot war"—World War II.*

FRANCE

France Liberated

THE LIBERATION OF THE COUNTRY

• With **the landings at Normandy on June 6 1944,** the liberation of France had begun. Corsica had already been liberated in 1943. After weeks of heavy fighting in Normandy, the Allies broke through the German lines at Avranches. From here, things accelerated rapidly, so much so that on August 15 **a second Allied landing** (French and American) took place in Provence. **On August 24 the capital was liberated by the Resistance**—where the *Francs tireurs* and the *Partisans français communistes* were numerous and influential—**and the 2nd tank division of General Leclerc.** At the end of November 1944, Strasbourg was liberated.

* Kirbyson, Ronald C. *Discovering Canada: Developing a Nation.* Toronto: Prentice Hall, 1992, 295–97.

- By this date, with the exception of a part of Alsace and some pockets of German resistance in the Atlantic ports, the vast majority of the country had been rid of the German presence. By providing information and performing acts of sabotage and guerilla warfare, **the interior Resistance participated in the combat as well,** frequently at a heavy price. Some regions, like Limousin, were liberated by the resistance fighters before the Allied armies arrived. The German army occasionally indulged in atrocious reprisals. For example, near Limoges the village of Oradour-sur-Glane was burned and its entire population massacred.

THE END OF THE VICHY REGIME

- **The Vichy regime did not survive the liberation of the country.** It receded with the withdrawal of the German army. Marshall Pétain was installed in Sigmaringen in southern Germany by the Germans in August of 1944. At the end of that month, General de Gaulle installed the provisional government of the French Republic in Paris. The collapse of Vichy and the victorious Free France allowed for France as a nation to participate in the end of the war and to take their place in the victors' camp on May 8, 1945 when Germany surrendered.

- Beginning in 1944 there began another phase, that of the *purge*. Those responsible for the "Revolution nationale" and the Collaboration were pursued. The ministers and prefects of the Vichy government found themselves in court and often condemned to harsh punishments. But the majority of government workers kept their posts and continued their careers. **Those prosecuted were the ones who had fought against the Resistance.** There were not, at this time, any trials for crimes against humanity because this legal concept wouldn't be defined until the Nuremburg trials of 1946. The few Jewish survivors of the camps coming home after 1945 did not attempt to prosecute those who were responsible for their deportation. At the beginning, they only wanted to forget the horrors of the camps.

- Nearly 10,000 people were executed, often without trial, during this transitional phase in the summer of 1944. The two most important trials were those of Laval, condemned to die by firing squad in October 1945, and Pétain. Brought to trial in July–August 1945, he was condemned to death. His sentence was commuted to life in prison by General de Gaulle; he died on the *île de Yeu* in 1951.

- Nearly 600,000 French died during the Second World War. The total cost was less than the toll taken in 1918, but **the scars were nonetheless profound** because beyond simply the horrors of those black years the French were divided over how to deal with defeat and occupation. What's more, with the Liberation the question of power became problematic: what would the communist attitude be? There was also the question of reconstruction and economic, social and institutional reforms proposed by the CNR* beginning in March 1944 and supported by the new authorities.†

★

ITALY

An Italian text highlights an often-overlooked effect of the war.

Europe faced the most tragic moment of its history in the winter of '41–2. With the intervention of the United States, moreover, the air raids on the cities were carried out on a scale much larger than what until then had been done by both sides. Europe's beautiful cities, cradles of civilization and keepers of immense treasures of art and culture, were subjected to intense air raids and often reduced to piles of rubble. It was all-out war: the unarmed civilian population suffered the gruesome consequences, often to a greater extent than the soldiers fighting on the fronts.‡

---

* *Conseil National de Résistance* (National Resistance Council).

† Lambin, Jean-Michel. *Histoire—T*ⁿˡᵉˢ. Paris: Hachette, 1998, 72.

‡ Villari, Rosario. *Storia Contemporanea.* Bari: Laterza, 1990, 571.

28

Resistance

Resistance during the war is not something ordinarily covered in depth in U.S. textbooks, in part because the United States was not occupied by an invading power. France, Italy, and even Germany, are just several of the countries that have had to come to terms with their complicity with Hitler during the war. Germany is considered the aggressor nation; Fascist Italy fought alongside the Germans while France's Vichy Regime willingly collaborated with the Third Reich. Every one of the following textbooks dedicates space to those who fought against tyranny, seeking perhaps to remind students that not everyone actively collaborated with the fascists.

★

FRANCE

The French are particularly adept at exploring the nuances of resistance and collaboration. Yet only since the last decade of the 20th century has the government even acknowledged the collaboration of the Vichy period.

France during the Resistance

THE REFUSAL OF GENERAL DE GAULLE

• From London on June 18, 1940—the day after Pétain's call for an armistice—de Gaulle called for the continuation of the fight over the British airwaves. This call on June 18 marked the historic origin of Free France. This gesture by de Gaulle sprang from both a refusal to quit and his vision of a worldwide conflict. He was convinced that the conflict was not limited to a simple fight between Germany and England. At the beginning, he was isolated in London. In July 1940, Free France numbered about 7000 men in Great Britain while only a part of the colonial empire rallied to his cause.

• In France, as well, the domestic Resistance appeared weak. The bombing of the French fleet at Mers-el-Kebir (Algeria) on July 3, 1940 by the British fleet provoked a wave of Anglophobia in France. **At the beginning the Resistance was the result of a few scattered efforts.** In the South, three movements eventually developed: "Libération-Sud" (1940), "Combat" (1941), and "Franc-tireur" (1942). The French Communist Party did not call for resistance against the occupiers until the USSR was attacked on June 22, 1941. Total opposition to Vichy France became an attitude shared by all, especially after 1942 and the first German defeats. In the North, the German occupation caused the rapid assembly of a network of Resistance from the beginning.

FREE FRANCE AND THE SHADOW WARRIORS

• To consolidate his influence, de Gaulle needed to have the domestic Resistance submit to his authority and have the Allies recognize his role. It was only in July 1942 that the relationship became clear between de Gaulle and the domestic currents of the Resistance. To demonstrate this new relationship, **Free France took on the name of "France combattante."** *

• A closer relationship between the French in London and the interior Resistance brought a greater degree of unity among the latter. On May 27, 1943 the first meeting of the *Conseil national de la Resistance*† was held in

---

* "Fighting France."

† [*National Council of the Resistance—CNR.*]

Paris under the direction of de Gaulle's special envoy, Jean Moulin. A motion was unanimously adopted which consolidated de Gaulle's position by supporting the Algiers constitution calling for a *"single strong"* government directed by de Gaulle. On June 3, 1943, the Comité français de libération nationale* was created in Algiers but de Gaulle had to share power with General Giraud who was supported by the Americans. Only in the fall of 1943 did de Gaulle become the lone head of Free France **(the provisional government of the French Republic).**

• During the four years of occupation, the interior Resistance evolved considerably. Born in 1940 of individual initiatives, it benefited from several subsequent contributions, mostly notably from the communists in 1941 and from numerous workers threatened by the STO† beginning in February 1943 (secondary students, university students and workers). The resistance fighters therefore came from all milieus, classes and party affiliations.

• While the **exterior Resistance** of the *Forces Françaises libres* (FFL)‡ fought the Axis armies in Africa alongside the Allies, **the direct military action** of the *Forces Françaises de l'intérieur* (FFI)§ was weak until 1944. The resistance efforts most often took other forms: aiding persecuted Jews and Allied pilots shot down, information on the German military forces or propaganda in the clandestine newspapers. Books were also published clandestinely such as *Le Silence de la mer* (1942) from the resistance writer, Vercors. Even these acts were gestures of refusal which could have meant death or deportation to their authors.‖

★

ITALY

Italy's examples of resistance include soldiers and officers "massacred by German troops" and a people who fought the Germans "bravely and victoriously."

---

* French Committee on National Liberation.

† [Service de Travail Obligatoire—mandatory work service organized in France under German pressure beginning in February 1943 to provide the Germans with workers.]

‡ Free French Forces.

§ French Forces of the Interior.

‖ Lambin, Jean-Michel. *Histoire—T^{sles}*. Paris: Hachette, 1998, 68.

Mass antifascist protest, which had already begun to manifest itself on a large scale before these events, fully revealed the abyss that had been dug between the nation and the regime, and the total lack of support of the war Fascism had imposed. [. . .] The allied troops from Sicily had landed on the peninsula in Calabria, while the Germans, who had allowed reinforcements to pour in, prepared themselves to take the situation in Central and Northern Italy under direct control. No measures had been taken to prevent the German reaction to the announcement of the armistice: the king and the government abandoned Rome, whose German occupation was briefly hindered by groups of soldiers and civilians who had spontaneously placed themselves in defense of the capitol. In various areas Italian troops refused to pass under German command and fought desperately, without provisions or leadership, before succumbing. One of the most important episodes of resistance was in Cefalonia, in the Ionian Islands, where thousands of Italian soldiers and officers who had refused to surrender were massacred by German troops. [. . .]

In the meantime in Naples, a city that had suffered in the most tragic ways the consequences of the war—the air raids, food shortages, and civilian casualties—the people, exasperated by the violence and aggravation of the German troops, rose up against them fighting bravely and victoriously in the streets for four days (September 27–30, 1943). It was one of the first episodes of the Italian Resistance, which coincided with the beginnings of a widespread antifascist awareness throughout the whole country, and with the transformation of antifascism from being confined to small groups to being a mass movement.*

*

GERMANY

Since the conclusion of World War II in 1945, few other nation's (with the possible exception of Japan) have been characterized with such negative images and stereotypes of their people as aggressive, brutal, and racist. In this text, German historians

* Villari, Rosario. *Storia Contemporanea*. Bari: Laterza, 1990, 559–60.

resist this widespread image by pointing out that not all Germans were Nazi sympathizers.

Resistance against National Socialism

FORMS OF OPPOSITIONAL CONDUCT

Under the leadership of National Socialism [NS] there was no unified and widespread political resistance against the regime. That was mainly because the security organs of the NS state, especially the Gestapo, were able to hinder the rise of an effective opposition by excluding the opponents of National Socialism early on in waves of imprisonment. In addition, the resistance lacked backing in the populace because the policy of Hitler was quite popular for a long time right up until the defeat on the Russian battlefield 1943. The resistance against National Socialism was therefore a **"resistance without the people."**

The **political resistance** was split into several small, independent groups, which were not unified in their strategy, did not know of each other, or because of conflicting worldviews, could not arrive at any sort of unified actions. Fundamentally the political opposition was formed by the members of the forbidden parties of the left (KPD, SPD), by the trade unions, and by circles within the Protestant and Catholic churches. But bourgeois-conservative circles also decided for opposition as they became aware that Hitler would lead Germany into catastrophe with his war policy. In addition, by 1938 a military opposition began to develop. In the face of persecution at the hands of the National Socialist regime, which remained in power, the different resistance groups eventually made contact with each other. Questions of the future order after the downfall of the NS regime were a dominant theme in these contacts. Underneath the political struggle ran distinctive currents of **societal protest,** in which individual persons or groups attempted to hinder the incursion of National Socialists in their occupational realms (military, church, bureaucracy). Another possibility of protest existed in maintaining the traditional customs in order to signal resistance against the National Socialists.

The rejection of the National Socialist ideology could express itself in multiple forms of **nonconformist conduct.** The spectrum spanned from the refusal of the Hitler greeting to nonparticipation in officially held NS celebrations and NS rallies, from standing up for Christian principles in everyday life to the maintenance of contact with Jews. Help for the persecuted or the supply of foreign compulsory workers with food stuffs also belonged to these small acts of resistance, which, like the assassination attempt on Hitler, were sometimes also punished by death.*

* Jager, Dr. Wolfgang, et al. *Kursbuch Geschichte*. Berlin: Cornelsen, 2000, 483.

29

World War II: Pacific Theater

In U.S. textbooks, the discussion of the Pacific war receives considerably less emphasis than the European war, with each major island conflict treated in a paragraph or less. Like the U.S. strategy itself, U.S. textbooks "island-hop" right to the end of the war. Often missing in U.S. textbooks is a discussion of the atrocities carried out in the Pacific; modern-day allies tend to get lighter treatment, and such notorious incidents as the Bataan Death March have been all but eliminated from U.S. accounts.

★

PHILIPPINES

This selection recounts a little known episode that took place between the Philippines and Great Britain before the start of the war. It reveals the more problematic aspects of U.S. power in the region prior to WWII.

Quezon's Secret Plan to Join the British Empire

The relations between the Philippines and the United States during the transition period were not always harmonious, as most vividly exemplified in President Quezon's secret approach to British authorities to join the British Empire as a self-governing dominion, like Australia and Canada.

As early as August 1933, then Senate President Quezon informed his British friend and adviser, Frank Hodsoll (also a prominent businessman in Manila), that if hostile pressure groups in Washington, D.C., successfully lobbied for the abandonment by the U.S. of the Philippines, "he (Quezon) would be prepared to go to London and, in the name of 14,000,000 inhabitants of the islands, ask for admission to the British Commonwealth of Nations."

In January 20, 1935, Quezon told Hodsoll to act as his secret liaison agent and contact British officials about the possibility of the Philippines joining the British Empire. By this time, President Quezon was concerned about the threat of a Japanese invasion and the apathy and disinterest of the United States in strengthening the military defenses of the Philippines.

The British Foreign Office seriously considered the implications of President Quezon's offer, and by December 1936, they expressed their approval for secret talks to be held in London between Quezon and the British Foreign Minister, Anthony Eden. However, on February 19, 1937, the proposed secret discussions were disclosed to the U.S. Charge d'Affaires in London, Ray Atherton, who immediately alerted the U.S. State Department about Quezon's contacts with the British authorities.

President Roosevelt and other high American officials were aghast, and the Assistant Secretary of State, Francis B. Sayre, was instructed to censure Quezon. Being an astute politician, Quezon denied that he formally made the offer and riposted that if the U.S. would not fortify the Philippines to make her impregnable to a Japanese invasion, it was his duty to seek protection from any other power for his country's survival, his first choice being Great Britain; but if Britain would not help he would turn to "another great power in the Far East". That "great power" was none other than Japan itself. Quezon earlier noted to his British adviser, Hodsoll, that he (Quezon) would consider a treaty of amity and alliance with Japan if the United States and Britain refused to protect the Philippines.

Ironically, U.S. war plans from 1937 onwards, which became their strategy during the Second World War, anticipated that the U.S. would concentrate on winning the war in Europe and was prepared to accept the initial fall of the Philippines, Guam, and possibly Hawaii, to Japan. Furthermore, U.S. authorities themselves considered the permanent declaration of the Philippines as a neutral country, like Switzerland, during the secret Japan-US diplomatic negotiations in 1941. Evidently, President Quezon, in toying with the idea of joining the British Empire or seeking appeasement with Japan, was acting as a fervent patriot, putting his country's interests first rather than maintaining perpetual allies of enemies of any other country.*

The Fall of Bataan was a military disaster for the United States, which resulted in the capture or death of thousands of U.S. and Filipino soldiers. This Philippine textbook takes the time to explain the sacrifice these soldiers made in defending the islands and then enduring the infamous Death March.

Bataan's Heroic Stand

On January 9, 1942, General Homma hurled his troops against the USAFFE (United States Armed Forces in the Far East) lines in Bataan. The Fil-American troops resisted with magnificent courage. The Battle of Bataan was on. Day and night, week after week, the fierce fight raged. On the blood-drenched, flaming peninsula of Bataan, the Filipinos and Americans, fighting side by side as brothers-in-arms, wrote a new epic in the annals of war, a new chapter in Philippine-American history.

But the Fil-American defenders faced a hopeless situation in Bataan. They had no air and naval support; they were insufficiently equipped and outnumbered; they were starved of food, medicine, and ammunitions; and the aid which they had expected from America never arrived.

The Fall of Bataan

Lt. Gen. Jonathan M. Wainwright succeeded MacArthur as commander of the Fil-American troops, now changed from USAFFE to USIP (United States Forces in the Philippines). He occupied MacArthur's headquarters in Corregidor, and from there he directed the gallant defense of Bataan. The Brave Filipino and American defenders reeled before the smashing onslaught of the invaders but they held their ground and fought on with tenacious courage.

* Zaide, Sonia M. *The Philippines: A Unique Nation.* Quezon City: All-Nations Publishing, 1999, 321–22.

Despite the terrible odds and the seductive propaganda of "Tokyo Rose" about America's inevitable defeat, the hungry, tired, and sick Fil-American defenders continued to fight. But theirs was a hopeless struggle. The much-awaited "miles of convoy from Australia" carrying reinforcements, armaments, and food supplies never came.

On April 3, 1942, Good Friday to the Christians and Jummu Tennon-Sai (Commemoration Day of Emperor Jimmu) to the Japanese, General Homma unleashed the full fury of an all-out Japanese offensive in Bataan—Bataan was doomed. The defenders, weakened by hunger, disease, and fatigue, fought fiercely, and died as heroes.

On April 9, 1942, Bataan fell. There was no other choice. General Edward P. King, American commander of the Bataan forces, surrendered in order to stop the carnage and prevent further killing of the helpless defenders.

The Death March

More than 76,000 USAFFE forces, including 66,000 Filipinos, laid down their arms in Bataan. This mass surrender, according to John Toland, American author, "was the greatest capitulation in U.S. military history". Aside from these war prisoners, there were 26,000 civilian refugees (men, women and children) who were trapped behind the USAFFE lines in Bataan.

The infamous "Death March" began in Mariveles and Cabcaben on April 10, 1942. The prisoners, weakened by hunger, thirst, sickness, and fatigue, painfully trudged at the points of Japanese bayonets along the road to San Fernando, passing through Limay, Balanga, Orani, and Lubao. Many perished on the way due to the Japanese who gave no food, water, or medicine to the war prisoners, in violation of the Geneva Prisoner of War Convention and brutally killed those who could no longer walk. Many more would have died were it not for the fact that Filipino townfolks who witnessed the suffering of the vanquished defenders of Bataan, surreptitiously furnished food, water, and fruits to the starving marchers and, at the risk of their lives, pulled hundreds of prisoners when the enemy guards were not looking and aided them to escape.

In San Fernando the weary and hungry marchers were herded like cattle into boxcars and were transported by railway to Capa. Before reaching their destination, hundreds of prisoners again marched on foot to their prison camp at Camp O'Donnell. Only some 56,000 reached the camp alive on April 15, 1942.

This prisoners' camp was a greater hell than the Battle of Bataan. According to the records of the War Crimes Convention, which tried the surviving Japanese military officers who were responsible for the atrocities committed in the Philippines, 22,155 Filipinos and 2,000 Americans died in Camp O'Donnell.

Corregidor

General Wainwright displayed superhuman efforts to defend the Island-fortress, but in vain. No general could save Corregidor then. And no army of the size that he had under his command could hold the place against overwhelming odds.

On May 6, 1942, Corregidor fell. Nearly 12,000 Fil-American soldiers were taken prisoner. Fortunately, unlike their comrade-in-arms of Bataan, the Corregidor prisoners did not undergo the rigors of a "Death March". With the fall of Corregidor, organized resistance against Japanese invasion of the Philippines came to an end.*

Although Americans usually remember the invasion of the Philippines only for its fulfillment of General MacArthur's pithy promise, "I shall return," for the Filipinos it is a far more significant event, in which they were able to free their nation from the control of the Japanese after nearly five years of oppressive occupation.

The Restoration of the Commonwealth

From August to October 1944, the tide of war decidedly turned in favor of the United States, as American planes began to bomb targets in the Philippines. On October 20, 1944, the main attack force of 174,000 American troops, ferried by an armada of 700 warships, landed at Leyte. After the first wave of Marine troops had made a beachhead, General MacArthur waded ashore, at Red Beach, near Palo, Leyte, accompanied

* Zaide, Sonia M. *The Philippines: A Unique Nation.* Quezon City: All-Nations Publishing, 1999, 327–331.

by President Osmena, General Carlos P. Romulo and General Basilio Valdez. "I have returned," MacArthur told the jubilant Filipino nation. On October 23, the Commonwealth Government was declared restored, with Tacloban as the temporary capital.

Japan's Collapse in Leyte

The liberation forces of General MacArthur encountered stubborn resistance in Leyte. Lt. Gen. Tomoyuki Yamashita rushed reinforcements to Leyte by ships and by planes. The Americans, using new carbines, flamethrowers, amphibian tanks, and faster fighter planes, smashed the enemy at all sectors of the island. In fanatical desperation, Japanese suicide pilots known as *kamikaze* crashed their planes on the American transports and warships at Leyte Gulf.

On January 9, 1945, General MacArthur struck at Luzon, landing in full force at Lingayen. The Filipino guerrillas and civilians, who had waited for three long years for his return, welcomed him. The liberating Yanks, reinforced by the fighting guerrillas, rushed toward Manila. All Japanese opposition on the way collapsed before the irresistible advance of the liberators.

Liberation of Manila

On February 5 the advance units of the First Cavalry crossed the river in amphibian tanks. They were reinforced by the infantrymen of the 37th Division, who had entered the city from the north. Elements of the 11th Airborne Division who had parachuted down on Tagaytay Ridge entered from the south. The Japanese forces in South Manila, trapped by the converging American columns, fought with fanatical courage. Crazed by their desperate situation, they plunged Paco, Ermita Malate, and Itramuros in a ruthless orgy of rape, destruction, and blood. They burned private homes, government buildings, beautiful colleges, and historic churches. They destroyed valuable books, documents, furniture, and art objects. They massacred hundreds upon hundreds of helpless civilians, men, women, and children. They spared nobody.*

---

* Zaide, Sonia M. *The Philippines: A Unique Nation.* Quezon City: All-Nations Publishing, 1999, 349–350.

★

JAPAN

U.S. history textbooks usually do not discuss Japan's position and motives prior to the attack on Pearl Harbor. These selections provide some of this information. Over the last few decades, there have been several international incidents involving Japanese history textbooks. Japan's Asian neighbors have objected to Japan's representation of its own history, specifically its "watered-down" version of atrocities committed by the wartime Japanese government and military. The government's approval of particularly conservative and nationalistic textbooks (though they represent very few of the textbooks in use overall) has been the cause of much controversy in the region. In 1995, the Japanese Ministry of Education printed a bilingual version of its history textbook in order to placate its critics—though the government's own version had rarely been the focus of concern.

Work toward Disarmament

In the postwar years, calls for a lasting peace mounted, with widespread expressions of antiwar sentiment in literature and art, and strong demands for disarmament. From 1921 into the following year, the Washington Conference was held in which Britain, America, and Japan agreed to restrict their capital ships, the total tonnage maintained by the three countries to be in the proportion of 5-5-3, and to prohibit the building of new vessels for ten years. Next, France joined these three nations in a Four-Power Treaty that pledged the maintenance of peace and the status quo in the Pacific area, and the Anglo-Japanese alliance was dissolved. In a Nine-Power Treaty pledging respect for the independence of China and its territorial integrity, as a result of negotiations between Japan and China, Japan returned to China its rights in Shandong Province. Further naval disarmament was pledged in London in 1930.

In Europe, too, Germany and other countries of Western Europe concluded the Lucarno Treaty aimed at collective security, in 1925. In 1928, Japan joined these countries in signing a treaty of nonbelligerence, which forswore resort to war.*

---

* *Japan in Modern History, Junior High School Textbooks.* Tokyo: International Society for Educational Information, 1994, 477.

To break the deadlock in the Japan-China War, the Japanese army attempted to occupy Southeast Asian countries as a new source of resources and also because it wanted to cut off the route by which the Allies were supplying aid to China. In 1940 Japan advanced to northern Indochina and also concluded a military alliance (the Tripartite Pact) with Germany and Italy.

In the following year, while securing the safety of the northern territories through a neutrality pact with the Soviet Union, Japan advanced into southern Indochina as well. These moves deepened the antagonism towards Japan by such countries as the U.S., Britain, and Holland, which then proceeded to impose restrictions on the export of war supplies to Japan. The U.S. held talks with Japan but eventually embargoed exports of oil to Japan while demanding the withdrawal of Japanese troops from Indochina and all Chinese territory.

Japan, which had been secretly preparing for war while continuing negotiations with the U.S., invaded the Malay Peninsula on December 8, 1941, and also attacked the U.S. forces base in Hawaii (Pearl Harbor). This was the start of the Pacific War. As a result of this, the whole world had become a battlefield, with the fascist countries of Germany, Italy, and Japan pitted against the Allied Powers of the U.S., Britain, USSR, and China, etc.

Southeast Asia becomes a battlefield: The Japanese army in a short period of time occupied Singapore, Burma (now Myanmar), Indonesia, and the Philippines. The people in the occupied territories were forced to cooperate with the Japanese army and had resources and food taken from them. They were controlled oppressively, and anyone who opposed occupation policies was severely punished.*

In the Pacific, the U.S. army came ashore on the main island of Okinawa in April 1945. Since the Japanese army regarded Okinawa as its front line for the defense of the Japanese mainland, it mobilized Okinawan people to hold back the attack, including junior high school boys and girls. About half of these boys and girls were killed in the battle. Many Okinawans were murdered by the Japanese army for disobeying orders or on suspicion of

---

* *Japan in Modern History, Junior High School Textbooks.* Tokyo: International Society for Educational Information, 1994, 329–331.

spying. Many others were forced to commit mass suicide. Some 66,000 soldiers from outside Okinawa Prefecture, plus 28,000 soldiers or military related people from Okinawa and a further 94,000 Okinawan civilians out of the 420,000 population of Okinawa lost their lives before Okinawa was finally occupied by the Allied forces.*

Whereas Americans joined the war effort at home with enthusiasm and patriotic zeal, this text describes the hardship endured by those participating on the Japanese home front. The last paragraph is this textbook's effort at explaining the forced labor of Koreans in Japan.

The U.S. army began its counterattack in the Pacific with the Battle of Midway in June 1942. With resources from overseas now dried up, Japan was not able to proceed with the production not only of war supplies, but also of everyday commodities, rice, and other foods. The government therefore put efforts into expanding the production of resources at home and the gathering of objects for recycling. It also recruited university students as soldiers to make up for the increasing loss of men at the front. And to replace farmers and laborers who were mobilized into the army, junior high school boys and girls were sent to work in the military factories.

In addition, the government brought about 700,000 Koreans to Japan and forced them to work in mines and elsewhere and rounded up the young women under the name of volunteer corps for the war. A conscription ordinance was also issued in Taiwan and Korea.†

Japan was occupied by U.S. military forces after its surrender aboard the U.S.S. Missouri in Tokyo Harbor. Most Americans would recognize the Nuremburg war crimes tribunal in Germany that followed WWII, but fewer are likely aware of the parallel war trials that took place in Japan at the time.

Shortly after Japan accepted the Potsdam Declaration, the Allied Forces, mainly of the United States forces, were stationed in Japan, and Japan signed the instrument of surrender. Japan's territory was confined to

---

* *Japan in Modern History, Junior High School Textbooks.* Tokyo: International Society for Educational Information, 1994, 341–343.

† *Japan in Modern History, Junior High School Textbooks.* Tokyo: International Society for Educational Information, 1994, 337.

Honshu, Hokkaido, Kyushu, Shikoku, and nearby small islands. The Japanese government was under the direction of the General Headquarters of the Allied Powers (GHQ), led by the U.S. General MacArthur as Supreme Commander (SCAP).

GHQ issued a series of orders to make extensive reforms. First it ordered that the military disband and arrested soldiers and politicians suspected of being war criminals, to bring them before a military tribunal. Professional soldiers and people who had occupied important positions during the war were ousted from public office. The Maintenance of the Public Order Act was abolished, and all those who had been imprisoned as political offenders were released from prison.

Freedom of speech, publication, and association was approved so long as it did not hamper Occupation policies. Thus, political parties, including socialist and communist parties, revived and started operation.*

[. . .]

The GHQ ordered the government to abolish the Maintenance of the Public Order Act, to recognize freedom of political activity, revise the election law, and give suffrage to all men and women aged twenty and over.

They further proceeded to democratize the country by establishing the Labor Union Law recognizing the right of workers to unite and the Labor Standards Act setting the minimum working conditions.†

As the antagonism between the United States and the U.S.S.R. intensified, the United States switched occupation policy towards helping Japan develop to support itself economically and become a power to cope with communism in Asia.

Thus, the United States instructed the Japanese government in 1948 to adopt tight money policies and a tax increase to stabilize the economy. Civil service employees were prohibited from striking and kept from engaging in the labor movement. With the strict indemnity plan and the antimonopoly policy relaxed, the economy started to grow, led by major corporations.‡

---

* *Japan in Modern History, Junior High School Textbooks.* Tokyo: International Society for Educational Information, 1994, 165.

† *Japan in Modern History, Junior High School Textbooks.* Tokyo: International Society for Educational Information, 1994, 363.

‡ *Japan in Modern History, Junior High School Textbooks.* Tokyo: International Society for Educational Information, 1994, 183.

30

The Atomic Bomb

The atomic bombs that were dropped on Japan were by far the most destructive weapons ever used. Today, the debate still rages over whether the United States was justified in using the atomic bombs on the populations of Hiroshima and Nagasaki—as evidenced by the varied perspectives of these excerpts.

★

JAPAN

Why the Atomic Bomb?

Was the atomic bomb really necessary in order to make Japan surrender? President Truman said that use of the atomic bomb saved the lives of tens of millions of American and Allied troops. An English scientist claimed that the dropping of the atomic bomb represented a cold-blooded sacrifice of the citizens of Hiroshima and Nagasaki as pawns in postwar strategy toward the Soviet Union. Another theory holds that the bomb was dropped in order to justify to American taxpayers the $2 billion spent in making the bomb.*

---

* *Japan in Modern History, Junior High School Textbooks*. Tokyo: International Society for Educational Information, 1994, 511.

As early as February 1945, the leaders of America, Britain and the Soviet Union had held talks at Yalta and secretly agreed that the Soviet Union should join the war against Japan. In July, the three leaders met again at Potsdam on the outskirts of Berlin, and issued the Potsdam Declaration, setting forth the conditions for Japan's surrender, but the Japanese government ignored it. As the day approached for the Soviet Union to join in the war in accordance with the Yalta agreement, America— partly out of a desire to have the edge over the Soviet Union in the postwar world—dropped atomic bombs on Hiroshima and Nagasaki on August 6 and 9, respectively. As a result, enormous numbers of people were killed or injured, and the towns were reduced to ruins. The number of dead, including those who died later from exposure to radiation and other causes, amounted to more than 200,000 in Hiroshima and more than 100,000 in Nagasaki.

On the 8th, between these two days, the Soviet Union abrogated its treaty of neutrality with Japan and sent forces into Manchuria, southern Sakhalin and the Kurils. Finally, on August 14, the Japanese government accepted the Potsdam Declaration and surrendered, the nation being informed of this fact the following day, the 15th, in a recorded broadcast by Emperor Showa. August 15 was to be the day of national liberation for people in Korea and Japan's other colonies. The number of dead among Japanese military and civilians in World War II was approximately 3.1 million, while the total number of dead in the war as a whole is said to have reached some 60 million.*

In July 1945, delegates from the U.S., Britain, and the Soviet Union met for talks in Potsdam, Germany. The Potsdam Declaration, made in the names of the U.S., Britain, and China, called for Japan to surrender and submit to democratization. However, the Japanese government ignored the declaration and urged the Japanese people towards a fight to the finish.

As a result, the U.S., which had succeeded in experiments to create the world's first atomic bomb and motivated also by the desire to come out of the war more powerful than the Soviet Union, dropped an atomic bomb

* *Japan in Modern History, Junior High School Textbooks.* Tokyo: International Society for Educational Information, 1994, 515.

on Hiroshima on August 6, and another one on Nagasaki on August 9. Both cities were annihilated in a flash. By 1950, it was estimated that more than 200,000 people in Hiroshima and 140,000 people in Nagasaki had died as a result of the atomic bombings, making this the worst tragedy in the history of mankind.

The radiation from those bombs was so great that its effects are still causing suffering to the victims of the bomb even today, and people are still dying from it. The names Hiroshima and Nagasaki have become symbols for people all over the world in their fight for the total abolition of nuclear weapons.

On August 8, two days after the atomic bomb was dropped on Hiroshima, the Soviet Union abandoned its neutrality pact with Japan and declared war on Japan based on the Yalta agreement. The Soviet army advanced into Manchuria, southern Sakhalin and the Kurils. The Japanese army continued to retreat, but while the army retreated, there were still Japanese people left behind in these places. Some committed mass suicide rather than be captured.

Under the circumstances, the Japanese government finally agreed to submit to the Potsdam Declaration and surrendered on August 14 after trying to gain assurance that the imperial system would be continued in Japan even after defeat. On the 15th, the emperor conveyed Japan's surrender to the Japanese people on the radio. This brought to an end Japan's war of invasion, which had lasted for fifteen years from the time of the Manchurian Incident, and also World War II. Victims of this war around the world numbered 60 million—10 million in China alone, and it left deep wounds on peoples everywhere.*

The greatest number of foreign victims of the atomic bombing in Hiroshima and Nagasaki were Koreans. It is said that some 25,000–28,000 Koreans were in Hiroshima at the time of the bombing, of whom 5,000–8,000 died; in Nagasaki there were 11,500–12,000 Korean victims, of whom 1,500–2,000 died. There are an estimated 20,000 atom bomb victims still living in South Korea, and the question of responsibility for their medical treatment and livelihood has become an issue.†

* *Japan in Modern History.* Tokyo: International Society for Educational Information, 1994, 343–353.

† *Japan in Modern History.* Tokyo: International Society for Educational Information, 1994, 355.

★

PHILIPPINES

What brought Japan finally to her knees were the horrible atomic bombs. The first atomic bomb was dropped on Hiroshima on August 6, 1945, and it wiped out 60% of the city. Two days later, the Soviet Union declared war on Japan. On August 9, Nagasaki felt the terrific explosion of the second atomic bomb; 40% of the city vanished. Unable to carry on the struggle and at the public behest of Emperor Hirohito, Japan finally surrendered unconditionally on August 15, 1945.*

★

CANADA

Canada's Role in Developing the Atomic Bomb

On August 6, 1945, the world was forever changed. On this day, the Japanese city of Hiroshima was obliterated by the world's first atomic bomb. Three days later a second Japanese city, Nagasaki, faced the same fate. About 110 000 people were killed and an additional 10 000 injured by the two bombs, known as "little Boy" and "Fat Man." The bombing had the desired result—Japan was forced to surrender, and the war was over. The nuclear age had begun.

Research into nuclear capabilities had been underway for several years before the 1930s, but the rise to power of Adolf Hitler and the re-arming of Nazi Germany stepped up research into harnessing nuclear power for war. The race to develop the nuclear bomb, officially known as the Manhattan Project, became the largest research project the world had ever seen. Requiring a staff of more than 200 000, the development of atomic weapons absorbed more funds than NASA later spent to reach the moon.

Most Canadians are unaware of the crucial role Canada played in the development of the atomic bombs that destroyed Hiroshima and Na-

---

* Zaide, Sonia M. *The Philippines: A Unique Nation.* Quezon City: All-Nations Publishing, 1999, 351.

gasaki. From the outset of the Manhattan Project, the Canadian government co-operated with the British and American governments to ensure that the Allies would develop the nuclear bomb before the Axis powers.

A key ingredient of an atomic bomb is uranium, a heavy radioactive metallic element. The Nazi conquest of Europe had the result that all European uranium refineries were under Nazi control. Only one uranium refinery was left for the Allies to use—the Eldorado Refinery in Port Hope, Ontario. It was here that all the uranium used in the Manhattan project was refined. Much of the uranium came from mines on the shores of Great Bear Lake in the Northwest Territories, and the heavy water used in the development of the plutonium bomb (Fat Man) was supplied by the Consolidated Mining and Smelting Co. in Trail, British Columbia. Canada's role in the development of the atomic bomb extended well beyond supplying raw materials. Canada provided a safe working environment, far from the battlefields, for British scientists working on the Manhattan Project. Also, Canadian scientists played a crucial role in the project from its beginning. They discovered uranium 235 (the basic element of the atom bomb), helped to create the first chain reaction using uranium 235, and discovered how to purify uranium 235. They also were part of the team working in New Mexico in 1945, which assembled the core of the first plutonium bomb.

Some Canadians were unwitting participants in the development of the atomic bomb. Men of the Sahtugot'ine people, a nomadic group of Aboriginal people who lived near Great Bear Lake, were hired as transporters for the uranium. Despite warnings from federal-government scientists about the dangers of radioactive substances, the Sahtugot'ine were allowed to carry tonnes of uranium without being provided with any protective clothing and were not warned about the dangers they faced. The men, covered in uranium dust brought the radioactive material into their tents, thereby unknowingly contaminating their families.

The long-term effects of their work in transporting the uranium have been devastating for the Sahtugot'ine community. Gina Bayha, from Deline, N.W.T. noted: "Men from my grandmother's generation regularly lived into their nineties or one hundreds. But we hardly have any men past the age of sixty-five. They all died of cancer." In August 1998, representatives of the Sahtugot'ine travelled to Hiroshima, Japan to meet with survivors of the nuclear bombing. There they apologized for the indirect role they played in the destruction of the cities of Hiroshima and Nagasaki in

1945. Some Canadians celebrate the country's role in the atomic bomb as a great technological accomplishment; many others are ashamed of Canada's contribution to the development of weapons of mass destruction. Whatever their opinion, it is important for Canadians to understand Canada's role in the birth of the nuclear age.*

★

GREAT BRITAIN

American scientists with the aid of British and European colleagues had developed a new bomb of unprecedented destructiveness. Two of these atomic bombs were dropped on the Japanese, ending their fanatical resistance and beginning a new nuclear age where the human species had, for the first time, the technological means of obliterating itself.†

★

ITALY

Japan put forth a desperate resistance to American advances in the Pacific islands and to incessant air raids. The widespread use of the kamikaze technique by the Japanese pilots [. . .] and the garrisons' desire to destroy themselves rather than surrender [. . .] demonstrated that a true victory would have caused even more losses. But the war's outcome had already been decided even in this sector, and there was no doubt that in very little time the Japanese, already at the end of their tether, would have had to surrender. In these conditions the American president Harry Truman [. . .] decided, after having made an ultimatum that was then rejected, to employ in Japan the weapon that had been newly completed in the American nuclear laboratories.

[. . .]

Unlike what had happened in Europe after Germany's surrender, this time any joy over recapturing peace was overshadowed by anxiety and worries,

* Newman, Garfield, et al. *Canada: A Nation Unfolding*. Toronto: MacGraw-Hill, 2000, 244.
† Roberts, Martin. *Britain 1846–1964: The Challenge of Change*. London: Oxford University Press, 2001, 255.

provoked by images of the atomic mushroom cloud at Hiroshima and of the destroyed city. This extreme product of the intense technological efforts brought about by war—along with the invention of missiles, whose innovative range could not be grasped at that moment yet—offered a preview of dangers that until that moment had been unimaginable. How was such an important turning point arrived at?

The use of the atomic bomb in the last phase of the conflict was not essential from a military point of view, and the reasons for why that terrible decision was made have not been entirely made clear. Among other things, there was not even full knowledge of the effects the explosion would have, especially concerning the biological consequences of the exposure of a large mass of people to the radiation, and the genetic damage that the fallout would cause. The atrocious consequences of the radiation on the survivors of Hiroshima and Nagasaki and their children revealed themselves over the course of the years that followed the explosions of August 6th and 9th.

What seems certain is that that show of force, made indiscriminately at the expense of unarmed people, increased the United State's weight in post-war tensions and decisions, especially concerning the Soviet Union. It is probable therefore that Truman's decision was inspired more by post-war prospects than by calculations on the most convenient method to put an end to the conflict with Japan. From then on the problem of nuclear armament has had a decisive influence on world history, and has conditioned more than anything else the relations between the great powers and their attitudes toward the rest of the world.*

* Villari, Rosario. *Storia Contemporanea*. Bari: Laterza, 1990, 565–67.

PART VI

The Cold War

31

The Origins of the Cold War

Behind the major political and military conflicts of the second half of the 20th century lay the ideological differences of two great superpowers. For years, U.S. textbooks treated the USSR, according to President Reagan's famous epithet, as the "Evil Empire." Naturally, other countries, most of whom found themselves uncomfortably situated between the two superpowers, were more nuanced in their judgment. Recent American textbooks tend to be more critical of excessive propaganda on both sides.

★

CANADA

A harsh critique of American Cold War policy, this text makes the case that the U.S. could have been just as guilty in starting the Cold War as the Soviets. The authors also emphasize that Canada, because of its geographic location, was often forced to go along with America's foreign and military policies.

The Cold War

The making of foreign policy could not be separated from domestic realities. With Britain weakened by the war, and the United States a growing influence in Canadian economic life, Canadian foreign policy began to mirror that of the Americans. In this respect, Canada was in step with the major European industrial powers, which depended on American aid to reconstruct their shattered economies and rarely questioned American foreign policy. That policy was dominated by a militant anti-communism.

The Soviet Union under Stalin appeared to be undermining the fragile democracies in Europe and using its position on the Security Council of the United Nations to frustrate efforts to keep the peace. Soviet agents seemed to be everywhere, including Ottawa. In 1946 Igor Gouzenko, a cypher clerk in the Soviet embassy, revealed that a Soviet spy ring had been in operation in Canada throughout the war. Given Canada's close involvement with research relating to the atomic bomb, this was perceived as a serious matter. Canadians were drawn into the so-called Cold War, which pitted communist states against capitalist democracies.

In dramatic contrast to its isolation in the interwar years, the United States became the champion of the so-called "free world." Its chief policy goal, trumpeted in classrooms, from the pulpit, and by the ubiquitous media, was the containment of communism at home and abroad. America's exclusive possession of nuclear weapons from 1945 to 1949, followed by a decade of clear nuclear superiority over the Soviet Union, encouraged American political leaders to enunciate a policy of so-called deterrence: the Soviets and their communist allies throughout the world would have to behave, or the Americans and their allies would drop nuclear bombs on their territory.

In Canada, most External Affairs officials, while appalled by Stalin and the police apparatus central to the Soviet state, regarded American claims regarding Soviet intentions in foreign policy as vastly exaggerated.

Publicly, however, Canada supported American views: "Given the importance of Washington's politics to Canada's economic future, a public declaration of a cautious, balanced assessment of Russian policy . . . would not in fact have served the Canadian interest."

In military terms, Canada and the United States were closely linked from 1940 when, in the wake of Nazi victories over France and Norway,

President Roosevelt and Prime Minister King established the Permanent Joint Board on Defence to co-ordinate the defence policies of the two nations. The Board continued to operate after the war and, while the Canadian government balked at its military planners' suggestions in 1946 that the two nations mesh their defence forces, Canada was increasingly drawn into American defence strategy. In 1949, Canadians joined the North Atlantic Treaty Organization (NATO), a military pact that included the United States and Britain as well as Western European nations. Despite Canada's insistence on the formal acknowledgement of NATO's goals of economic as well as military integration, the organization soon became primarily an American instrument for co-ordinating the defence policies of its allies, rather than a club of equals that could restrain American initiatives. [. . .]

Nuclear superiority was, in the 1950s, the strategic key to American foreign policy. In 1954, John Foster Dulles, the hawkish Secretary of State in the administration of President Dwight D. Eisenhower, proclaimed that Americans would resort to "massive retaliation," including possible use of nuclear weapons, against aggression. That year NATO agreed to make nuclear deterrence the mainstay of defence strategy. Ignoring the likelihood that a nuclear war, once begun, would not be contained, NATO decided to build up stocks of "tactical" nuclear weaponry, intermediate-range weapons designed for battle in a particular region, as opposed to "strategic" weapons designed for a full-scale nuclear war. In December 1957, in line with this NATO policy, Canada agreed to play a role in surveillance of possible military strike plans by the Communists. In 1959 and 1960, Canada ordered a variety of aircraft and missiles meant to serve this role. In 1959, Canada agreed to permit storage of American nuclear weapons at Goose Bay and Harman Air Force bases, which, though on Canadian territory, were controlled by the Americans. That same year, Canada received a reward for its close co-operation with American defence policies: under the Defence Production Sharing Agreement, Canadian companies won the right to bid for American military contracts on an equal basis with American contractors. Canada offered the Americans the same privileges for this country's rather less impressive military procurements.

Despite its co-operation in American military policy, Canada attempted to cultivate an image as a peacemaker. When Britain, France, and Israel attacked Egypt to undo its efforts to seize control of the Suez Canal,

Minister of External Affairs Lester Pearson's role in ending the conflict won him a Nobel Peace Prize. Canada was one of a number of nations that sent peacekeeping forces to the region and, in subsequent years, Canada proved more than willing to send peacekeeping troops to hot spots. In retrospect, it seems clear that Canada was able to play the peacekeeping role only when the Americans did not feel their vital interests were at stake. This was not the case in Vietnam, a French colony since the nineteenth century. In 1954, Communists under Ho Chi Minh forced the French out and established control over the northern half of the partitioned country. Negotiations in Geneva that year produced an accord calling for reunification of North and South Vietnam after elections to be held in 1956. An International Control Commission (ICC), with Canada, Poland, and India as its members, was established to monitor the implementation of the provisions of the Geneva accord. But the Americans decided to violate the accord in order to provide time for the new, pro-American rulers of South Vietnam to gain popular legitimacy. In practice, this regime oversaw a reign of terror, murdering suspected sympathizers of the Communists and uprooting peasant villages.

In monitoring the developing conflict in Vietnam, members of the ICC were guided more by their own political views than by attempts at neutrality. Poland seemed able to see only South Vietnamese violations, while Canada, after briefly trying to prevent breaches of the accord, came to notice only violations by the North Vietnamese side.

In Vietnam and elsewhere, makers of foreign policy argued that they had to publicly support the broad outlines of Washington's external policies if they hoped to moderate these policies via "quiet diplomacy." Ottawa would have no moderating influence on the White House if Canada were not seen as a reliable ally. Scholars are divided as to whether this perspective reflected a sober assessment of geo-political realities or was simply a self-serving rationalization for kowtowing to a nation whose ability for economic retaliation was painfully clear. The foreign policy community was, in any case, not monolithic: a minority within the Department of External Affairs prodded their colleagues to support nationalist objectives in the Third World and not to reduce all issues to Cold War polarities.*

* Finkel, Alvin, et al. *History of the Canadian Peoples: 1867 to the Present, v. 2.* Toronto: Copp Clark Pittman, 1993, 400–401.

WHO STARTED THE COLD WAR?

In retrospect, Soviet ambitions in the postwar period appear to have been more conservative than the Americans claimed. Scholars have revised analyses of various Communist and left-wing revolutionary insurrections to suggest that nationalism, rather than Soviet-sponsored communism, was the determining factor in grass-roots struggles against western-supported regimes. But the Americans, despite having had their own revolution against foreign control, distrusted nationalist forces elsewhere.

Historians will long debate the degree of blame to be attached to the United States and the Soviet Union for launching and continuing the Cold War. Defenders of American behaviour stress Stalin's bloody-minded policies and the bellicosity of the Soviets. Defenders of the U.S.S.R point out that the Soviets had lost over twenty million people to the Nazi war machine and were understandably paranoid about the postwar intentions of a nuclear West that had refused to share the secrets of the atom bomb with its wartime ally. They claim that American ideological blinkers made impossible an appreciation of Soviet demands for security and destroyed the possibilities of peaceful relations with a nation that might have enjoyed greater liberalism at home if it were not forced to become a militaristic state. Some opponents go further and claim that America's Cold War posturing reflected "free-trade imperialism"—the need of its capitalist economy for untrammelled access to cheap resources and unprotected markets. Nationalism within former colonies threatened the success of American imperial objectives and therefore had to be snuffed out. It has also been noted that military pump priming of the economy was more ideologically acceptable to American business than welfare pump priming.*

* Finkel, Alvin, et al. *History of the Canadian Peoples: 1867 to the Present, v. 2.* Toronto: Copp Clark Pittman, 1993, 401.

★

RUSSIA

Soviet history textbooks were highly centralized in content and distribution. On any given day, one could expect to find history teachers covering the same material in every school across the entire Soviet Union. All this changed after 1991. The presentation of Russian history since the end of the Cold War has been mostly a reaction against this highly dogmatic approach. In Russia, the one Soviet history textbook, based on Stalin's 1944 account of Bolshevik history, has been replaced by a selection of textbooks published by several private publishing firms recognized by the Ministry of Education of the Russian Federation. In nearly all the new textbooks, Soviet history is replaced by Russian history, in which the central protagonist has reverted from the Communist party back to the Motherland. This holds true for all the former Soviet satellite countries, where the collective identity of Soviet-Marxism has been replaced by respective versions of nationalism.

This particular textbook comes from Prosveshchenie Publishers, which was founded in 1930 and held the monopoly in educational publishing in the USSR until the end of the Cold War. They still produce more than 45% of educational material in Russia.

After the end of the Second World War, two great superpowers, the USSR and the USA emerged as the most powerful in both the military and economic senses of the word and obtained the most influence of any nations in the entire world. The split of the world into two systems and the polarity of political ideologies and platforms of the two superpowers could not help but affect international relations of this time period. The ideological stand-off that divided these two nations gave rise to an atmosphere of hostility in the world arena, and to a never-ending search for the enemy within the two nations. Nonconformity of thought was considered an act of anti-government activity and was persecuted. As a result, an ugly movement appeared in the United States that became known as McCarthyism—the accusation of persecution of American citizens suspected of engaging anti-American activity. In the Soviet Union this atmosphere was one of the characteristics of the totalitarian regime.

The two great superpowers became entrenched in the state of a bipolar world and perpetual confrontation. An influential American journalist christened this conflict "The Cold War." Media picked up on this name, and it came to refer to the entire period in international politics all the way through the 1980s.

In historical works relating to the period in question it is common to consider a speech made by Winston Churchill to be a turning point in the course of foreign policy of the United States and other Western nations. This speech was made on March 5, 1946, in a small town in the middle of America, with President Truman in attendance. Truman's presence had to emphasize the special importance of this event. Why else would the President of the United States fly to the middle of the country to listen to a speech, the content of which he was already familiar with? It was also not a coincidence that, at the same time, Soviet agents went on trial for spying in Canada. Churchill proclaimed that an "iron curtain" separated Eastern Europe from European civilization, and that the Anglo-Saxon world should unite in the face of the Communist threat.

The diametrically opposed interests of the two superpowers became increasingly clear during the process of making post-war decisions and redrawing national boundaries in Eastern Europe. The coming to power of Communist parties throughout Eastern Europe in 1947–1948 and the partisan movement in Greece were viewed by the United States as acts of Communist expansion. This resulted in the appearance of the American foreign policy doctrines of "containment" and "pushing back" of Communism. Soviet propaganda held its own and proclaimed the aggressive expansion of American imperialism.

The arms race was the most important spot of contention and potential conflict between the superpowers and their allies. There exists a widespread opinion that the atom bomb dropped on Hiroshima in August 1945 was not only the final act of World War II, but also the first act of the Cold War, giving rise to the back-and-forth arms race.

The Soviet Union started pushing towards obtaining an atom bomb of its own, and conducted the first tests as early as 1949. The United States tested a hydrogen bomb in 1952, with the USSR just a year behind. The USA created its first strategic bombers at the same time as intercontinental missiles appeared in the Soviet Union. Anti-aircraft and anti-missile defenses were perfected and modernized. The competition between the two sides in the sector of military production escalated until the moment when it became clear to the leaders of both nations that the amount of armaments was far more than necessary for any defense or act of war. The stockpiled bombs were sufficient in power and number to destroy the earth several times over.

The creation of military-political blocs (or alliances) of nations also became an area of competition between the superpowers. This started with military assistance from the United States to Turkey and Greece in 1947 to help out the nations which faced "Communist pressure." The Marshall Plan that allocated billions of dollars in economic aid to nations of Western Europe served as a method of maintaining the stronghold of capitalism on the region. The Soviet Union and socialist nations refused this aid, citing the unwillingness to be indebted to American imperialists. Simultaneously, a propaganda campaign against Anglo-American warmongers escalated in the USSR. Churchill's speech from March 5, 1946, became known as the declaration of war from the side of "Anglo-American imperialism."

In 1949 the North Atlantic Treaty Organization (NATO) was created to supposedly provide security to Western nations against a possible rebirth of Nazism in Germany. West Germany itself joined NATO in 1955. That same year a military-political alliance headed by the Soviet Union was created by the Warsaw Pact. Thus, the stand-off between the two superpowers became a stand-off between two blocs of nations. The increasing polarization of the entire world and its gradual division into two camps was leading the globe towards a growing threat of nuclear war.*

★

GREAT BRITAIN

Great Britain was arguably the staunchest ally of the Americans during the Cold War. This selection, taken from a larger chapter on British imperial and foreign policy through 1964, reflects the diminished role of the former power.

Britain and the Cold War

At Potsdam in 1945, the Allies failed to agree about the settlement of Europe. By 1947, relations between the 'Western' allies (the USA, Britain

---

* *The World in the XXth Century.* Moscow: Prosveshchenie, 1999, 199–202.

and France) and the Soviet Union had deteriorated into a 'Cold' War, where there was such fear and suspicion that both sides might have been at war except they were not actually fighting. The Soviet Union took control of virtually all the countries of Europe which her armies had reached in 1945; set up pro-Moscow governments in them; and erected a barrier of barbed wire fences and minefields (which Churchill christened the 'iron curtain') to cut this 'Soviet bloc' off from the West.

One of Bevin's greatest achievements was to persuade the USA that Russian Communism was a danger to Europe and the world and that the Americans must stay involved in European affairs and not retreat into isolation as in 1919. The USA-Western Europe link was forged in three stages.

The first stage was linked to the situation in Greece. There, British forces had restored the Greek monarchy and then stayed to defend it in a civil war against Communist republicans. The economic problems which Britain faced in 1946–47 convinced the government that it could no longer shoulder the anti-Communist responsibility in Greece. However, it was able to persuade the US President, Truman, to take it over. Truman announced the Truman Doctrine, that the USA could be counted on to support anti-Communist forces throughout the world. Marshall Aid then followed which helped in the economic recovery of Western Europe.

The second stage was a crisis over Berlin. West Berlin was a non-Communist island surrounded by the Communist-controlled East Germany. In 1948, the Russians tried to force West Berlin, by a blockade, to become part of the Soviet bloc. The American and British airforces airlifted vital supplies into the city for more than a year until Stalin ended the blockade.

The third stage was the creation, in 1949, of the North Atlantic Treaty Organization for the defence of Eastern Europe against the Soviet Union. The USA dominated NATO and, for the next 40 years, the USA had military bases all over Europe, many of which were in Britain.

Between 1950 and 1953, Britain fought alongside American troops in Korea to prevent South Korea falling under Communist control. The costs of this war were an untimely extra burden for the Attlee government.*

* Roberts, Martin. *Britain 1846–1964: The Challenge of Change*. London: Oxford University Press, 2001, 278.

32

The United Nations

The United Nations is not a major topic of interest in most U.S. history textbooks. Most make an initial comparison with the failed League of Nations and explain that with U.S. support, this organization would succeed where the League had failed. But after a brief explanation of its internal structure and role in international politics, the UN more or less disappears, resurfacing only when the textbooks look at events in which the U.S. operated within the parameters of, or agreed with, the UN: creation of Israel, the Korean War, the Persian Gulf War, etc. There is virtually no discussion of dissent between the U.S. and the UN Security Council historically, for example, and little debate about the role the U.S. has had and should play in the organization.

★

GREAT BRITAIN

This British text shows a rarely mentioned connection between the disbanded League of Nations and the newly formed United Nations.

When Churchill and Roosevelt spoke of the need for 'a wider and more permanent system of general security' at the Atlantic Charter summit conference in 1941, they had in mind the failure of the League of Nations to provide any such security in the years before the war. To all intents and purposes, the League of Nations was already dead. It was finally disbanded in April 1946 when all its assets and property were transferred to the United Nations.

By 1941 the United Kingdom was the only great power still technically a member of the League. The United States never joined the League. The Soviet Union was expelled in 1939. Italy, Germany and Japan all resigned in the 1930s. Vichy France was no longer a great power. Any future world organisation could only work if it included both the United States and the Soviet Union.

This didn't mean that the League had little influence on the shaping of the United Nations. Far from it. The structure of the UN—with its Secretariat, Security Council, General Assembly, International Court of Justice and Specialised UN Agencies—bears a very strong resemblance to that of the old League of Nations—with its Secretariat, Council, Assembly, Court of International Justice and Specialised Organisations. The Covenant setting up the League of Nations also influenced the officials who drew up the UN Charter. But the United Nations is much more than a League of Nations, as you will see.

Dumbarton Oaks

In January 1942, Britain and America were joined by 24 other nations in confirming the principles enshrined in the Atlantic Charter. They included the Soviet Union, China and the Commonwealth Dominions. Roosevelt called this grouping The United Nations.

The Allied foreign ministers, Molotov (USSR), Eden (UK) and Hull (USA) took the first steps forward when they met in Moscow in October 1943, a month before the Teheran Conference. At these discussions, they agreed on the desirability of setting up a United Nations Organisation.

Accordingly a special conference, to draw up the Charter and decide the structure of the UN, was called for the autumn of 1944. It met at Dumbarton Oaks near Washington DC. Only the United States, the United Kingdom and the Soviet Union met initially to draw up this Charter.

They decided that the UN would have a General Assembly and a Security Council consisting of permanent representatives (the three great powers) and other representatives appointed for a fixed term from the

other member-countries of the UN. Later, China took part in discussions
with the UK and the USA but not with the Soviet Union, which was neutral at that time in the war between the Allies and Japan.

Although much of the Dumbarton Oaks Conference went well, there
was one crucial sticking point. This was the proposed right of any of the
great powers to veto proposals which affected their own interests. The Soviet Union was adamant that decisions of the great powers should always
be unanimous. The British delegates, on the other hand, were equally determined that a country involved in a dispute should not be able to vote on
any course of action proposed by the UN. They argued that no other
country in the world would agree to the great powers having privileges
which they were not allowed to share. Without such an agreement, there
could be no United Nations, they warned.*

★

RUSSIA

*A common enemy during WWII was enough to ensure cooperation between Russia
and the United States. Once Hitler was defeated, it would take an organization like
the United Nations to keep any dialogue going.*

An important part of the international peace movement that followed
the conclusion of World War II was the creation of the United Nations.
This organization was created towards the end of the war at a conference
in San Francisco (April 25–June 26, 1945). United Nations was originally
created by 51 nations, all members of the anti-Hitler alliance, and its constitution was approved on October 24, 1945. The main branches of the
UN are its General Assembly, the Security Council, the International
Court, a number of specialized councils, and other intergovernmental organizations. The General Assembly convenes annually, but the Security
Council is always in action, as its main responsibility is to uphold world-
wide peace. The Security Council has five permanent members (United
States, Russia, Great Britain, France, and China) and six temporary mem-

---

* Sauvain, Philip, *The Modern World: 1914–1980*. Cheltenham: Stanley Thornes, 1989,
305–06

bers, which change every two years. An important principle of the Council's activity, which allowed this organization to remain in existence despite constant conflicts between its members throughout the Cold War, is the requirement of a unanimous vote from the five permanent members of the Council when a decision to stop aggression and uphold the peace is being made. This is the so-called right veto, which allows any one member nation to reject any decision with which it does not agree. The United Nations also created groups aimed at creating and maintaining international economic stability, such as the International Monetary Fund and the International Bank of Reconstruction and Development.

In this fashion, a foundation for postwar cooperation among members of the Allies was laid at the end of World War II. Despite the frequent and often major conflicts of interest between the Soviet Union and the United States in the first years following the war, they were forced to conduct their struggle within the framework of international organizations and collectively made decisions.*

★

CANADA

Canada is the only country in this section that represents a non-Security Council country. This selection is more representative of the "middle powers" who benefit from the egalitarian structures of the representative bodies and who actively participate in the many UN operations around the world. In many ways, it provides the perspective of the role player who actively carries out the decisions of the main players.

The lesson of the Second World War seemed obvious. Canada would become involved in international conflicts regardless of their location. This being the case, then Canada's interests lay in trying to influence the events of the world around it.

[...]

Canadian delegates had a chance to carve out an appropriate activist role when they went to San Francisco in April 1945. Many nations, large and small, had gathered there to discuss the formation of another interna-

* *The World in the XXth Century.* Moscow: Prosveshchenie, 1999, 198.

tional organization that would be more effective in dealing with disputes than the old League of Nations had been.

The conference was dominated by the great powers—the United States, the Soviet Union, France, Britain, and China. They had littlie inclination to share or give up their authority. Nevertheless, the Big Five met with opposition from middle powers like Canada, Brazil, and Australia, which felt that they had a role to play in creating world peace and stability. They wanted the structure of the new United Nations to reflect their presence and ideas.

To some extent the middle powers got their way. All nations, regardless of size, got a seat and a vote in the General Assembly of the UN. The General Assembly was a forum in which discussion and debate took place. It could not take action on its own but could make recommendations to the Security Council. Unlike the earlier and weaker League of Nations, the Security Council could name aggressors and had the power to call for an international force to come to the assistance of any nation in trouble. The Security Council was the most powerful body of the whole UN, and here the great powers dominated. Each of the Big Five had a permanent seat on the council and had the right to veto any decision that went contrary to its interests. Middle and lesser nations were entitled to six (later ten) seats on the council. They served two-year terms and had no right of veto.

[...]

The United Nations did not fulfil the great expectations it had raised for bringing about world peace. Its successful operation depended on co-operation among the great powers, and this, sadly, did not happen.*

---

* Francis, Daniel and Sonia Riddoch. *Our Canada: A Social and Political History.* Scarborough: Pippin, 1995, 465–467.

33

The Cuban Revolution

U.S. textbooks often ignore the period in Cuba leading up to the Castro era. When Castro merits mention it is because of the perceived Communist threat that he represented right next door. Castro's government was born in opposition to the Batista regime, a government supported by the United States. So while the United States considered Fidel Castro a menace, the following Cuban texts argue that the menace was, at least in part, created by the United States.

★

CUBA

The undeclared war against Cuba. The bloodbath that never was— No matter how just, humane, and necessary the measures adopted by the Revolution, imperialism and the oligarchy were not ready to accept them, since they alter the foundations of the oppression and exploitation system that guaranteed their domination over the country.

From the very first days of January, 1959, the United States opened its doors, and gave shelter and protection to war criminals, embezzlers, and other notorious characters who had served as their instruments in Cuba during the bloody tyranny of Fulgencio Batista. These elements immediately began to organize and arm themselves, with the complicity of the US's Federal Bureau of Investigation(!), the Central Intelligence Agency, and US authorities in general. On January 28th, a group of henchmen and spokespersons for the ousted dictatorship founded their first counterrevolutionary organization outside Cuba: *La Rosa Blanca* (the white rose).

Also in early January, the United States began a huge campaign against Cuba's decision to try and exemplarily punish torturers, murderers, and informers at the service of the Batista dictatorship. The US tried to portray actions connected with the rulings of the Revolutionary Tribunals as barbaric acts and assassinations, and accuse the Cuban government of conducting a bloodbath. Their chief aim was saving the lives of those who had unconditionally served their interests until a few days before; interfering with popular justice; and discrediting the Revolution. This campaign showed to what extent criminal, corrupt, pro-annexation elements of the Batista dictatorship were part of the imperial design against Cuba and an extension of the US government. Those anti-Cuban campaigns would never stop thereafter.

By the end of January, in a fraternal, friendly visit to Venezuela, Fidel Castro announced the creation in Cuba in a short time of [a] news agency that would defend peoples of the world against the slander campaigns of their enemies. Shortly after, and with that aim, the Prensa Latina news agency was established.

During gigantic popular rallies in Havana, the nation protested with indignation the US complicity with local criminals and thieves, and the so-called Operación Verdad, or Operation Truth, began, aimed at countering the powerful imperialist campaign that was going on against Cuba.

The US government initially avoided a public involvement in plans against Cuba. One of its tactics then was using those running away from revolutionary justice, and the dictatorship of Rafael Trujillo, in the Dominican Republic, much like the US had used it before to send weapons to the Batista regime. So with the participation of US officials and Cuban counter-revolutionary elements, the Dominican dictator turned his country into a base for aggressions against Cuba.

By mid-January, 1959, news from the Dominican Republic spoke of mercenaries being recruited to launch an invasion on Cuba "as soon as its discontent with the Revolution brewed". For seven months, numerous aggressions, against Cuba [were] conducted from Dominican soil. Attacks were carried out against the Cuban embassies in Haiti and the Dominican Republic, and the Cuban ambassador in the latter, and raids conducted into Cuban waters and airspace, aimed at supplying weapons to alleged counter-revolutionary groups operating out of the Escambray mountains.

The Cuban government denounced the conspiracy to the world. In late June, Cuba had been forced to break diplomatic relations with the Dominican government. But by August, Trujillo's plans ended in total failure with the capture in Cuban territory of pirate planes, their crews, and their cargo of weapons.

Plots to assassinate Fidel Castro and other leaders of the Revolution began to feature high in aggressions against Cuba. As early as February 2nd, 1959, a US citizen was captured after he had illegally entered Cuba with the purpose of murdering Fidel. Hundreds of similar attempts would follow, with their organizers resorting to the most diverse of means, from long-range, high-precision rifles to poisons to bomb-pens to lethal germs and others.

One other early way of trying to destroy the Revolution was the training of cells of saboteurs, spies, and conspirators of different kinds, for their introduction in Cuba. The first of these groups was discovered and annihilated in the city of Regla, on the outskirts of Havana, in April of 1959. It was demonstrated that they had connections with US espionage agencies and were financed by supporters of the Batista dictatorship. That same month, two US nationals were caught while carrying out espionage and taking photos of the inside of the La Cabaña Military Fortress.

As the revolutionary process consolidated, the activity of the subversive groups increased. Sectors of Cuban society affected by the new measures, like the big landowners and real estate proprietors, members of the medical trust, and those involved in the casino and gambling business, in association with former military officers and Batista supporters, began to conspire. These were joined by people who turned their backs on the Revolution after they realized it was not going to help them to fulfill their selfish ambitions. The hierarchy of the Cuban Catholic Church, with its close ties with the oligarchy, also played an active role against the Revolution during those early years.

US espionage agencies found in those circles excellent allies for their anti-Cuba efforts, and began training them, organizing them, and financing them. By mid-1959, they had set up numerous rings of conspirators and recruits for armed uprisings in Pinar del Río and other provinces.

Those early days of February, 1959, also saw the beginning of one of the most dangerous forms of aggressions against Cuba: the violation of its airspace and territorial waters by boats and planes coming from the United States—including US military boats and planes—manned by US citizens or by mercenaries of Cuban origin. Many could be the purposes of those raids: bombing and shelling towns, sugar mills, factories, power plants and other facilities; setting cane fields and oil refineries on fire; dropping weapons, explosives, and supplies to armed groups, espionage and sabotage rings; picking enemies of the Revolution and taking them to Miami; planting panic among the population; or simply triggering a violent reaction inside Cuba.

Great importance was attached to anti-Cuba propaganda and misinformation, an area in which the United States played a most active role. On May 12th, 1959, US ambassadors to South American nations met in Chile to coordinate a regional campaign against the Cuban Revolution. On the 17th, when the Agrarian Reform law was passed, the first US financed and sponsored radio station of the Cuban counter-revolution abroad, Radio Swan, began its broadcasts.

With the passage by Cuba of the Agrarian Reform law, the United States realized that diplomatic pressures, veiled threats, and political and propaganda campaigns were useless. Washington then decided to prepare a military operation against Cuba. In late May, a secret meeting took place in the US capital between Vice-president Richard Nixon and representatives of the Mafia and several US monopolies, in which Nixon pledged to overthrow the Cuban government.*

---

* Navarro, José Cantón. *History of Cuba: The Challenge of the Yoke and the Star.* Havana: SI-MAR, 2000, 216–218.

34

The Korean War

What is often referred to as "the forgotten war" has, until very recently, received relatively little attention in the United States. Most U.S. textbooks place the Korean War squarely within the context of U.S. containment policy during the Cold War. Occasionally, it is placed alongside Vietnam in an effort to explain the "domino theory." The war is rarely discussed without mentioning the United Nations, as it was a coalition of UN forces (under U.S. command) that fought against the Communist forces on the peninsula.

★

CAUSES OF THE WAR

NORTH KOREA (SENIOR HIGH)

Upset by the fast and astonishing growth of the power of the Republic, the American invaders hastened the preparation of an aggressive war in order to destroy it in its infancy. [. . .]

The American imperialists furiously carried out the war project in

1950, the 39th year of the Juche calendar.* The American imperialist called the traitor Sungman Lee to Japan and gave him the order to hurry the war, while frequently sending warmongers to the South in order to survey the preparation of the war. [...]

The American invaders who had been preparing the war for a long time, alongside their puppets,† finally initiated the war on June 25th of the 39th year of the Juche calendar. That dawn, the enemies unexpectedly attacked the North half of the Republic, and the war clouds hung over the once peaceful country, accompanied by the echoing roar of cannons.

Having passed the 38th parallel, the enemies crawled deeper and deeper into the North half of the Republic. A grave menace drew near our country and our people. His Excellency, the great leader of the Republic, had a crucial decision to make—the invading forces of the enemies had to be eliminated and the threatened fate of our country and our people had to be saved.‡

★

NORTH KOREA (JUNIOR HIGH)

The American invaders who had been preparing the war for a long time, accompanied by their puppets, finally waged the war against the North half of the Republic on June 25th of the 39th year of the Juche calendar (1950). The bastards who crossed the 38th parallel at dawn were stoking the flames of war, jumping around like mad men, yearning to invade the North under any pretext. And so our peaceful homeland was surrounded by the roar of cannons and the clouds of war.

His Excellency, the great leader Kim Il-sung, summoned immediately an emergency council of the Cabinet. The great voice of his Excellency echoed in the room:

---

* The Juche calendar uses the year of Kim Il-sung's birth as its starting point (1911). It was implemented after the death of the emperor in order to honor him as a great hero, revolutionary figure, and shining example of what the North Koreans "aspire" to become. The calendar was implemented on September 8, 1997, three years after the leader's death. One Juche year equals one year on the Julian calendar.

† Literally, "cat's paws."

‡ *History of the Revolution of our Great Leader Kim Il-sung: High School.* Pyongyang: Textbook Publishing Co., 1999, 125–27.

". . . Those bastards are unparalleled in their ignorance. The American bastards were mistaken regarding our Chosun People."*

"The American bastards look down upon Chosun People. As the saying goes wolf-dogs† should be conquered with clubs, we should show to those ignorant invaders what our true color is." [. . .]

Actually, the war between our newly founded country and the US—recognized worldwide as the world's most powerful country—was a tremendously unfair conflict. So the people around the world worriedly watched us, wondering how our people would fight against the US.

"We have to fight firmly against our enemies in order to defend the independence of our country, the freedom and honor of our people. We have to respond to their barbarous invasion by a war of independence. Our People's Army will have to disable the attacks of the enemies and set out immediately a defense combat in order to get rid of the forceful invaders."‡

★

SOUTH KOREA (JUNIOR HIGH)

The North Korean communists hastened the war against the South after setting up their government. Having entered into a secret military treaty with the Soviet Union, they strengthened their own military forces. Just before the June 25 War, the North Korean army included 200,000 soldiers and was equipped with modern Russian planes and tanks. Meanwhile, the South was in a chaotic situation created by the riots and strikes. With the sudden growth of the population and the resulting famine, its economy was suffering greatly. Furthermore, the political situation was very fragile

* The term *Chosûn People* comes from the Chosôn Dynasty, which ruled the peninsula from 1392 to 1910, the year of the Japanese occupation. North Korea's use of the title intends to show their heritage rooted in this deep history. They consider themselves, therefore, the true Koreans.

† "Wolf-dogs" is another name used to refer to Americans in North Korea. It is an insult because of the hybridity of the animal, which is why the adjective "bastard" most often precedes the substantive "Americans."

‡ *History of the Revolution of our Great Leader Kim Il-sung: Junior High.* Pyongyang: Textbook Publishing Co., 2000, 56–58.

due to the overabundance of political parties and social constitutions. The armed forces were also in very poor condition. The South Korean army comprised less than 100,000 soldiers whose arms and equipment were also outmoded.

The North Korean communists, while preparing for the war, approached the South under the pretext of a peaceful policy all the while hiding their true intentions to attack. On June 25th 1950, they finally launched the war against the South, attacking from every point along the 38° parallel.*

★

SOUTH KOREA (Senior High)

When the overthrow of the South Korean government through social confusion became too difficult, the North Korean communists switched to a stick-and-carrot strategy: seeming to offer peaceful negotiations, they were instead analyzing the right moment of attack and preparing themselves for it. The North insisted on political negotiations between the leaders of the South and the North aiming toward a constitution of a unified government, and openly publicized their policy. By that time the American forces stationed in the South withdrew and announced that the peninsula would be excluded in America's first line of defense in the Far East. Taking advantage of this situation, the North Korean communists prepared themselves for war. Kim Il-sung secretly visited the Soviet Union and was promised the alliance of the Soviets and China in case of war. Finally, at dawn on June 25th, 1950 the North began their southward aggression along the 38° parallel. Taken by surprise by these unexpected attacks, the army of the Republic of Korea (South Korean) fought courageously to defend the liberty of the country. But with the lack of soldiers and equipment, Seoul had to surrender and the South Korean forces were forced to retreat to a battle line south of the Nak-dong river. The armed provocation of the North Korean communists brought the UN Security Council around the table. A decree denounced the North Korean military action as illegal and as a threat to peace, and a decision was made to help

---

* Kim, Hongsoo. *Korean History: Junior High*. Seoul: Dae Han Textbook Co., 2000, 172.

the South. The UN army constituted of the armies of 16 countries—among them the United States, Great Britain and France—joined the South Korean forces in the battle against the North.*

★

GREAT BRITAIN

When Japan was defeated in 1945 the Allies were faced with the problem of deciding the future of the old Japanese empire. The Korean peninsula had been Japanese since 1910. The Allies (but not Stalin) promised it would become independent after the War. But in 1945 it was partitioned along the 38th parallel with the Japanese forces surrendering to the Red Army in the north and to the Americans in the south.

Plans to unite the two halves failed, so in 1948 both occupation zones were granted their independence. The Republic of Korea (formerly the American zone in the South), led by Syngman Rhee, came into being on 15 August 1948. The Korean People's Democratic Republic (formerly the Soviet zone in the North), led by Kim Il Sung, was founded on 9 September. The Soviet forces left North Korea by the end of 1948. US forces left South Korea by June the following year.

Neither of the two Korean governments was happy with the partition of their country. Both claimed to be the rightful government. The United Nations tried in vain to unify the two Koreas as both sides built up their armed forces. Not surprisingly, there were frequent skirmishes on the frontier between the two Koreas. In 1949, the UN Commission in Korea warned of the danger of civil war.

An uncomfortable peace kept the two sides apart until 4:00 a.m., Sunday, 25 June 1950. A large North Korean army led by Marshal Choe Yong Gun, supported by tanks, crossed the border and rapidly moved south. Its seven divisions easily outnumbered the four poorly equipped South Korean divisions which faced them.†

---

* Kim, Doojin. *Korean History: Senior High*. Seoul: Dae Han Textbook Co., 2001, 199.

† Sauvain, Philip. *The Modern World: 1914–1980*. Cheltenham: Stanley Thornes, 1989, 314–18.

★

RUSSIA

Originally, the division of Korea into two parts at the 38th parallel was designed as a temporary measure, intended to prevent clashes between Soviet and American troops fighting against the Japanese. Subsequently, the division was meant to designate the zones in which the two sides were responsible for normalization of civilian life and for the preparation of Korea's population for self-government. Despite the temporary nature in which the break-up of Korea was designed, different approaches of the USA and USSR to post-war organization of life in their respective spheres of influence and the beginning of the Cold War and the conflicts between the superpowers that accompanied it led to a long-term change of the Korean peninsula into an area of competition between two ideologies and the forces that lay behind them.

Immediately after Korea's liberation, numerous political parties and social organizations appeared and became active alongside Korea's governing bodies—the so-called People's Committees. In North Korea, the communists were most active, uniting in October 1945 into the Labor Party of Korea. In 1946, many social measures and reforms were passed and carried out in North Korea, including a land reform, the nationalization of industry, transport, communications and banks as well as foreign trade and laws dealing with gender equality. These measures, especially the land redistribution, influenced the people of South Korea where most of the governing was still done by the American military administration. From the very beginning of the administration's activity, Americans committed a series of mistakes that turned the general population's sentiment against them. As a result, an atmosphere of civil protest permeated the South complete with mass demonstrations that were put down by military force.

In 1948 elections to the National Assembly were held in the South and the Republic of Korea was declared with a new constitution and president and Seoul as its capital. In response, elections were held in the North to the Supreme Public Assembly a few months later. These elections were given an air of encompassing all of Korea through the inclusion of several representatives of the population of South Korea. The Supreme Public Assembly proclaimed the creation of the Democratic People's Republic of Korea (DPRK) with its capital in Pyongyang. Shortly thereafter the Soviet Union removed its troops from the territory of North Korea at the request of DPRK's government.

The existence of two Korean states, each of which claimed to be the only lawful government of the whole peninsula, clearly created grounds for conflict between them. The 38th parallel became the site of frequent armed confrontations, which numbered 1,836 in 1949 alone and often included large quantities of troops on both sides.*

★

JAPAN

One reason American leaders gave for sending troops to Korea was an early version of the "domino theory": namely, that if South Korea fell to the Communists, then Japan might do so next. From the Japanese standpoint, Japan received a long-term economic benefit from the United States' going to war.

While the Cold War was worsening, war finally broke out in 1950 between the Republic of Korea and the Democratic People's Republic of Korea (the Korean War). As the North Korean army advanced southward rapidly, the U.N. Security Council, with the Soviet Union delegate absent, decided to give military support to South Korea. The United Nations forces, consisting mainly of United States troops, advanced northward to near the Chinese-Korean border. China sent a powerful volunteer army to North Korea. Subsequently, fierce battles raged around the 38th parallel; in 1953, a cease-fire agreement was concluded at long last.

During the Korean War, American bases on the main islands of Japan and on Okinawa were used, and a vast amount of military supplies were procured in Japan. The effect was an upswing in the Japanese economy and a speeding of recovery.†

---

* *The Newest History of Foreign Nations: 20th Century.* Moscow: Vlados, 1998, 99–100.

† *Japan in Modern History, Junior High School Textbooks.* Tokyo: International Society for Educational Information, 1994, 183, 185.

★

THE FIGHTING

American textbooks generally portray the fighting in Korea as a three-year see-saw battle fought primarily along the 38th Parallel. Considered within the context of the U.S. containment policy, the Korean War pitted the U.S.-led UN forces against an aggressive Communist North Korea and China, which, in colloquial terms, turned the Cold War hot.

It is worth noting here that the North Korean reference to the battle over Heartbreak Ridge is quite different from all other accounts of the event.

★

NORTH KOREA (Senior High)

Leading the Battle of the 1211 Plateau into Victory

The ravages of war had been going on for a year already.

Meanwhile, after a year of bitter crushing defeats, the American invaders could not but stay at the 38th parallel—the line at which, the year before, they set fire to the war. Nevertheless, the bastards would not give up their evil intention.

Pretending to attack from the West, the enemies secretly placed a great number of their forces in the East and the middle of the battle line. On the other hand, the bastards furiously hurried an attack from the East coast.

The situation at the front became extremely tense.

His Excellency, great leader, **Kim Il-sung** called a council to work out a countermeasure for the situation.

Numerous opinions were presented regarding the situation at the front.

Our greatly adored* leader who was listening attentively to every opinion slowly moved in front of the map.

---

* The words that directly precede "leader" in this passage could be translated *greatly* or *dearly and loved, adored,* or *worshiped. Adored* was chosen because of its original Latin sense meaning to love to the point of worship, a sense that aptly describes the supposed relationship between the North Korean people and their leader.

As he stood in front of the map, our greatly adored leader, pointing to the East of the battle line, said in a loud voice: "The enemies are targeting this place."

Our greatly adored leader immediately gathered great forces on the East side of the battle line and mapped out measures to defend the plateau.

Our greatly adored leader instructed that the 1211 plateau be defended with special care and the enemies were slaughtered en masse.

The 1211 plateau was a very important spot. To lose this spot would mean the loss of a great amount of land in the North and certain defeat in sea combat.

In September of the 40th year of the Juche calendar, our great leader, **Kim Il-sung,** left for the extreme front to fortify the defense system of the Eastern battle line where the 1211 plateau was located.

Finally the American invaders attacked the 1211 plateau like a flood. The bastards were dropping 30,000–40,000 bombs and shells on that spot every day.

While the ravages of war were going on day and night, our greatly adored leader called one night to the commanding officer of the 1211 plateau.

Our greatly adored leader asked first about the health of our forces and wanted to make sure that the war supplies were arriving well. He was concerned about the lives of our soldiers. Then he said: "Every soldier is a priceless treasure. Everyone is a precious comrade in this revolutionary war. How many times did we regret not having enough soldiers when we were fighting against the Japanese military and police? We have to take good care of our soldiers. [. . .] we have to provide them with hot rice and soup and with warm beds. And we have to prevent them from catching colds."

The brave soldiers of our People's Army swore to defend the 1211 plateau until the end in order to repay him for his great love and grace. They presented a vow of fidelity to our greatly adored leader and displayed peerless courage and heroism in every battle.

While the young civil forces soldier, Li Subok, was blocking the enemy's fire with his body, sacrificing his only soul for the sake of his unique motherland, a signalman ensured the communication of his unit by replacing a broken communication line with his blood vessel.

The brave soldiers of our People's Army slaughtered countless enemies in this combat and stole or destroyed a great number of fighter planes.

The enemies named the 1211 plateau "Heartbreak Ridge"* since they felt regret every time they saw the spot. They also called it "The Valley of Entrapment"† because going there meant not coming back alive.

The shining victory of the 1211 plateau proved to the world the excellent strategies of our dearly adored great leader and showed that our People's Army always wins.‡

★

RUSSIA

With the conditions of the conflict escalating, war finally broke out on June 25, 1950. The fighting took place with limited success for both sides. Large forces of American paratroopers and other soldiers were brought in to fight on the side of the South while Soviet military strategists and fighter pilots fought for North Korea. Furthermore, in October 1950, large units of Chinese "People's Volunteers" also appeared to help the North.

By the end of 1950 both opposing armies situated the bulk of their forces along the 38th parallel. After that most of the fighting was contested bitterly along the parallel without major sustained territorial gains for either side. On July 27, 1953 a truce agreement was signed in Korea halting the three-year conflict between the two sides. Both Chinese and American troops remained on the Korean peninsula.

After the conflict, the two Koreas continued to follow their respective paths dictated by the superpowers that influenced them.§

---

* [sang-shim-ryung].

† [ham-jung-gol].

‡ *History of the Revolution of our Great Leader Kim Il-sung: High School.* Pyongyang: Textbook Publishing Co., 1999, 69–73.

§ *The Newest History of Foreign Nations: 20th Century.* Moscow: Vlados, 1998,

★

THE ARMISTICE

Despite initial victories on both sides, the Korean War quickly bogged down along the 38th Parallel. In 1953, Eisenhower kept his campaign promise and went to Korea. Soon after, talks resumed over how to bring about an end to the war.

U.S. history textbooks usually refer to the Korean War as "the Forgotten War," owing in part to the fact that there was no clear-cut victor, and little, if any, territory was gained by either side.

★

NORTH KOREA (JUNIOR HIGH)

The troops of the People's Army defeated the American bastards over and over again on every battlefield. Cornered in a dead end, the American bastards didn't know what to do. The quick-tempered Americans finally signed the armistice on July 27th of the Juche calendar (1953) and kneeled down before the Chosun People. His excellency our great leader **Kim, Il-sung** gave the following instructions:

> "The American invaders finished by kneeling down before our Chosun People. We bent the pride of the Americans who used to boast of being the world's most powerful nation and for the first time in history, we brought the beginning of their decay. This victory will forever shine in the Chosun People's combat history, and will be an inspiration to the combat of all people around the world."

The great victory of having beaten the Americans, this proud triumph and honor of our people, was the glorious accomplishment of our great leader.*

---

* *History of the Revolution of our Great Leader Kim Il-sung: Junior High.* Pyongyang: Textbook Publishing Co., 2000, 76.

★

SOUTH KOREA (Junior High)

The National Army pushed the battleline beyond Ab-rok and Du-man river, and the unification of the country seemed to have come near. But with the unexpected intervention of the Chinese communists' army, they couldn't but draw back. The Chinese communists' army, backed up by their numerous forces, was fighting with the human sea tactics. Seoul was again temporarily invaded by the enemies, but the National Army and the UN forces soon fought back having regrouped their fighting power. Seoul was recovered again and the enemies were pushed back behind the 38° parallel. Since then, violent offensive and defensive battles followed. Meanwhile, exhausted by the war, the communist army, foreseeing their defeat in the war, asked an armistice to be signed through the mediation of the Soviet Union. Negotiations followed during two years between the UN forces and the communist army. The people of the South disagreed with the armistice, which was a renunciation of the re-unification of the country; but nonetheless the armistice was signed in 1953. *The June 25 War,* waged by the North Korean communist army, was a threat to liberty and peace and a crime, a fratricidal war. Numerous people lost their lives and fortunes and factories, power plants, bridges and railroads were destroyed.*

★

SOUTH KOREA (Senior High)

The National Army and the UN forces began to fight back beginning in August of 1950, turning the tide of the war in our favor with the success of the Inch'eon landing operations. On the 28th of September, Seoul was recovered and soon after the battle-line was pushed beyond the 38° parallel northward. The National Army and the UN forces invaded Pyong-yang, and that winter marched onward toward the Ab-rok river. The dearest wish of unification was about to be realized when the Chinese communists' army

* Kim, Hongsoo. *Korean History: Junior High.* Seoul: Dae Han Textbook Co., 2000, 174.

intervened, forcing the National Army and the UN forces to draw back to an area south of the Han river. But a counterattack was soon prepared and the war came to a deadlock around the 38° parallel. [. . .]

The struggle see-sawed to and fro and in the midst of it the communists' army asked for an armistice through the mediation of Soviet UN representatives. Our government and our people, fearing that such a treaty would lead to a perpetual division of the Korean peninsula and its people, disagreed to this offer of the communists. Consequently, nationwide demonstrations condemning the armistice were held. But against the desire of our people to unify our country, an armistice was signed between the UN forces and the communist army in 1953.*

★

CANADA

By the time NATO was established in 1949, the cold war had extended beyond Europe into Asia, where a communist government headed by Chou En-lai had taken over China. Communism made gains in other places like Indochina and Korea, which had been partitioned after the war. The United States always saw these communist governments as mere extensions of international communism rather than as movements of legitimate national liberation. In 1950 North Korea invaded American-supported South Korea. The Americans took advantage of a temporary Soviet boycott of the Security Council of the United Nations to invoke universal collective security. The Canadian government was in a quandary. It had neither a peacetime military nor enthusiasm about collective security under the American aegis. Eventually a Canadian Army Special Force of 20,000 volunteers served in Korea, suffering 1,557 casualties and 312 fatalities. Most of the Canadians were involved after the Chinese had intervened on behalf of North Korea. Canada was more eager than the United States for an armistice, but usually supported the Americans in public.†

* Kim, Doojin. *Korean History: Senior High*. Seoul: Dae Han Textbook Co., 2001, 199–200.
† Bumsted, J.M. *A History of the Canadian Peoples*. Toronto: Oxford University Press, 1998, 407.

35

NATO

The North Atlantic Treaty Organization was one of the most influential organizations established during the Cold War. It was an elite club of European and North American countries resolved to mutual defense in the face of "Communist aggression." Its founding spurred the Soviets to form their own alliance among Eastern European Communist countries, called the Warsaw Pact. The two superpowers now had their respective camps.

★

GREAT BRITAIN

When the Berlin Blockade ended on 12 May 1949, the future course of Europe had changed irrevocably:

- the Western Allies had formed a defensive alliance—NATO.
- plans for the creation of the German Federal Republic had been finalised and came into being 11 days after the lifting of the Blockade.

Both these results had an important 'knock-on' effect, since the Russians and their allies regarded the formation of NATO as a hostile act, as an endorsement of the Cold War and a threat to their own security. This led, inevitably, to the formation of their own Warsaw Pact alliance in 1955.

The founding of the Federal Republic made it possible for Germans in the three Western occupation zones to start rebuilding their country. But it also ensured that Germany would now be split permanently in two.

The German Democratic Republic (East Germany) came into being on 7 October 1949, little more than four months after the foundation of its rival the Federal Republic, on 23 May 1949. When the Federal Republic joined NATO on 9 May 1955, it was followed five days later by the signing of the Warsaw Pact. The North Atlantic Treaty Organization came into being on April 1949. The most significant feature of the Treaty was not so much the fact that it was an alliance of 12 powers—ten in Europe and two in North America—but the fact that it committed the United States, bigger than all the other countries put together, to the defence of Europe. This was a convincing answer, at last, to Churchill's worries, in May 1945 at the end of the war, about the future defence of Europe.*

★

RUSSIA

In 1949 the North Atlantic Treaty Organization (NATO) was created to supposedly provide security to Western nations against a possible rebirth of Nazism in Germany. West Germany itself joined NATO in 1955. That same year a military-political alliance headed by the Soviet Union was created by the Warsaw Pact. Thus, the stand-off between the two superpowers became a stand-off between two blocs of nations. The increasing polarization of the entire world and its gradual division into two camps was leading the globe towards a growing threat of nuclear war.†

---

* Sauvain, Philip. *The Modern World: 1914–1980.* Cheltenham: Stanley Thornes, 1989, 311–12.

† *The World in the XXth Century.* Moscow: Prosveshchenie, 1999, 202.

*

CANADA

This Canadian text gives quite a different reason for why and how NATO was formed, as well as the Canadian vision for its structure and purpose.

The North Atlantic Treaty Organization

After the Communist coup in Czechoslovakia, five nations in Western Europe signed a treaty that committed each member to assist the others in the event of an attack. Canadian officials envisioned another, larger organization, bolstered by the superior resources of the United States. They were successful in persuading the Americans to become part of an organization known as the North Atlantic Treaty Organization (NATO).

NATO was primarily a military alliance, but Canadian delegates hoped that, in addition, it might lead to the creation of a close-knit North Atlantic community, which might act as a counterweight to American influence in Canada. Largely because of Canadian insistence, Article Two was inserted into the NATO charter; according to its terms, members promised to build up economic and cultural connections between themselves. Very little came of this article, however, and NATO became basically a defensive military alliance.

As a result of its commitments to NATO, Canada sent an air squadron to France and an army division to Germany, along with naval units to serve under NATO command. Because the United States was the largest member nation in the organization, an American commander was given overall charge of NATO forces. Not all Canadians approved of this structure; some [. . .] complained that **Person and St. Laurent** were "selling Canada down the river to the U.S." But most Canadians did not agree; they were anti-Communist and distrustful of Soviet motives. They favoured any action that would counter that threat. James Eayrs, a historian specializing in defence matters, even suggested that Canada might have to merge with the United States if that were necessary to fight communism. *

---

* Francis, Daniel, and Sonia Riddoch. *Our Canada: A Social and Political History.* Scarboroug: Pippin, 1995, 467.

36

McCarthyism

During the 1950s U.S. Senator Joseph McCarthy of Wisconsin took the foreign policy of then-Secretary of State John Foster Dulles and applied it domestically. The Communist threat abroad became the perceived Communist menace at home. McCarthy brought America's hunt for Communists to the American government itself, claiming to have a list of 205 Communists in the U.S. government. He succeeded in raising the level of public fear by casting suspicion on anyone who questioned his methods. In foreign textbooks, McCarthy is often held up as the example of American excesses during the Cold War.

★

CANADA

The Domestic Cold War

The Cold War was, in part, an ideological battle, and its participants, hoping to impose their values on other countries, would not countenance defeat on the home front. The Soviets and their allies crushed dissent ruthlessly. Western countries claimed that they allowed completely open discussion, but McCarthyism in the United States suggested otherwise. Though Senator Joseph McCarthy was hardly the first important American politician to equate dissent with treachery, his pursuit of communists and critics of his rabid brand of anti-communism was so relentless, that he gave name to the witchhunts of the early 1950s.

McCarthyism in Canada was less virulent than in the United States but it infected Canadian institutions nonetheless. Anti-communism became a key ingredient in immigration policy. While restrictions on former Nazis were lifted to the point where the RCMP* complained that war criminals were being admitted to Canada, no such tolerance was extended to communists and ex-communists. Communists were not only deported and kept out as permanent immigrants, they were even prevented from making visits to Canada. The federal government meanwhile attempted to root radicals out of the civil service. After all, it was just such people who had passed information to Soviet Embassy officials about nuclear programs during World War II. The civil libertarian argument that individuals ought to be judged by their actions and not their beliefs or associations was rejected in such an environment.

Communists who had been democratically chosen to head unions were denounced so stridently by editorialists and their non-communist union opponents that the state confidently persecuted them and, in cases, destroyed their unions. In 1946, [Quebec Premier Maurice] Duplessis jailed Kent Rowley and Madeleine Parent, organizers for the Trades and Labour Congress local of textile workers in Valleyfield. In 1949, the RCMP helped to force striking seamen who belonged to the Canadian Seamen's Union into the Seafarers' International Union, headed by convicted American thug Hal Banks. A year later, the Canadian Labour Relations Board revoked the CSU's certification, claiming a Communist-led union could not be recognized under the Industrial Relations and Disputes Investigation Act.

Communists and ex-communists faced constant surveillance and harassment. Roscoe Fillmore, active from the early 1900s with the Socialists and Communists, and later a founding member of the Labour Progressive Party, was a prominent horticulturalist in Nova Scotia. Even though he gave up his LPP membership in 1950, years later the RCMP was still fol-

---

* Royal Canadian Mounted Police.

lowing him to horticultural conferences and filing reports, complete with licence plate numbers, on the cars stopping by the Fillmore Valley Nursery on summer weekends. RCMP agents even spied on the funerals of Fillmore's comrades, sitting in the back row, noting the names of those attending.

The suicide of a veteran Canadian diplomat, E.H. Norman, in Cairo in 1956, after repeated but unsubstantiated charges that he was a Soviet agent, demonstrates the tragic side of McCarthyism. Lives could be ruined if individuals were suspected of being communists or being soft on communism. Representatives of the peace movement, such as the Women's International League for Peace and Freedom, founded in 1915, also suffered severely from red-baiters who smeared anyone who opposed them. In such an atmosphere those leery of the Cold War philosophy or of particular actions that flowed from such a philosophy generally kept their mouths shut. Both in Canada and the United States, fundamental criticism of Canadian and American foreign policy or of red baiting was rare, both in scholarly and journalistic media. The notion that democracy versus communism was a simplistic assessment of a complicated world situation would take hold only in the late 1960s.*

★

FRANCE

France has long had an active Communist party (PCF), one which actively participated in the French Resistance during the Second World War. The government's relationship with the Communist Party historically has been one of acceptance, tempered by political suspicions ranging from mild to serious. It has never reached the fevered pitch of the McCarthy years in the United States.

The Leader of the Liberal Democracies

Advocating neo-liberalism, the United States placed itself in the lead in the fight against Communism, both domestic and foreign.

---

* Finkel, Alvin, et al. *History of the Canadian Peoples: 1867 to the Present, v. 2.* Toronto: Copp Clark Pittman, 1993, 404–05.

A MODEL TO RIVAL THE COMMUNIST SYSTEM:

The Americans planned to expand their economic idea of Free Trade across the globe. They identified their interests with those of the world, a fact which concerned the Soviets who worried about American influence in areas they considered vital for their own security. The two Giants began a battle for influence in order to prove the superiority of their respective political and economic systems. The Soviet vetoes in the UN and their control of Eastern Europe led the Americans, well aware of their own military and economic supremacy, to assume the responsibility of organizing the rest of the "free world" against the communist threat.

THE BATTLE AGAINST COMMUNISM FROM WITHIN:

President Truman took the initiative in the fight against communism in the United States. He ordered an investigation into the loyalty of the government employees, which resulted in 2000 reassignments and 200 dismissals. But it was quickly overtaken by a demagogue, Senator McCarthy, who denounced the alleged infiltration of communist agents in the American administration and unleashed a psychosis of fear and suspicion.

This McCarthyism quickly became a "witch-hunt," which the majority Republicans in Congress exploited politically. The most spectacular aspect was the 1953 execution of the Rosenbergs who had been accused of spying for the USSR despite their protests of innocence and a global campaign in their defense. Even President Truman, who tried to use his veto against laws which would tarnish the image of America (Land of the Free), found himself accused of sympathy for the communists. Republicans exploited the accusations to block his social programs (civil rights for Blacks, mandatory health insurance), which they considered inspired by communism. It was President Eisenhower who in 1953 finally put an end to McCarthyism while still remaining vigilant toward the USSR.*

---

*Berstein, Serge, and Pierre Milza, et al. *Histoire—T^{ales}*. Paris: Hatier, 1998, 162.

37

Suez Canal

The Suez Canal crisis in 1956 marked a changing of the guard in the Middle East: the end of the Europeans' influence in their former colonies, and emergence of a new theater in which the Cold War powers would confront one another.

★

GREAT BRITAIN

The United States and Great Britain have historically been strong allies, and they have only rarely sharply disagreed on serious issues. The Suez Canal crisis was just such an event.

At the beginning of the First World War, Britain had declared a protectorate over Egypt. The unpopularity of British rule persuaded Britain to make a unilateral declaration of Egyptian independence in 1922. This apparent easing of imperial control was qualified by Britain's retention of control of a number of important areas of government, including the conduct of Egyptian foreign and defence policy. While the 1936 Anglo-

Egyptian Treaty formally ended Britain's military occupation of Egypt, British forces were permitted to garrison the Suez Canal zone for a further twenty years.

In 1945, Egypt requested a revision of the 1936 treaty. Subsequent discussions focused on the circumstances in which Britain could use military facilities in Egypt. Bevin and the Egyptian premier, Ismail Sidky, were on the verge of agreement towards the end of 1946 when negotiations foundered on Britain's refusal to countenance an Egyptian reunification with the Sudan. The failure to reach an accord obliged Britain to rely on the discredited 1936 treaty to justify her continued military presence in the Canal zone. Egypt's growing resentment towards Britain was fuelled by the latter's role in the creation of Israel.

Referring to the impact of Egypt's defeat at the hands of Israel in 1948–49, John Darwin has argued that 'Nothing could have been better calculated to . . . redouble Egyptian hostility to Britain on whose "betrayal" of the Palestinian Arabs the catastrophe could conveniently be blamed'. This feeling was given tangible expression in October 1951 when the Egyptian premier, Nahas Pasha, unilaterally abrogated the 1936 treaty. This dramatic gesture failed to save his unpopular government, which soon fell from power. A succession of weak governments followed. Against this unstable background, a group of army officers, led by General Muhammad Neguib and Colonel Gamal Abdel Nasser, staged a successful coup on 23 July 1952. In the power struggle between Neguib and Nasser which followed, the latter emerged triumphant, becoming prime minister in April 1954 and president from June 1956. It was the Suez Crisis which elevated Nasser from leader of Egypt to leader of the Arab world.

Initially Anglo-Egyptian relations experienced a marked improvement. In July 1954 an agreement was reached under which all British forces were to leave Egypt by 18 June 1956. Anglo-Egyptian harmony was short-lived, however. The formation in February 1955 of the Baghdad Pact, a defensive alliance between Iraq and Turkey which Britain subsequently joined, infuriated Nasser, who perceived it as a threat to his regional leadership ambitions. In September, he announced a deal to purchase arms from the Soviet Union, via Czechoslovakia, thus breaking the Western monopoly on the supply of weapons to Egypt. In an attempt to administer a sharp rebuke to the Egyptian president, the United States withdrew its financial support for the construction of the Aswan Dam, a project which Nasser claimed to be vital for the economic development of his country. On 26 July 1956 Nasser's response came with the announcement of the nationalisation of the Suez Canal.

The Canal, which still carried a vast amount of British trade, especially oil, was seen as vital to Britain's prosperity and economic well-being. The British prime minister, Anthony Eden, even described Nasser as having "his hand on our windpipe." Eden also told the American president, Dwight D. Eisenhower, that "The removal of Nasser and the installation in Egypt of a regime less hostile to the West must . . . rank high among our objectives". Despite Eisenhower's refusal to support the use of force, Eden moved towards military confrontation with Nasser. During secret discussions between representatives of the British, French, and Israeli governments, at Sevres, Paris, on 22 October, it was agreed that Israel would attack Egypt, thus providing Britain and France with a justification to dispatch their own troops to Egypt under the guise of separating the combatants and protecting the Canal.

Following the Israeli assault on Egypt on 29 October, Britain and France issued an ultimatum, described by the US secretary of state as 'about as crude and brutal as anything he had ever seen', demanding that Israel and Egypt withdraw 10 miles either side of the Canal to allow an Anglo-French occupation. The Egyptians rejection of the ultimatum led to the first wave of Anglo-French attacks on 31 October. This action provoked a storm of international criticism, not least from the United States, which not only condemned its allies in the United Nations, but also refused to provide assistance to stabilise Britain's deteriorating financial situation. A week after the attack on Egypt had begun, British forces were ordered to cease fire. On 23 November, Eden flew to Jamaica for rest and convalescence, prompting his former principal private secretary to remark: "The captain leaves the sinking ship which he has steered personally on to the rocks." On 9 January 1957, Eden resigned from office, ostensibly on health grounds.

THE IMPACT OF SUEZ

The long-term impact of the Suez episode on Britain's international and imperial relations is a complex question. Anglo-American friendship and co-operation were restored following a meeting between Eisenhower and the new British prime minister, Harold Macmillan, at Bermuda in March 1957. Nevertheless, the Suez Crisis underscored the real limits to Britain's freedom of action on the international stage. Britain, as Eden's private secretary, Guy Millard, pointed out, 'could never again resort to military action, outside British territories, without at least American acquiescence'.

On the question of the consequences of Suez on Britain's standing in the Middle East, no simple picture emerges. Certainly Britain's attack on Egypt, in apparent collusion with Israel, shocked the Arab world. In March 1957, the traditionally pro-British regime in Jordan succumbed to pressure to repudiate the 1948 Anglo-Jordanian military alliance. The loyalty of the oil-bearing sheikhdoms of the Persian Gulf was also stretched. Referring specifically to Kuwait, the British representative there, known as the political agent, confessed that 'it is difficult to see how, in the face of an accepted and unquestioned view that we acted in collusion with Israel, we can hope to maintain our previous close relationship of confidence and trust'. The prestige of the monarchical regime in Iraq, upon which Britain had so heavily depended for the maintenance of her regional interests, was severely undermined by Suez. At the beginning of 1957, the British ambassador in Baghdad warned that 'The action of Her Majesty's Government, because it was linked with action by Israel, placed . . . the King and Crown Prince and all those in Iraq who had so actively pursued a policy of friendship with Her Majesty's Government, not only in the gravest political difficulty but in danger of their lives, and imperiled the continued existence of the regime and the monarchy'. This warning proved prophetic. On 14 July 1958, the Iraqi monarchy was swept aside in a bloody revolution.

It would be dangerous, however, to regard Suez as a watershed separating a period of British regional supremacy from one of impotence. On the one hand, Britain, while remaining the dominant power in the Middle East after 1945, had seen her influence progressively eroded. In Saudi Arabia, the United States assumed the political and economic sway once enjoyed by Britain. It can be suggested, moreover, that the nationalisation of the British-owned Anglo-Iranian Oil Company in 1951 by Iranian premier Mohammed Mossadiq was even more damaging to British prestige than Nasser's actions five years later. In the aftermath of Mossadiq's nationalisation of Anglo-Iranian, for instance, the British political agent in

Kuwait identified the emergence of a belief . . . that it was merely necessary to bark loudly and lengthily enough to make the British let go anywhere.*

★

FRANCE

France's mention of the Suez Canal crisis comes within the context of the Algerian crisis in France, and the Cold War in general. As an event in French textbooks it receives attention not only because of French participation, but because it also represents the final moment of France's former glory and influence.

- In July 1956, the Colonel Nasser, incarnation of Egyptian nationalism, decided to nationalize the company that operated the Suez Canal. France and Great Britain, their interests affected, decided to react with force. France hoped to thus weaken the State which supported the nationalists that it was combating in Algeria. The operation conducted in conjunction with Israel was stopped in December 1956 by Soviet threats and American pressure.
- Thus the two Great powers demonstrated their desire to control the planet.†

[. . .]
- The year 1956 was marked by two events:
  - The 1956 Suez Crisis (July–November 56) resulted from the will of Egyptian leader Nasser to set himself free from the tutelage of the West and develop his country by nationalizing the Suez Canal. Joint pressure from both the United States and the USSR forced the British, the French, and the Israelis to withdraw from the area of the canal which their troops occupied. This brought Nasser considerable prestige. The crisis also marked the decline of both France and the Great Britain which were no longer able to act without the agreement of the two Great Powers.

---

* Smith, Simon C. *British Imperialism, 1750–1970.* Cambridge: Cambridge University Press, 1998, 189–191.
† *Histoire—Iʳᵉ*. Paris: Nathan, 1994, 65.

• In October and November 1956, the Hungarians rose up against the Soviet domination. The Russian tanks crushed this Hungarian uprising with much bloodshed. The intervention of the Red Army was mildly condemned by the West which was too concerned by the Suez Crisis.*

The following text is taken from a supplemental history book used by many students in the French school system. The format is similar to American textbooks in it's use of an extended narrative. (In contrast the current French textbooks are more resource-oriented, with short, informative summaries and primary source documents, graphs, and images.)

The Suez Canal crisis

The aggravation of the Arab-Israeli conflict offered the two superpowers the opportunity for a changing of the guard in the Middle East. While France was forced to concentrate on its problems in the Maghreb†, the British, facing the rise of Arab nationalism, found it more and more difficult to maintain control in the region. Their most important problem was the Suez Canal, symbol of their ancient imperial power and a new strategic economic outpost (of 15,000 ships—two thirds being petroleum tankers—passing through the canal in 1955, 35% were British ships). However, on July 26, 1956, Colonel Nasser, who had taken the reigns of power in Egypt two years earlier and wished to unite the Arab population in his country, decided to nationalize the canal company, the majority of whose shares are held by the French and English. Beforehand, he had obtained important military aid from the Soviets as well as the promise to help finance the work on the Assouan Dam situated on the Nile. This would raise the energy output for the entire country and, more importantly, extend the limits of irrigation. The Kremlin's diplomacy, which since the death of Stalin had reoriented itself toward providing aid to "national bourgeois states" in its struggle against imperialism, made its first move in the Near East. From their side, following the US Secretary of State, Foster Dulles, and his strategy of containment toward the USSR,

---

* Lambin, Jean-Michel. *Histoire—T^{ales}*. Paris: Hachette, 2001, 206.
† North(west) Africa.

the United States supported the countries in the Baghdad Pact (Iran, Iraq, Turkey).

The Suez Canal Crisis, 19th century Europe's final manifestation of gunboat diplomacy, found its outlet in the autumn of 1956. During the summer, the French and English had led parallel negotiations with Egypt while making preparations for a military intervention; the French saw in Nasser's demise one of the conditions of their victory in Algeria (Cairo had been supporting the rebels), while the British wanted simply to save what rested of their prestige and influence in the Arab world. Israel, who saw the new Russian arms in Egypt as a shift in the balance of power, felt threatened by its neighbor. Israel decided to join the French-English alliance and on October 29, 1956, Israeli troops attacked Egypt, invading Sinai. One week later the French and British, who had 60,000 troops at Cyprus, landed in the Canal Zone.

Just as the three allies appeared to have an easy victory, Moscow and Washington reacted with extreme vigor toward an initiative that could have prevented them from substituting their own influence for that of the former colonial imperialists. While the Soviets threatened to send nuclear missiles over Paris and London, the Americans (Eisenhower was reelected November 6) exerted political and economic pressure on Eden's cabinet. The French government under Guy Mollet was obligated, by the British defection, to accept the cease-fire ordered by the UN. Operation "Musketeer" ended in failure. While Nasser transformed his military defeat into political success, the two superpowers found each other face to face in the Middle East.*

★

ISRAEL

This Israeli text provides extensive detail about Israel's arrangement with Great Britain and France, as well as the fighting over the canal. It was, after all, mainly Israeli soldiers who faced the Egyptian army.

---

* Berstein, Pierre, and Pierre Milza. *Histoire du XXe siècle: 1945–1973, Le monde entre guerre et paix.* Paris: Hatier, 1996, 258–59.

The Suez Crisis

On July 6, 1956 Gamal Abdel Nasser, President of Egypt, announced his plans to nationalize the international joint stock company that operated the Suez Canal in Egypt. This announcement resulted in one of the most serious crises the world had known since World War II. The crisis brought a serious rift between the Western powers—France and Britain vs. the United States—and war (the Sinai War)—Israel, France and England against Egypt. The War brought with it a threat by the two superpowers of the time: the United States and the Soviet Union were opposed to the military operation. The crisis ended only in March 1957 after France, Britain, and finally Israel evacuated the territory they had conquered during the Sinai War.

The Suez Canal was and still is one of the most important water passageways in the world. It significantly shortens the distance from Europe to the Southern African continent, the Indian subcontinent, the center of Eastern Asia and to the South. Britain, a declining world power, still had essential interests in the region such as oil in the Persian Gulf. They were also active in blocking the dangerous southern expansion of the Soviets. In June 1956 Britain finished evacuating its forces from the canal where they had had a presence since the 1880s. The "slap" the British received from Nasser moved the British Prime Minister Anthony Eden to decide for removal of the Egyptian president and a return of his own forces to the canal.

France, which also held stock and interests in the canal, concluded that Nasser was deeply involved with the Algerian uprising against France. The uprising, which broke out in 1954, accelerated and the frustrated French blamed Nasser for actively aiding the uprising. The Suez crisis presented the perfect pretext to go to war with Nasser and his regime.

The United States, ally to both Britain and France, refused to accept the "old imperialistic" approach that allowed itself to punish leaders in the developing world for actions that it deemed unacceptable, and was thus adamantly against the French and British plan to strike at Suez. The two were forced to work secretly to avoid the ire of the United States. This secrecy brought Israel into the war. The French-Israeli alliance, the big weapons deal that came as a result, and Israel's principle of war-readiness made Israel the ideal candidate for a combined operation with France and England against Egypt.

The Sinai War

The Sinai War broke out on Monday, October 29th, 1956. According to the clandestine agreement between Britain, France and Israel (known also as "the Collusion"), Israel would strike at the Suez Canal. France and Britain would give an ultimatum that both Israel and Egypt would have to evacuate the canal area. Israel would accept the withdrawal and her allies would arrive at the Suez Canal to ensure secure passage despite the Egyptian threat. From without, it was essential that the operation give off no impression of being pre-coordinated or preplanned.

In exchange, Israel received from France additional weapons, French Aircraft carriers operating in its territory and war ships protecting its ports and skies. Britain in turn promised that it would not side with Jordan, with whom it had a defense contract, if Israel were to strike Jordan in light of the continuous unrest across the eastern border. Finally, given the agreement with France and the weakness of Israel, [Israeli Prime Minister] Ben Gurion could not refuse such an accord, although it was questionable to him.

The IDF* sent Paratrooper Battalion 890 under the command of Major Refael Eitan to the Mitla Pass in the Western Sinai peninsula. By parachuting in close proximity to the Mitla pass Israel opened the joint war. The Israelis part was called "Kadesh" and the Anglo-French part was called "Musketeer." According to the agreement that was prearranged, Israel's allies were supposed to begin air bombing against Egypt 24 hours after Israel's initial move. But the bombing never came due to organizational difficulties and internal arguing amongst the allies, thus leaving Israel to face Egypt by itself.

The situation became even more complicated when Chief of Staff Dayan's senior officers, who were not made aware of the secret agreements, operated quickly, as Dayan himself taught them. As a result, the head of Southern Command, Colonel Asaf Simchoni, did not know why he had to wait 48 hours, per Dayan's instructions, until he would be allowed to move his forces from the Negev to the isolated Paratroopers in the western side of the Sinai Peninsula. Although Dayan asked him to wait for full war—according to the agreement with the allies—Simchoni instructed his troops to press forward.

---

* Israeli Defense Forces.

Only on the evening of October 31 did the French and British air forces begin to operate. The War was now at its climax. The Egyptian army had spread its forces thinly across the Sinai after the nationalization decision of Nasser in order to defend the Suez Canal. This fact, coupled with the surprise operations of the allied forces in Egypt, meant the IDF had to contend mostly with rough terrain, supply chain problems previously unknown, and a political time table that was quickly running out.

The land strike of the allies in Egypt began only on November 5, when Israel was on the verge of finishing its operations in the Sinai after it had captured the entire peninsula. This strike by the allies was too little, too late.

Prior to the completion of the landing and the full arrival of the Anglo-French forces (they had only arrived as far as Kantara on the northern part of the canal), the two superpowers each issued a separate ultimatum that blocked Britain and France. As early as November 6–7, the invading forces were halted for fear that World War III would break out. The invaders held the city of Port Said that sat at the northwestern entry of the canal and the city of Port Fuad that sat at the eastern side, as well as the canal, as mentioned, as far as Kantara. On 22 November the withdrawal of the British and the French was concluded.

Israel made a huge attempt to keep in its hands something from the conquest of the war, but what was made clear to the important powers such as France and Britain, was made clear to Israel as well. Immediately after the war Ben Gurion announced that Israel was ready to withdraw. He asked that that the Gaza strip and the Gulf of Eilat remain in the hands of Israel, but after attempts to reach this agreement failed, an agreement was reached wherein the UN forces and not the Egyptian army would occupy the Gaza strip. The powers, headed by the United States, guaranteed the free movement of Israel in the straits of Tiran. In the beginning of March 1957, the IDF concluded its withdrawal from the Suez Canal.

What did Israel achieve in this war? Territorially nothing was achieved. Even the Gaza Strip was returned to its prewar state with the entry of the Egyptian army and the inability of the UN to prevent it. With that, Israel achieved two clear objectives: First, it stood by the commitment to its French ally. (The nuclear facility in Dimona was the clear expression of the French trust in Israel during this time), and secondly, it saw an improvement in relations with Britain on the one hand and a reduction in the environment of fear on the other.

Beyond this Israel was perceived as a state that could act with force and its deterrent ability was restored, at least temporarily. In contrast, many developing countries saw Israel as a country that was collaborating with the hated old imperialistic guard, a fact that did not prevent many of them from getting aid help from Israel in the next decade.

In addition, the Sinai war encouraged the feeling in Israel that problems could be solved by war. This fact would have a significant impact on the political and security landscape in the future. As Ben Gurion expected, the conclusion of the Sinai War was another step towards the third round that took place during the Six Day War in 1967.*

★

SAUDI ARABIA

This Saudi Arabian selection offers an Arab perspective on the crisis. It is decidedly more critical of the motives for intervening, but gives more credit to the role played by the United Nations. There is a certain compression of history in this account. The Crusades do not represent a topic of contemporary historical currency in the West, but they still hold a strong influence in contemporary Middle Eastern historical accounts.

The Second Confrontation

It took the form of a treacherous tripartite aggression on Egypt and the Gaza Strip on the part of Israel, France and Britain in 1376 AH [1956].† Thus, the forces of Imperialism, Crusadism and Zionism cooperated in pouring their hidden malice on the Arabs and the Muslims. What irritated the English and French was the nationalization of the Suez Canal in 1376 [1956]. France was [also] irritated by the help of Egypt to the Algerian re-

---

* Domke, *The World and the Jews in the Past Generations: Part B, Volume 6: 1920–1970.* Jerusalem: Merkaz Zalman Shazar le-toldot Yisra'el, 1995, 288–90.

† The Muslim calendar was created by Caliph Umar I in 639 AD. Since it dates from the *Hijrah*, it is labeled as AH from the Latin, *Anno Hijrah* (in the year of the Hijrah). Dates are written according to the Muslim calendar and are translated in brackets to correspond to the Julian calendar for the reader. CE here represents the Common Era, which corresponds to the commonly used AD (*Anno Domini*—in the year of our Lord).

volt in weapons as well as by training the Jihad fighters. Israel was angry at Egypt for the latter's closure of the Gulf of Aqaba to vessels making their way to Israel, whatever their type was. England and France resorted to the methods of military invasion of the nineteenth century. Planes hit Port Said with bombs while Israel swept through the Sinai Peninsula. The Security Council asked the aggressor states to withdraw. UN emergency forces were deployed on the border of the Gaza Strip, on the Egyptian-Israeli border and along the Gulf of Aqaba . . . *

* *Biography of the Prophet and History of the Muslim State,* Grade 10. Kingdom of Saudi Arabia: Ministry of Education, 2001, 113–15.

38

The Cuban Missile Crisis

The Cuban Missile Crisis is ubiquitous in history textbooks worldwide. Presented most often as a defining moment of the Cold War, most countries discuss it as the height of the nuclear confrontation between the superpowers, and the catalyst for arms reduction.

★

CUBA

This textual portrait of the history of Cuba describes a nation that has fulfilled its destiny through its revolution, despite the continuous meddling of "imperialist" forces.

The Missile Crisis—The defeat of the mercenary Brigade at Bay of Pigs made the US think that the only way of crushing the Cuban Revolution was through a direct military intervention. The US immediately embarked on its preparation.

But this did not go unnoticed for the Cuban government. On April

23rd, 1961 four days after the Bay of Pigs victory, Fidel Castro warned that a direct US aggression was all the more likely after the failure of their indirect attack; then on April 27th, President Osvaldo Dorticós met with the diplomatic corps to denounce that danger and ratify the island's determination to resist till the end.

The US stepped up its aggressive actions. On April 25th, Washington established an embargo on exports of any kind of products to Cuba, even those that had already been purchased and were waiting in US harbors.

Groups engaging in sabotage, espionage, and diversionist actions increased, as also did US support for the armed bands. New assassination attempts were plotted against Fidel Castro, other Cuban leaders, and supporters of the Revolution. An attempt to murder Carlos Rafael Rodríguez was aborted, but others claimed the lives of several members of the Rebel Army and the Militia in various parts of the country. The media campaign to make the US public opinion believe that by international law the US was allowed to send troops to Cuba intensified.

As part of their hostile plans, the US considered a self-inflicted aggression in connection with the Guantánamo Naval Base that would allow them to blame Cuba and provide a pretext for invading the island. With this aim, constant provocations took place from the US side of the base: Marines shooting toward Cuban territory, some times for several hours; the murder of a fisherman.

The number of violations of Cuba's airspace and territorial waters increased. In one single day—July 9th, 1962—US planes flew over Cuban territory 12 times. On another occasion, they launched rockets against eastern Cuba territory. US pirate boats attacked units of the Cuban Revolutionary Navy: three Cubans died during one of those attacks; 17 others were lost in another one.

Meanwhile, Washington stepped up its pressures on Latin American governments so they unconditionally supported US plans against Cuba. It accompanie[d] its pressures with bribes: an assistance program for Latin America, the so-called Alliance for Progress, portrayed as a solution for the region's problems. In late 1961, Venezuela and Colombia broke diplomatic relations with Cuba; in January, 1962, the 8th Consultative Meeting of OAS Foreign Ministers, in Punta del Este, Uruguay, suspended Cuba's membership in the organization for its "incompatibility with the inter-American system".

From late 1961 to early 1962, the US designed the so-called Operation Mongoose, approving 33 tasks to be carried out against Cuba in a graded way. The plan was expected to end with an internal rebellion in October of 1962, the pretext for the US military intervention. Hundreds of CIA officials were involved in the plan. In late September, the US Congress passed a "joint resolution" authorizing the President to use force against Cuba— an invasion if necessary—to put an end to "the aggressive and subversive work" of the Cuban Revolution in the western hemisphere.

In late September and up to beginning of October, military forces were concentrated near Cuba; US President John F. Kennedy called 150,000 reservists into active duty; an additional 150,000-strong force comprising several divisions was regrouped in Florida and Texas; and a hemispheric meeting convened by the Secretary of the US State Department was held in Washington, to impose the anti-Cuba plan on Latin American countries.

The Cuban government denounced the offensive to the world since it began, and responded to each aggressive US action. As Cuba was being expelled from the OAS, a Peoples Conference was being held in Havana, with the participation of relevant political and intellectual personalities of the hemisphere. The meeting denounced the US government as the disrupter of peace on the continent, and proclaimed that Cuba's fate was the fate of 200 million oppressed people in Latin America.

Also in response to the OAS agreement, more than one million persons met in Havana in a new National General Assembly of the Cuban People, and approved the Second Havana Declaration, a document of an extraordinary political and ideological value that analyze[d] the serious situation in Latin America, its main causes, and the way to solve it. The Declaration asserted that where all peaceful ways were closed for the peoples, the armed insurrection was indispensable, and that "the duty of every revolutionary is to do the revolution".

In 1961, the Cuban Revolutionary Armed Forces began streamlining and improving their structures and composition, and the government appealed to the Soviet Union to speed up its shipments of weapons and combat equipment necessary to guarantee the island's defense. On May 29th, 1962, the USSR proposed to deploy in Cuba medium and intermediate range missiles, an offer that was accepted considering its significance for the general strategic strengthening of the Socialist block, and what it meant for Cuba's own defense. It was decided that the signing of this military agreement be announced in November, during a visit to Cuba of Soviet Prime Minister, Nikita S. Khrushchev. In August, the deployment of 42 medium range nuclear missiles began, together with the sending to Cuba of IL-28 medium range bombers and a 43,000-strong Soviet military contingent. The Soviet troops would be directly subordinated to the government of the USSR, their mission being to support the Cuban Revolutionary Armed Forces in case of a foreign aggression, in full respect of the island's sovereignty and legal order, and without the right to occupy Cuban territory or carry out any other actions not connected with their cooperation role.

But before the Soviet-Cuban military agreement was announced, when US forces were ready to launch their aggression against the island, evidences were presented to President Kennedy of the missiles' presence in Cuba. The situation changed altogether, since it was no longer an issue of a military operation against Cuba but an international conflict in which the Soviet Union, a nuclear power, was involved.

The US immediately mobilized its army, navy, and air forces, not only in the western hemisphere but also in Europe and the Far East. It increased its reconnaissance flights over Cuba; activated its nuclear bomb carrying B-27 bombers; considerably reinforced Guantánamo Naval Base; and, on October 22nd, ordered a naval blockade of Cuba. US planes began flying low over Cuban territory.

Fidel Castro, Commander in Chief of the Cuban Forces, ordered a nation-wide military state of alert. Cuba requested an immediate meeting of the UN Security Council; denounced before the world the new and dangerous US adventure; and stressed the island's sovereign right to repel any enemy aggression and ask any friendly nation for assistance. The Soviet government placed its armed forces in full combat readiness; issued a declaration condemning the naval blockade and the rest of the US's aggressive measures; and warned Kennedy about the possible consequences of those aggressions.

Cuba declared that it would not allow its ships to be inspected by US forces, and that it would shoot against enemy planes entering its territory. On October 27th, the batteries of an anti-aircraft rocket group at Banes, in eastern Cuba, shot down a U-2 plane that was violating the island's airspace.

A wave of solidarity with Cuba was generated world-wide, while UN Secretary General, U Thant, intervened, in an effort to find a solution to the conflict. Exchanges took place between the Cuban and the Soviet governments, and Khrushchev maintained an active correspondence with President Kennedy. As a result of that Soviet-US correspondence, the USSR accepted to withdraw its missiles from Cuba in return for the expressed US commitment not to attack Cuba and stop its allies from doing it. And so, the Missile Crisis came to its end.

The very same day that the agreement was known in Cuba, on October 28th, Fidel Castro made a public statement expressing the position of the Cuban government, [that it] had not been consulted with regards to the compromise. Cuba set forth five conditions as a true guarantee against a US aggression. These conditions, which came to be known as "the five points", were the following:

- End to the economic blockade and all measures of commercial pressure against Cuba by the US in the world.
- End to all subversive activity, the dropping and infiltration of weapons and explosives, the organization of mercenary invasions, the infiltration of spies and saboteurs, all of them actions originating in the United States or in other countries that acted in complicity with the United States.
- End to pirate raids from bases in the United States and Puerto Rico.
- End to all violations of our naval and airspace by US warships and planes.
- US withdrawal from Guantánamo naval base, and return of that occupied territory to Cuba.

The Missile Crisis once more showed the world the US arrogance, and its disregard for the sovereignty of other nations. It also demonstrated the Cuban and Soviet interest in the peaceful solution of conflicts, preserving Cuban sovereignty and preventing a world nuclear catastrophe. It also proved that Fidel Castro was right when he said that the defense of the Cuban Revolution could not be trusted to external forces but had to rely on readiness and patriotism of Cubans. Lastly, the conflict evidenced the high morale, serenity, unity, and courage of the Cuban people, who did not yield before the dangers, and were ready to fight and die for the defense of their dignity and freedom. Cuba showed, again in the words of Fidel Castro, that it may not have had nuclear missiles, but it had "long range moral missiles that cannot be dismantled, that will never be dismantled".*

★

RUSSIA

Shortly after the success of the Cuban Revolution on January 1, 1959 Premier Khrushchev officially announced the recognition of the new Cuban government by the Soviet Union. While this became an instant cause for concern for President Kennedy and Congress, the real crisis was still ahead. In 1960 the United States took severe economic sanctions against Cuba, refusing to supply oil to the island and cutting back on the purchases of sugar, Cuba's largest and most important export. Forced to make a choice, the Cuban government nationalized the oil industry, sugar processing plants, and other American-owned businesses in Cuba in the summer of 1961. In response, the United States set up an economic blockade of Cuba, stopping trade and prohibiting American tourism to the island. In September 1960 Congress passed a law denying American foreign aid to any nation that assisted Cuba economically or militarily. The ban of tourism alone deprived Cuba of 60 million dollars in annual income and left tens of thousands workers in the service industry unemployed. Finally, in January 1961, USA broke off all relations with Cuba. In this dire situation the Soviet Union and other Communist nations stepped in to purchase Cuban sugar and provide the country with oil and other essential goods. By the end of 1960 the Cuban government nationalized most industry, trade, banking, and transportation, taking another step towards becoming a Communist state. Meanwhile the United States pressured and forced other Latin-American nations to break off relations with Cuba. Further anti-Cuban measures were in the works.

By 1960 a large group of exiles, opposed to Cuba's Communist government, was concentrated around Miami, Florida. In March 1960 President Eisenhower issued a secret order to the CIA to assist the Cuban

---

* Navarro, José Cantón. *History of Cuba: The Challenge of the Yoke and the Star.* Havana: SI-MAR, 2000, 229–32.

immigrants with preparations for a military invasion of their homeland. In the early morning of April 17, 1961 Cuban counterrevolutionaries, carried to Cuba by American ships, landed at the so-called Bay of Pigs. At the same time, American military planes entered Cuban airspace. It only took the Cuban military 72 hours to crush the invasion, with over 1,200 people taken prisoner. Despite this failure, Cuban contras continued to be trained by the Americans at over 50 military camps and bases throughout USA and Central America. In accordance with a treaty regarding mutual military assistance signed by the two nations, the Soviet Union sent military technology, transport, weapons, and specialists to Cuba in the summer of 1962. Some of these weapons, including strategic medium-range nuclear rockets, were installed in Cuba in complete secret. The Soviet Union pursued two major goals in carrying out this military assistance. It attempted to preserve Socialism in Cuba, hoping that it would be a spark setting off a series of revolutions throughout Latin America, and at the same time hope to create an immediate threat to the major cities of the United States. The nuclear missiles were spotted by an American observation satellite from space on October 16, 1962. The existence of Soviet nuclear rockets, capable of reaching most major American cities on the Eastern seaboard, became known in the White House.

In these conditions President Kennedy conducted an emergency meeting in which he demanded an immediate removal of the Soviet rockets from Cuba. At first the Soviet delegate to the United Nations denied the presence of Soviet rockets on Cuba, but he was proved wrong when the Americans produced a series of photographs undeniably proving the rockets' existence. Several days later Kennedy announced a complete naval blockade of Cuba. This blockade was carried out by 183 vessels of the US Navy, manned by over 85,000 marines. The Cuban airspace was monitored by American strategic bombers, equipped with nuclear bombs. This blockade was meant to provide a "quarantine" of armament shipments to Cuba by stopping and inspecting any foreign ships approaching the island. Cuba and the USSR refused to accept such a quarantine. As the possibility of a direct confrontation between the two superpowers loomed large, the world stood on the brink of a nuclear war.

Thus began the so-called Cuban Missile Crisis. The United States put all of its military forces, including troops stationed in Europe, and most of the Pacific Fleet, on high alert. The USSR and other Eastern bloc nations did the same. Cuban forces were mobilized and positioned throughout the country ready for action. Women and children took the places of drafted workers at the factories. Both sides were considering different courses of action, and meetings went on almost continuously behind closed doors in both Moscow and Washington. Despite great pressure from military leaders and high ranking government officials to begin military actions against Cuba, President Kennedy finally took a realistic position, and began negotiating with Khrushchev. The Soviet government acknowledged the presence of the weapons in Cuba, as well as their attacking and destructive capabilities. USSR promised to dismantle all the rockets in Cuba, in return for which the United States guaranteed Cuba's security and promised to dismantle its own nuclear rockets located in Turkey. Agreement was reached in the end of October, and by November 20 Kennedy announced the conclusion of the military blockade of Cuba.*

The peaceful resolution of the Cuban Missile Crisis appeared to give a push to the process of ridding the world of immediate nuclear danger. A major success of most of the world's major powers (with China as the notable exception) became the signing in Moscow of a treaty that banned nuclear testing in the atmosphere, in space, and under water. It was signed on August 5, 1963.†

★

CANADA

As Soviet ships carrying the missiles cruised westward towards Cuba and Kennedy threatened war if they did not turn back, NORAD automatically ordered DEFCON 3, the state of readiness just short of war. Neither [Canadian PM] Diefenbaker nor his ministers were consulted— much less informed—about the decision. The prime minister was furious that a megalomaniac American president could, in effect, push the button that would destroy Canada.‡

---

* *History of Russia: XX Century,* Moscow: Drofa, 1998, 380–81.

† *Newest History of Foreign Nations: XX Century.* Moscow: Vlados, 1998, 247.

‡ Bumsted, J.M. *A History of the Canadian Peoples.* Toronto: Oxford University Press, 1998, 409.

In 1959, troops led by Fidel Castro toppled a corrupt military regime in Cuba and ushered in a socialist revolution. The Kennedy administration in the United States supported a military expedition to undermine Castro in 1961, but it was decisively repulsed at the Bay of Pigs. In the aftermath of the attempted invasion, Soviet missiles were sent to Cuba. Still rankling from the defeat at the Bay of Pigs and determined to keep the western hemisphere free from communism, Kennedy demanded, in October 1962, that the Soviet Union remove its missiles from Cuba. He also called upon his Canadian allies to put their NORAD forces on alert in the event the Soviets refused to back down.

On the evening of 22 October, Lester Pearson rose in the House Commons to demand a statement from the prime minister concerning President Kennedy's television broadcast announcing the missile build-up in Cuba. Pearson was not the only one wondering about Canada's official response in the dramatic developments that threatened to pre-cipitate a third world war. Concerned that Kennedy was being too belligerent with the Soviets, Diefenbaker waited three days before an-nouncing that Canadian forces were on alert. No one had any way of knowing that the defence minister had secretly placed Canada's forces on alert immediately after Kennedy's request. As events unfolded, Canada's half-hearted public response was of little immediate conse-quence: the Soviet Union agreed to withdraw the offending missiles. However, Diefenbaker's truculence annoyed the Americans who were now determined to topple a Canadian prime minister who refused to do their bidding.

In the months preceding the 1963 federal election, statements from the American State Department and from a retired American NATO leader attempted to discredit Diefenbaker's admittedly inconsistent for-eign policy. Diefenbaker decried American interference in a Canadian election and finally made a commitment to reject nuclear weapons for Canada, but his unpopular government went down to defeat by Lester Pearson's Liberals, who had abruptly changed their position on the nu-clear question following the missile crisis. Once in office, the Liberals fol-lowed through on their commitment to the controversial nuclear warheads. Pearson's secretary of state for external affairs, Paul Martin, had made it clear that Canada's acceptance of nuclear weapons for its

NATO and NORAD forces helped the country obtain special consideration from the Americans on economic issues.*

★

CARIBBEAN

The Missile Crisis

On 29 August 1962, high-altitude flights over Cuba by American spy planes showed what might be surface-to-air nuclear missiles being installed in the western provinces by Soviet technicians. Premier Khrushchev assured President Kennedy that his intelligence reports were wrong. But on 14 October, photographs were delivered to the White House which proved that Khrushchev had lied. They clearly showed launching pads and missiles in western Cuba. Why Khrushchev had gone ahead with plans which were bound to endanger the safety of the whole world is not clear. Perhaps the blunders of the Bay of Pigs and the unpopularity of the United States in Latin America had led him to think there was no risk. If so, he was wrong.

Kennedy spent some time discussing his course of action with advisers. He then acted decisively. He informed the OAS of the danger from the missiles to both the United States and the Latin republics. He demanded and got OAS support for a plan to stop and search all Soviet ships heading for Cuba. He then contacted Khrushchev and demanded the removal of the missiles. Without waiting for a reply, he ordered 145,000 American troops to stand by in Florida and Nicaragua. Faced with the possibility of clashes which could lead to all-out war, Khrushchev backed down. On 29 October he ordered ships heading for Cuba to turn back and work to start on dismantling missiles on the island.†

---

* Finkel, Alvin, et al. *History of the Canadian Peoples: 1867 to the Present, v. 2.* Toronto: Copp Clark Pittman, 1993, 603–04.

† Claypole, William, and John Robottom. *Caribbean Story, Bk. 2: The Inheritors.* Kingston: Carlong, 1994, 195–96.

39

The Pueblo Incident

★

NORTH KOREA

The following event rarely figures in U.S. history textbooks, but like many such incidents, it is included here because of its importance for the other countries involved. In this case, the recounting of the Pueblo Incident goes a long way toward explaining North Korea's desire for nuclear capabilities.*

On January 23, 1968, naval vessels of the KPA captured the US armed spy ship Pueblo (1,000-ton class) in the very act of espionage. It had entered deep into the DPRK's territorial waters, at 39° 17.4' North Latitude

---

* This text comes from a history of North Korea published by the government in Pyongyang and distributed in English by the Democratic People's Republic of Korea mission to the United Nations in New York City. When the authors of *History Lessons* approached the mission about acquiring secondary school textbooks, they were instead offered a collection of five official versions of Korean history, including this one.

and 127° 46.9' East Longitude, 7.6 miles away from Ryo Island off Wonsan.

On the orders of the US CIA, the Pueblo, attached to the US Pacific Fleet, had been given the task of spying on the Far East of Russia and the territorial waters of the DPRK. On January 15 it reached the waters of the latter through the former's Maritime Territory. The spy ship intruded into DPRK waters on 17 occasions, on full alert each time, and engaged in espionage off Chongjin, Wonsan and other places, using radar and various other monitoring instruments.

It performed thorough reconnaissance on the radar network of the KPA, the movement of the DPRK navy vessels, the depth of water, the tide, salinity and transparency, as well as the capacity of harbour accommodation and displacement of vessels at anchor. This was admitted in a statement of Captain Lloyd M. Bucher and other crew.

Nevertheless, asserting that "it was an unjust capture on the open sea," the United States demanded that north Korea return the ship and its crew at once, apologize to the US government and compensate for damages. Its demand being rejected, the United States was foolish enough to threaten military action.

US President Johnson convened the National Security Council on January 24 and 25 and made a decision to launch "military retaliation."

The "working group of the Korean peninsula" was established by the US Departments of State and Defence and the CIA, and measures were proposed to address the situation. These included blocking the entrance to the port of Wonsan with mines, the capture of DPRK vessels, air raids on the KPA air bases, a "limited punishment attack" by US troops and the south Korean army, the intensification of reconnaissance flight, and so on.

In line with the plans, huge ground, naval and air forces of the United States were concentrated in and around the Korean peninsula. The peninsula was threatened with the danger of a sudden outbreak of war.

In February Kim Il Sung declared that "We do not want war, but we are not afraid of it. Our people and People's Army will retaliate for any retaliation of the US imperialists, return all-out war for all-out war."

Following this declaration, a statement of the Government of the DPRK was published and the entire army and all the people maintained combat readiness.

As evidence of their acts of espionage was laid bare and the DPRK took a firm and resolute stand, the United States signed a letter of apology on December 23 recognizing the intrusion of the Pueblo into the territorial waters of the DPRK for the purpose of espionage and guaranteeing that it would not repeat such behaviour.

In consideration of the request made by the US Government to deal leniently with the Pueblo crew, all 82 members of the Pueblo were expelled from the DPRK on that day. The corpse of a crewman who had been killed while recklessly resisting capture, was handed over to the US side. But the ship and its equipment and weapons were all held.

Instead of drawing a lesson from the incident, the US imperialists sent a large-sized reconnaissance plane, the EC-121, belonging to the US Pacific Fleet into the air space of the DPRK on April 15 the following year. The plane was destroyed in the air by the gunfire of the planes of the KPA as soon as it was detected. It was a justified punishment. However, the United States again distorted the facts, claiming the spy plane had been shot down during "reconnaissance activities over the open sea." Further aggravating the situation, it threatened to continue such reconnaissance flights and said that the development of situation depended on the "reaction" of the DPRK Government.

The DPRK Government did not hesitate to publish a statement which exposed and condemned the provocative act of the United States, and proclaimed solemnly its self-defensive stand. The United States was forced to back down.*

---

* Am, Jo, An Chol Gang (ed), and Kim Yong Nam (trans), et al. *Korea in the 20th Century: 100 Significant Events*. Pyongyang, Korea: Foreign Languages Publishing House, Juche 91 (2002), 180–83.

40

Vietnam War

Shortly after World War II the United States quietly entered a conflict that would escalate dramatically in the 1960s & 1970s. The Vietnam "quagmire" proved very unpopular within the United States and was almost unanimously condemned by other nations around the globe, including America's allies. It has been called unnecessary, and is widely considered the United States' most controversial and disappointing war.

★

FRANCE

This French selection offers some background to the Vietnam War, highlighting the international dimensions of the conflict and its origins in French colonialism.

B. The Indochina War

• During their occupation of Indochina, the Japanese encouraged anti-French feelings. **In September 1945,** the Vietminh, led by **communist Ho Chi Minh,** declared the Independence of the Democratic Republic of

Vietnam. France reacted by sending troops commanded by General Leclerc who regained control of Cochinchina by the end of 1945. In March 1946, France finally agreed to recognize the Republic of Vietnam, while keeping it within *l 'Union Francaise*. But against the wishes of Ho Chi Minh, the French High Commissioner, Thierry d'Argenlieu, proclaimed a Republic of Cochinchina. To deal with the unrest which resulted from this tougher stance, the French bombed Haiphong (November 1946), resulting in hundreds of dead. The following month, as a reprisal, Europeans were slaughtered in Hanoi—this was the beginning of the Indochina War.

• A difficult war was fought against guerilla forces well-armed by the USSR while in France, where communist propaganda called it *"une sale guerre"* [a dirty war], people were indifferent. Moreover, France did not have the support of the United-States who considered it a backward colonial fight. But everything changed in 1949–1950 when the Chinese revolution and the Korean War brought fears of communism sweeping through Asia. The Indochina War then lay within the framework of the Cold War. The USSR and China increased their support to the Vietminh while the United States gave financial aid to France.

• However, this aid was not enough to defeat the Vietminh. After the death of Stalin in 1953, the Americans wanted to settle the whole of the problems in Asia with a conference expected to take place in Geneva. France then tried to put herself in a position of strength and concentrated her troops around the entrenched camp of Dien Bien Phu so the Vietnamese army could be lured and crushed. But the trap closed on the French who were forced to surrender by May 7, 1954, after a 54 day fight. In July during the Geneva Conference, France recognized the independence of Laos, Cambodia and Vietnam, which was divided into two parts.*

★

VIETNAM

This Vietnamese selection resembles textbooks from both Communist Cuba and North Korea in its vocabulary and style, despite the normalization of relations between Vietnam and the U.S.

*Lambin, Jean-Michel. *Histoire—T^{ales}*. Paris: Hachette, 2001, 224.

Chapter 13

After the failure of the French Army at Dien Bien Phu, when they saw that they could not realize their prolonged conspiracy, they widened and internationalized the Indochina War. Not abiding by the Geneva Accords concerning Indochina, America under Eisenhower "filled the vacancy" in southern Vietnam.

General Collins, who was appointed ambassador in southern Vietnam, went to Saigon on November 7, 1954 bringing with him a plan sketched out in Washington that included six main points:

- Dismiss the French and the French forces that are still in southern Vietnam.
- Kill revolutionary forces, destroy the Geneva Accords, cut Vietnam into two.
- Help Diem to build a legal/judicial administration, with three branches: political, economic, and military.
- Help Diem build a National Army including equipment and leadership.
- Advance many economic policies aimed at transforming southern Vietnam into a market economy.
- Provide incentives for American companies to come in and develop the southern Vietnamese economy.

Through the puppet administration and puppet army America was able to realize the plan and change South Vietnam into a new kind of colony and an army base, then use South Vietnam as a springboard to attack the North to prevent the revolutionary wave for liberation of our people and socialist revolution in Southeast Asia.*

After the "General Uprising" (1959–1960) in the South, there continued more uprisings coupled with political battles and artillery battles against the American enemy. During that time, world wide, ethnic liberation movements were getting stronger, directly threatening the colonial system of imperialism. In order to counter this, Kennedy—who had just been in-

* Lam, Dinh Xuan, et al. *Lich Su 12: tap hai,* Vietnam: Nha Xuat Ban Giao Duc, 1997, 126–27.

augurated in Washington (the beginning of 1961)—established special forces to fight "reactionary activity" and to carry out the war of invasion in southern Vietnam. America started a new method of war in Vietnam, a "special war." *

"Special war" was a new form of a war, carried out by a puppet army, directed by the American army and dependent on American artillery, equipment, technology and transportation and meant to fight against our revolutionary forces and our people. The basic ploy of the "Special War" was to "use Vietnamese people to fight Vietnamese people." †

Chapter 14

Beginning in March 1965, facing the danger of the total destruction of its "Special War" forces, violent America brought its expeditionary forces and vassal army with its artillery and war technology into South Vietnam to strengthen its war of invasion. It had become an occupying force. The "total war" in South Vietnam widened into a "War of Destruction" in the North.

"Total war" in reality began from the middle of 1965 in the form of a new kind of war of invasion by the American army and the vassal‡ and puppet armies. Among them, the American army held the most important role and did not stop increasing its numbers and equipment, to fight our revolutionary forces and our people. §

The Vietnamization of forces and Asianization of the American War took place at the beginning of 1969, having just elected a president who just stepped into the White House, Nixon. Nixon came up with a theory that carried his name—"the Nixon theory"—that offered a new strategy of "practical prevention." Following a new path, America decided to "Vietnamize" the war [or "Laotianize" the war, "Khmerize" the war].

"Vietnamizing" the war was a new American form of invasive war car-

---

* "Special War" has to do with the United States training armies in other countries to fight their own wars.

† Lam, Dinh Xuan, et al. *Lich Su 12: tap hai.* Vietnam: Nha Xuat Ban Giao Duc, 1997, 137–38.

‡ A footnote in the original text lists five countries that participated alongside and supplied the "vassal" army: Korea, Thailand, Philippines, Australia, and New Zealand.

§ Lam, Dinh Xuan, et al. *Lich Su 12: tap hai.* Vietnam: Nha Xuat Ban Giao Duc, 1997, 142.

ried out mainly by a puppet army that would be coordinated with American forces. America would still call the shots through a network of advisors, giving dollars, artillery, technology and transportation to fight against our revolutionary forces and our people.

In accordance with this "Vietnamization" of the war, the American army and vassal armies extricated themselves from the war to lessen the flow of American blood in the war, at the same time increasing and taking full advantage of the flow of blood of the puppet army, to make the Vietnamese blood flow. That was the new goal and meaning of America in the war. In reality, there was a plot to use Vietnamese people to kill Vietnamese people.*

Chapter 15

Concerning the Paris Accords and Vietnam, we "drove the Americans out" and still the enemy "did not fall completely." On March 29, 1973, the American army finally left our country completely. But because the enemy still did not fully "surrender" America continued to maintain administrative power over their "double agents" or "minions" in southern Vietnam, so they still kept more than 20,000 army consultants masquerading as civilians who established an undercover army command post, which continued to assist the army and economy for the enemy.

Continuing to receive the advice and direction of the Americans—though not as before—the enemy leadership proudly destroyed the Paris Accords. They mobilized all the forces to carry on a campaign to submerge our native land, continued to launch new operations in already liberated areas, and erased the whole form of the Paris Agreement. In reality those activities were strategies to "Vietnamize" the war and were aimed against the revolutionary forces and our people in South Vietnam.†

The War of Resistance against the Americans to rescue our country ended with the Spring Battle of 1975: the historical Battle of Ho Chi Minh.

It was a great patriotic war, a war of national liberation to protect our nation. The war had lasted more than two decades (7-1954 to 4-1975),

* Lam, Dinh Xuan, et al. Lich Su 12: tap hai. Vietnam: Nha Xuat Ban Giao Duc, 1997, 151–52.
† Lam, Dinh Xuan, et al. Lich Su 12: tap hai. Vietnam: Nha Xuat Ban Giao Duc, 1997, 168–69.

longer than any war in history, and we had to fight one of the most power-ful nations, America.

Five generations of American presidents with their legs bound to-gether oversaw four different American plans of imperialist attack and in-vasion. They directly invested almost $676 billion in the war in Vietnam (compared with $341 billion in the Second World War and $54 billion in the Korean War), and if you include the indirect costs it comes to almost $920 billion. At its peak, they mobilized 550,000 active workers, along with workers from five other countries that totaled 70,000. There were more than 1 million enemy puppet soldiers in southern Vietnam either di-rectly fighting or in supportive roles. On both sides of our country (North and South) they dropped more than 7 or 8 million tons of bombs, more bombs than were dropped in any previous war.*

Our victory is a source of inspiration to all revolutionary movements in the world, for all nationalities who are fighting imperialism.†

★

CANADA

U.S. textbooks have often portrayed Canada during this period as simply the main destination for American draft dodgers. The Vietnam War did indeed have a signifi-cant impact on Canada, but as this text explains, it went far beyond accepting those who refused to serve in the U.S. military. These Canadian texts portray a Canada deeply conflicted by its own policies and unsuccessful in its efforts to distance itself from U.S. foreign policy.

It was not only the configuration of world politics that had altered by the 1960s. So had the policy of the United States. President Kennedy and his successor, Lyndon B. Johnson, were actually more hard-bitten and confrontational Cold Warriors than their predecessors, Truman and Eisenhower. Kennedy authorized dirty tricks by the CIA in foreign coun-tries with no compunction or apology when they were exposed. His only

* Lam, Dinh Xuan, et al. *Lich Su 12: tap hai.* Vietnam: Nha Xuat Ban Giao Duc, 1997, 176–77.
† Lam, Dinh Xuan, et al. *Lich Su 12: tap hai.* Vietnam: Nha Xuat Ban Giao Duc, 1997, 179.

regret about the abortive 1961 Bay of Pigs invasion of Cuba by US-backed Cuban exiles, for example, was that it had failed. Most important, however, both Kennedy and Johnson permitted their governments to become ever more deeply involved in the quagmire of Southeast Asia. Like Korea, Indochina had been partitioned into communist and non-communist states after the Second World War. When the French government proved incapable of retaining its colonial control against armed 'insurgents' from the Democratic Republic of Vietnam (North Vietnam, governed by Ho Chi Minh), Canada in 1954 had become involved in attempts at international control. From the outset Canada had deceived itself into believing that it had a free hand to carry out its work without either upsetting the Americans or appearing to act merely as a lackey of the United States.

When the American administration gradually escalated both US involvement and the shooting war in Vietnam after 1963, Canada's position became increasingly anomalous, both on the commission and outside it. Lester Pearson was still hoping to mediate in April 1965 when he used the occasion of a speech in Philadelphia to suggest that the American government might pause in its bombing of North Vietnam to see if a negotiated settlement was possible. He was soon shown the error of his ways in no uncertain terms. In a private meeting with Lyndon Johnson shortly thereafter, the American president shook Pearson by his lapels and criticized Canadian presumptuousness with Texas profanity. Canadians now sought to distance themselves from the policies of the "Ugly Americans", although never by open withdrawal from the American defence umbrella.*

In English Canada, what really ignited the revolt of youth was the war in Vietnam. In retrospect, the extent to which Vietnam dominated the period becomes even clearer than it was to contemporaries. The war became the perfect symbol for the sixties generation of everything that was wrong with mainstream American society. It was equally exportable as an emblem of American evil, representing everything that the rest of the world hated about the United States, including its arrogant assumption that it was always morally superior. Vietnam was central to the Canadian counterculture in a variety of ways. Hostility to American policy in Vietnam fuelled

* Bumsted, J.M. *A History of the Canadian Peoples.* Toronto: Oxford University Press, 1998, 411–12.

Canadian anti-Americanism, as a paperback book about the United States entitled *The New Romans: Candid Canadian Opinions of the U.S.* demonstrated in 1967. This hostility also connected young Canadians with the burgeoning American protest movements. Many Canadian university faculty members recruited during the decade were Americans, most of them recent graduate students critical of American policy. They were joined in their sympathies by an uncounted number of American war resistors (some said as many as 100,000 at the height of the war), the majority of whom sought refuge in communities of university students or hippies in large Canadian cities.*

During the Pearson years, the only episode that jeopardized Canada's status in Washington was a speech made by the prime minister in 1965 at Temple University in Philadelphia. Pearson advocated that the American temporarily cease bombing North Vietnam in an effort to seek diplomatic solutions in Indochina. President Lyndon Johnson, meeting Pearson afterwards, grabbed him by the shirt collar and shouted, "You pissed on my rug." It was a rough reception for a prime minister whose country had compromised its role in the International Control Commission to defend America's view of the Vietnamese conflict and to spy on North Vietnam for the Americans. A report in 1962 prepared by Canada and co-signed by India, desperate for American goodwill because of border wars with China, was regularly produced by American officials wishing to demonstrate North Vietnamese atrocities, of which there were no doubt many. That the report ignored the equal or greater human rights abuses in South Vietnam appeared to be of as little interest to official Canada as it was to the United States.†

---

* Bumsted, J.M. *A History of the Canadian Peoples.* Toronto: Oxford University Press, 1998, 336–37.

† Finkel, Alvin, et al. *History of the Canadian Peoples: 1867 to the Present, v. 2.* Toronto: Copp Clark Pittman, 1993, 604–05.

41

The End of the Cold War

1989–1990 brought an end to the Cold War, as the Soviet Union gradually dissolved and then suddenly collapsed. *Perestroika* and *Glasnost* were the proverbial final straws; together they had brought down the wall that divided East from West.

FRANCE

The Collapse of the Soviet Union

1989, THE FALL OF THE BERLIN WALL

• The year 1989 marked a turning point in History. Gorbachev believed he had obtained his objectives; meanwhile the USSR was ready to collapse. **Eastern Europe went through a period of upheaval,** first of all in Poland. April 5, General Jaruzelski, who governed his country with an iron fist, signed an agreement with the directors of the non-communist union, Solidarity. The USSR encouraged him and the Catholic Church, very influential in Poland, approved. Free elections were organized and a new government was formed, led by a non-communist.

- Hungary opened the "iron curtain" in May of 1989, abandoned Marxist-Leninism and announced free elections. There was worse in store for the cohesion of the Soviet bloc; Hungary allowed the East Germans hiding out in the West German embassy in Budapest to reach neighboring Austria. It was a breach in the "iron curtain." The East German regime was deeply destabilized; its leaders **opened the Berlin wall on November 9** and announced free elections. The USSR only watched; the Soviet troops stationed in East Germany did not intervene. An unbelievable emotion seized the public watching the spectacle of the crowd crossing the rest of the wall. It marked a new era for Europe and for the world, an unbelievable turn of events.

- In November and December, Czechoslovakia, Bulgaria and Romania each did away with communism. The Romanian communist dictator, Ceaucescu, was executed. The "popular democracies" were hereafter engaged on the path of true democracy; **the Soviet model was swept from Central Europe.** The Soviet Empire had lost its strategic buffer zone.

1991, THE END OF THE USSR

- The USSR took little time to implode. Gorbachev, who had refused to use force to maintain Soviet domination, was criticized by many Soviets who reproached him for having sold out communism. The nationalists reappeared in the Baltic States and in the Caucuses. March 13, 1990, the People's Congress, elected one year earlier, abolished the directing role of the communist party. To save a dying regime, Gorbachev tried to accelerate the economic reforms. On May 29, **Boris Yeltsin,** an old member of the communist party recently converted to democracy, became president of the Russian Federal Parliament. Next to Gorbachev's declining power, he represented a new alternative.

- During 1990, several Soviet republics proclaimed their independence. The disintegration of the regime accelerated in 1991. On June 12, Yeltsin was elected through universal suffrage as Russia's new president. A **coup attempt** by those nostalgic for the old Soviet dictatorship failed in August. **In December 1991,** ten republics of the old USSR—including Russia and the Ukraine—announced that *"the Soviet Union no longer ex-*

ists," and formed a Commonwealth of Independent States (CIS), which replaced the former USSR. On December 25, Gorbachev was forced to resign.

• The USSR and the Soviet model disappeared. It remains without a doubt the major historical event of the 20th century. **The exterior explanations** of this collapse are numerous. The economic crisis persisted and was actually worse than that envisioned in the West. Gorbachev could not attempt further economic reforms without some corresponding political reforms. In stimulating the first, he provoked the latter, all without popular support. In a world more or less open, thanks to new information technologies, **the will toward democracy** was both universal and irrepressible. Nationalism, which everyone considered disappeared, resurfaced.*

★

RUSSIA

The Unification of Germany

By the end of the 1980s the situation in East Germany worsened. Although government-controlled press wrote about successfully reached economic goals, in reality huge disparities were developing in the economy, the budget deficit grew annually and the national debt surpassed 20 billion dollars. Exodus and migration of young qualified and educated workers to the West reached catastrophic proportions. In addition to the 2 million people who escaped to West Germany in the preceding years, 350 thousand more made it across the border in the first half of 1989 alone. New political and community organizations were appearing, signaling the rise of a revolutionary movement. On the day of the 40th anniversary of the creation of East Germany an anti-government demonstration was dispersed by force. This triggered massive and widespread demonstrations throughout the nation. The "velvet revolution" began in the German Democratic Republic.

The way out of political crisis could only be found after a change of authority. Chancellor Erich Honecker resigned on October 18, 1989. The

---

* Lambin, Jean-Michel. *Histoire—T^{ales}*. Paris: Hachette, 2001, 250.

Berlin Wall fell on November 9 that year. The process of merging of East and West Germany was becoming faster and more uncontrollable almost daily. In the East political structures came tumbling down, and the economy was in shambles. The first free elections in East Germany took place on March 18, 1990. A party that favored a unified Germany and that was created with the help of Helmut Kohl, the chancellor of West Germany, emerged victorious. The results of the election showed that the unification of East and West Germany was inevitable. A treaty on economic cooperation introduced the West German mark as the official currency of East Germany. The two nations officially united on October 3, 1990.

The first all-German elections took place in December of that year. The Christian Democrats Party, led by Kohl, won again, and stood at the forefront of the force that brought the two Germanies back together.

A number of international treaties and documents made the unification of Germany official. On September 12, 1990, representatives from the United States, Great Britain, France, and the USSR, as well as of East and West Germany signed a treaty that put an end to the regulation of Germany by countries victorious in World War II. A cooperation and partnership treaty between the Soviet Union and Germany was signed shortly thereafter, limiting the size of the German military and prohibiting the nation from building weapons of mass destruction. The same treaty also guaranteed the removal of Soviet troops from the territory formerly known as East Germany. Finally, on October 1, 1990 a treaty was signed in New York that stopped the international control over Berlin and Germany as a whole that had persisted since the conclusion of World War II.

This was the conclusion of the direct results of World War II in Europe. An entire era in the history of Germany, Europe, and the world was over. A new geopolitical situation emerged.*

★

CANADA

In 1984 Mikhail Gorbachev became Chairman of the Communist party in the Soviet Union, a position that made him the most powerful

---

* *The World in the XXth Century.* Moscow: Prosveshchenie, 1999, 268–69.

person in its government. The slogans of his government were *glasnost* and *perestroika.* *Glasnost,* meaning openness, also translated into less media censorship, more freedom of expression, and a less dominant role for the Communist party. *Perestroika,* or rebuilding, signified rapid modernization and, more importantly, moving away from a state-controlled economy to one that was more market-oriented. In foreign affairs Gorbachev spoke of the need for "new political thinking." The Soviet Union relaxed its control over its Eastern European neighbours, allowing them more freedom in running their affairs. Gorbachev proposed radical reductions in both nuclear and conventional armaments. Three successive summits (1985–87) with President Ronald Reagan established cordial relations between the two superpowers and led to an important series of arms limitations talks. The tensions of the early 1980s, resulting from the Soviet invasion of Afghanistan in 1979 and from Reagan's anti-Communist speeches, were evaporating.*

* Francis, Daniel, and Sonia Riddoch. *Our Canada: A Social and Political History.* Scarboroug: Pippin, 1995, 479.

PART VII

Modern Times

42

The Hostage Crisis in Iran

The hostage crisis in Iran represented a major shift in the perception of American policy in the Middle East. The Iranian confrontation shattered the aura of American invincibility and became a model for later engagements. Many American history textbooks view this crisis in the context of three major issues facing the U.S. in the Middle East in the 1970s: a growing American dependence on oil, the U.S.'s diplomatic backing of Israel, and the rise of Islamic fundamentalism.

★

IRAN

In sharp contrast, this excerpt shows a dramatically different Iranian view of the Revolution. As one U.S. history textbook put it, "[T]he dictator of Iran who replaced the Shah was Ayatollah Ruhollah Khomeini, a fanatical Muslim who tried to return the country to the Middle Ages." *

---

* Boorstin, Daniel J., and Brooks Mather Kelley. *A History of the United States.* Upper Saddle River, New Jersey: Prentice Hall, 1996, 894.

From the Victory of the Islamic Revolution Until the Resignation of the Interim Government

An important event that occurred in October of 1979 was the overthrow of the American Embassy in Teheran, which later came to be known as the *American Den of Spies*. The shah, after he ran away from Iran for a few months, wandered in several countries. Throughout the world he was famous for being a corrupt dictator so that no country was willing to accept him on a permanent basis. But the Americans, who thought of the shah as an obedient servant and thought they could restore him to power, invited him to their country under the pretext of treatment for his illness. Considering America's previous intrusions and conspiracies in Iran's internal affairs and the hostility of the American government against Islam and the Islamist Revolution, the shah's going to America signaled that the US was explicitly supporting the enemy of the Iranian people and it meant a conspiracy against the Revolution. The Iranian foreign ministry formally complained to the US, but it was futile. In November 1979, on the occasion of the anniversary of the exile of Imam Khomeini, from Qum to Turkey and Iraq, and on the first anniversary of the killing of high school and university students in Teheran University, the students gathered in the university and had demonstrations. These students from that day on called themselves the Muslim Students following the path of the Imam. They left the university as a group and headed toward the American embassy. When they reached the door of the embassy, they attacked it, and in a short amount of time and without any weapons, they conquered the embassy. They took the Americans who were there as hostages and announced that until the US surrendered the shah to Iran for trial, they would not release the hostages. From the documents that fell into the hands of the students at the embassy it became clear that the US, with the help of its elements inside Iran, had a hand in many of the anti-Revolutionary plots that were occurring in Teheran and other parts of Iran.

The names of several of the people, who had secret contacts with the American spies in order to hurt the Revolution, were also obtained from these documents. The news of the takeover of the American embassy in Teheran and the taking of dozens of its workers as hostages exploded in the world like a bomb. America was completely taken by surprise. Imam Khomeini and the assembly of experts approved of the students' actions.

The people as well, by gathering and demonstrating in the streets around the *Den of Spies,* announced their support of this action. But the interim government of Vazargan was unhappy with these events.

From the Resignation Until the Beginning of the Imposed War

In the beginning, the most important issue in the country was the issue of the *American Den of Spies* in Iran. On the one hand, the Imam, the government, and the people were supporting the students who were holding the hostages inside the embassy and condemning America. On the other hand, America was trying to release the hostages through any possible means. From the beginning, the Imam did not accept any negotiations with America and asked his nation not to be scared of America's threats. In those days and weeks, Iran was the most newsworthy part of the world. The United States and the servile governments supporting them throughout the world were propagandizing against the Revolution and making threats. On the other hand, Iranian Muslim students living in America and Europe and also the Revolutionary and oppressed people of other countries were approving the Islamist country of Iran through demonstrations. Iran's position was clear, but American policy was similar to a knot that cannot be opened.

American Failure in Tabas

Another important event in the spring of 1980, was the American military attack in order to rescue the hostages. America's plan was to bring their forces into Iran with airplanes and helicopters via the Gulf and to reach Teheran secretly at night. They meant to attack the American embassy in which the hostages were being held and to take them with them. But this attack failed because of the sandstorm in Tabas. American helicopters caught on fire and some of their forces were killed. The Americans ran away disgracefully, without reaching Teheran, leaving behind several helicopters, airplanes and other things in the desert.

From the Beginning of the Imposed War
Until the Presidency of Ayatollah Khomeini

In this period one of the issues in the country was the American hostage situation. Imam Khomeini left the decision about the hostages to the parliament. Because the Islamic Republic of Iran was not willing to negotiate directly with the US, the Algerian government was selected to act as a go-between. Finally after 444 days the hostages were released and the US pledged to return the Iranian money that they had frozen in their banks.*

---

* *History for Iran in the Modern Age,* 4th year. Tehran: Ministry of Education, 1996, 201–205.

43

Nicaragua in the 1980s

The 1980s saw sharply increased U.S. activity in Latin America. Particularly after Ronald Reagan's election, any government on good terms with the Soviets was seen as a potential threat. Because Nicaragua's Sandinistas were recipients of Soviet aid during the 1980s, U.S. aid flowed to the enemies of the Sandinistas until Congress cut off the official sources.

★

NICARAGUA

Beginning in 1982, the revolutionary government found itself besieged by an armed offensive (Nicaraguan Resistance) which was organized in the mountains to the north. At its core it was composed of the dispersed elements of the old National Guard. Progressively, the ranks of the insurgents were filled, especially after 1984. In 1989 they had an army of 20,000 soldiers, the majority of which were peasants between 17 and 24 years old. They were sufficiently armed and well-trained to confront the Popular Sandinista Army and its 100,000 soldiers. The Resistance like the

PSA relied on the aid of foreign governments, the former on the United States and the latter mainly on the Soviet Union and Cuba.

In order to face the Resistance, the government was obligated to establish mandatory military service for youth between 16 and 24 years old, as well as place on military reserve all men between 25 and 40 years. The population in the country and city reacted against the mandatory military service.

The war lasted several years causing great damage to the country. Thousands of youth were killed or left disabled; the majority of them were of humble origins. Thus, it was the poorest population that paid the highest price for the war.

Under the influence of the Central American presidents and with the goal of finding a peaceful solution to the armed conflict, representatives from the Revolutionary Government and from the Resistance met in Sapoá. The two parties arrived at several accords during these talks, among them free and supervised elections. In 1984, the revolutionary government had called elections in which the FSLN candidates won: Daniel Ortega as president and Sergio Ramírez as vice-president.

Once again elections were called in 1989. A considerable number of political parties registered to participate in the electoral contest. The two most important parties were the FSLN and the Unión Nacional Opositora (UNO).* There were huge manifestations for both candidates during the election campaign with many of the opinion polls showing victory for the FSLN. However, on February 25, 1990 on the day of the elections, the popular majority voted for the UNO.

Economic Aspects

The revolutionary government, established in 1979, followed a political plan that provided for a mixed economy: part state, part private, part co-operative.

The new revolutionary state intended to develop the country's economy in order to accomplish the social objectives that it had proposed. But state-ownership dominated, pushed on by the confiscation of private property administered by the civil servant apparatus. In its eagerness to

---

* National Union Candidate.

control foreign and domestic trade, the state created new organizations, which resulted in the reduction of production and trade.

On the other hand, the financial system had become totally state-controlled. It resulted in numerous devaluations between 1979 and 1990. Due to the discrepancy between the artificial value of the dollar and its real value, a huge black market appeared.

Consequently, relations deteriorated between the Sandinista government and the United States, which ultimately declared a trade embargo against Nicaragua. The economic consequences were disastrous.

The intervention of the State in the economy, the lack of administrative capabilities in many of the civil servants, the North American embargo and the exile of thousands of Nicaraguans brought an economic decline that manifested itself in rationing, a black market and a decline in exportations. In 1978, one year before the Revolution, Nicaragua exported $646 million. In 1984, exports had fallen to $226 million. It was a reflection of the economic deterioration of the country.*

★

CANADA

Canada offers the perspective of a concerned third party who wanted to help but was constrained by the policies of its neighbor. Here it views the unrest in Latin America as rooted in economics instead of the "communist elements" blamed by U.S. officials.

During the 1980s much world attention was focused on Central America and its violent conflicts. In Nicaragua, Sandinista rebels overthrew the government of Anastasio Somoza, but the Sandinista regime itself soon faced opposition from a rebel group known as the Contras. There were continuing civil wars in Guatemala and El Salvador. Most Latin Americans believed that the social unrest was rooted in long-standing social, economic, and political problems. But the American government of President Reagan was convinced that Communist agitation, inspired by the

* Romero Vargas, Dr. Germán. *Nuestra Historia*. Managua, Nicaragua: Editorial Hispamer, 1995, 124–26.

Soviet Union and Cuba, was responsible for the violence in the region. The Americans supported anti-Communist groups and governments by giving them a great deal of military and economic assistance.

The Canadian government was caught in a squeeze. Privately, Canadian government officials were inclined to accept the views of Latin Americans regarding the causes of conflict in Central America. A very vocal segment of Canadian public opinion consisting of non-governmental organizations, church agencies, labour organizations, and academic experts also agreed with this position. These individuals and groups did not hesitate to lobby the government in support of their views; in fact, public concern pushed Latin American issues high on the government's agenda. Some American actions, such as mining the harbours of Nicaragua, which violated international law were also contrary to the general principles of Canadian foreign policy, such as using peaceful methods to resolve problems. On the other hand, the Canadian government did not wish to antagonize Washington, especially when the free trade negotiations were under way.

Torn between these conflicting pressures the Canadian government adopted a policy of "quiet diplomacy." Prime Minister Mulroney avoided direct criticism of American actions in Central America. When the American government cracked down on the numbers of refugees fleeing from Central America, the Canadian government in its turn adopted policies making it harder for such refugees to enter Canada. Canadian foreign aid continued to flow to countries such as El Salvador, Honduras, and Guatemala, even though they did not have good human rights records. But at the same time the Canadian government expressed quiet support for the Contadora Peace Group. (This was a group of nations including Argentina, Brazil, Mexico, and Venezuela that were working to resolve the war between the Sandinistas and the Contra rebels.) At the United Nations, Canada voted in favour of a resolution requiring the United States to stop sending aid to the Contras and to pay reparations to Nicaragua. In addition, Canada refused to go along with an American embargo on trade with Nicaragua.*

---

* Francis, Daniel, and Sonia Riddoch. *Our Canada: A Social and Political History.* Scarborough: Pippin, 1995, 480.

44

Apartheid

The U.S. approach to apartheid in South Africa, like many other issues during the 1980s, played out according to Cold War alliances. For many years, South Africa had been a strategic ally for the West. As long as this remained true, the U.S. could turn a blind eye to its racist government. In the 1980s however an international antiapartheid movement increasingly made this policy untenable.

★

ZIMBABWE

This text comes from a Zimbabwean history textbook that looks not only at Zimbabwe but at all of southern Africa. This textbook offers a small glimpse of how U.S. policies in South Africa were perceived by Black Africa.

The International Community and Apartheid

Both the United Nations (UN) and the Organization for Africa Unity (OAU) condemned apartheid. However some Western members of the UN had different opinions. For example, the Conservatives in England backed the apartheid regime although there were many Englishmen and women who worked tirelessly for the elimination of apartheid. The same was true of the Republicans in America. Most Democrats were opposed to apartheid but did not agree on the measures to be taken against apartheid. Some talked about what they called 'limited sanctions,' even when these were not effective. Almost all Western countries were opposed to the armed struggle as a means of bringing down apartheid. This is quite ironical when one considers that America owes her independence to the armed struggle; so do many countries in and outside Africa. In any case, when every possible peaceful avenue has been exploited and has failed, should a people sit down and accept their oppression? One writer has said, "a time comes when the evils of submission are greater than those of resistance". Such a time came to South Africa during the sixties, seventies and eighties.

In the 1980s many countries voted to placed [sic] a total ban on trade with South Africa. Many American companies and banks disposed of their assets and left South Africa as a result of international pressure. Many anti-apartheid organizations were formed the world over. The 'Free Mandela' campaign reached almost every corner of the globe.

South Africa's Response

South Africa responded to international pressure and to the crisis at home by tightening the screws and by exporting terror and genocide to neighbouring African countries. At home, the press was gagged, African activists were incarcerated or murdered and new laws to deprive the masses of any form of freedom or expression were promulgated. According to the Front Line States, South Africa's destabilization cost them an estimated US$10 billion by 1980. Reactionary groups were sponsored by the regime to fight wars of destabilization in Angola, Mozambique, Zimbabwe, Zambia, Bostwana, Lesotho and periodically Jonas Savimbi's UNITA in Angola and Alfonso Dhlakama's bandits in Mozambique wreaked havoc in those countries. In this, South Africa was supported by the USA administration which had publicly admitted giving aid to Jonas Savimbi.

The unholy alliance between South Africa and Reaganism in America gained strength during the early 1980s when the Reagan era began. The

Black American Republican, Jeane Kirk Patrick [*sic**], believed that right-est authoritarian regimes, no matter how oppressive, were natural allies of the USA as they were useful in combating the spread of communism.

The appointment of Dr. Chester Crocker as assistant Secretary of State with responsibility for Africa did not make things any better. He had previously backed the Ian Smith Internal Settlement and seemed more interested in backing reactionary regimes in southern Africa such as the South Africa regime, UNITA and others. Ronald Reagan once asked of South Africa:

> Can we abandon a country that has stood by us in every war we have ever fought, a country that is essentially strategic to the free world?

One might ask, "how free a world was that of the South African blacks?" The point being made was clear. Thereafter, the USA vetoed every resolution that was intended to bring down apartheid at the UN. In Namibia, the US Government linked the granting of independence to Namibia with the withdrawal of Cuban troops from Angola. This gave South Africa the excuse to continue its occupation of Namibia. As if this was not enough, Jonas Savimbi, the UNITA leader commonly known to independent Africa as 'renegade Savimbi' arrived in Washington in December 1981 to seek US aid for the destabilization of Angola. From then, he was backed by both South African and the USA and caused a trail of terror among the peasant population of Angola. The USA and South Africa wished to force the Angolan Government to accommodate Savimbi so that they could use him as their neo-colonialist agent. This was the same tactic used in Mozambique where certain countries sponsored the RENAMO bandits to try and force the Frelimo Government to accommodate the Renamo leaders in Government.†

---

* Jeanne Kirkpatrick served as U.S. Ambassador to the United Nations under President Reagan from 1981 to 1985. She was a Republican, but not black.

† Sibanda, M., and H. Moyana. *The African Heritage: History for O' level Secondary Students, Book 3*. Harare, Zimbabwe: Zimbabwe Publishing House (Pvt) Ltd. 1999, 115–16.

45

Free Trade

Since the end of the Cold War, free trade has practically become synonymous with American-style capitalism. What the U.S. government, the International Monetary Fund (IMF) and the World Bank promote as globalization, the rest of the world understands as Americanization. Nevertheless, U.S. textbooks ignore the subject almost without exception.

★

CANADA

Canada is the United States' largest trading partner, sharing with it the longest undefended international border in the world. Canadian interest in economic treaties with the United States rests on this idea of proximity and free flow.

American Participation in the Canadian Economy

Many Canadians welcomed the flow of American money into Canada in the 1950s. But by 1967, 81 percent of the $34.7 billion worth of foreign investment in Canada was from American sources. Public opinion shifted: a 1967 poll showed that two thirds of Canadians wanted their government to control American investment in Canada. Several government reports, including the Watkins Report of 1968 and the Crey Report of 1971, raised concerns about the extent of the foreign ownership of Canadian firms.

Securing Markets for Canadian Products

Making investments in Canada was not the only way in which the United States played a major role in the Canadian economy. Seventy percent of all Canada's exports went to the United States. Canada was also the biggest customer for American goods. Any change in American economic policy sent major shock waves through the Canadian economy. In a famous comment, Pierre Trudeau described Canada's uncomfortable dependence on the U.S. economy: "Living next to you is in some ways like sleeping with an elephant: no matter how friendly and even-tempered the beast, one is affected by every twitch and grunt."

Just a few months after Trudeau's comment, the elephant twitched and Canadian businesspeople trembled. In 1971 U.S. President Richard Nixon ordered a 10 percent tariff on goods imported into the United States. This came to be known as the Nixon shock. As a result, Canadian-made goods cost more in the United States, and Canadian businesses faced the prospect of losing $300 million in exports. Although worldwide pressure forced the United States to cancel the 10 percent tariff a few months later, Canadians were shocked to discover how economically dependent they were on the United States and how badly they could be hurt by changes in American economic policy.

The Third Option

After the "Nixon shock," Canada had three choices: it could maintain its present relationship with the United States, move toward even closer relations, or try to create a more independent Canadian economy. Trudeau's government chose the third option. Canada began to look for new trading partners around the world as a way of lessening its dependence on the United States.

During the 1970s, Canada tried to forge new trade links in Europe,

Asia, and Africa, but by the mid-1980s it looked as if the only important market willing to take Canadian goods was the United States. The United States, however, was thinking about creating its own trade barriers to keep out goods from other nations.

Ottawa began to worry that Canada would be locked out of global markets, including the American market. Trudeau seriously considered developing closer trade ties with the United States. In September 1985 the Royal Commission on the Economic Union and Development Prospects for Canada called for a "leap of faith" into free trade with the United States. By this time Prime Minister Trudeau had retired, and it would be up to Brian Mulroney and the Progressive Conservatives to steer Canada into free trade.

MAKING THE "LEAP OF FAITH" INTO FREE TRADE

Once he was in office, Prime Minister Mulroney proposed a full-fledged free-trade deal between Canada and the United States. Because of **GATT** (General Agreement on Tariffs and Trade) negotiations since World War II, about 80 percent of the tariff barriers that had existed between the United States and Canada in 1935 had been removed. The Free Trade Agreement (FTA) gave Canada and the United States open access to each other's markets for most goods, and committed the two countries to dropping crossborder tariffs by the end of 1998. It also dealt with other trade concerns, including energy, the movement of people for business purposes, investment, and financial services. Free trade became the issue of the 1988 federal election, just as it had been in the 1911 election. Arguments for and against free trade raged across the country. In the election the Progressive Conservatives won a majority government, and the FTA became law on January 1, 1989.

What was the outcome of free trade, ten years later? Was the "leap of faith" justified? The results were uncertain. Statistics from 1998 showed an increase in Canadian exports to the United States. The greatest increase in exports was from Ontario, followed by Quebec and Alberta. It should be noted, however, that the surge in exports was also due to a low Canadian dollar. Except in Ontario and Quebec, where automotive parts were the major export, the exports continued to be from the resource sector. In other words, a longstanding pattern in Canadian economic history remained the same. There was an increase in north—south trade for all regions, integrating the Canadian economy more closely into that of the United States. Only Prince Edward Island exported more to the rest of Canada than it did abroad. Manufacturing increased, though not as much as the FTA's supporters expected. Nor was it clear that the NAFTA led to an increase in the number of jobs; wages had not risen as a result of the agreement.

NAFTA may also limit a country's power to protect its environment. A controversial provision in the agreement allows a company to sue if it loses.

FROM FTA TO NAFTA

Shortly after the FTA came into effect, Mexico wanted to become a close trading partner of Canada and the United States. In 1992, after another round of trade talks, the leaders of Mexico, the United States, and Canada signed the North American Free Trade Agreement (NAFTA), which included Mexico in the free-trade region created by the FTA. It created a large free-trade bloc linking 370 million people in three countries, with 31 percent of the world's wealth, into a single trade region. Again Canadian public opinion became polarized over free trade. Opponents of the deal claimed that the United States would be the main winner, because American employers would take advantage of cheap Mexican labour and Canadian raw materials. Despite opposition, however, NAFTA came into effect in 1993.*

★

MEXICO

Mexico, the other major participant in the regional NAFTA accords, has been racked by instability since 1993, a fact alluded to only subtly in this selection.

Beginning in 1982 political leaders began to completely open the country toward the international market, reducing customs tariffs to the point of nearly abolishing them. 1994 saw the beginning of the Free Trade

* Newman, Garfield, et al. *Canada: A Nation Unfolding.* Toronto: McGraw-Hill, 2000, 360, 361, 363, 365.

Agreement with Canada and the United States, facilitating the flow of products and capital between the three countries. From 1990 to 1994 there was economic growth, but at the end of this growth was a new crisis with another harsh devaluation of the national currency.

The government, the investment companies and many experts affirmed that the applied politics would lead to a short period of healthy growth and economic stability and would give way to a general improvement of the population. Other sectors did not share this opinion and wanted to change the adopted orientation. Debates and the like arose in several countries including those with strong economies like France, Italy, Great Britain and the United States.*

★

JAPAN

Western economic aid and Japanese ingenuity worked together to rebuild a Japan devastated by World War II. Forty years after the war, Japan found itself rebounding economically and spiritually. This rebound came at a price, though, since many in the international community openly expressed fears about a rebuilt Japan. But unlike the Japanese threat of the 1930s and 1940s, which was military, the threat of the 1980s was economic.

Japan in the World

In the 1980s, with a strong yen and a cheap dollar, not only did Japan's trade surplus continue to grow, but there was also a rapid expansion in overseas investment by Japanese firms. In 1988, the balance of Japan's external assets had overtaken that of Britain, and Japan became the world's largest creditor nation. As a result, the other developed nations began to point the finger at the trade imbalance and the problem of access to Japanese markets and [to] demand solutions.

With the developing nations of Asia problems also arose over the profit-oriented, indiscriminate exploitation of resources by Japanese enterprises as well as over Japan's methods of economic cooperation.

* Brom, Juan. *Esbozo de Historia de México.* Mexico City: Grijalbo, 1998, 349.

Looking at overseas relations, while friendship with the U.S. has long been at the core of Japan's overseas diplomacy, recently the government has also been promoting diplomatic negotiations with the Russian Federation to solve the Northern Territories issue. Japan has also started talks with the Democratic People's Republic of Korea for the restoration of diplomatic relations.*

---

* *Japan in Modern History, Junior High School Textbooks.* Tokyo: International Society for Educational Information, 1994, 407.

46

U.S.-Philippine Relations

After the events of the Spanish-American War and World War II, U.S. history textbooks all but ignore the Philippines. This lack of attention in no way suggests a lack of actual influence in the islands, since the United States maintained a very large military presence there and significantly influenced the Philippine economy and politics throughout the 20th century. This selection expresses a special satisfaction in the importance of the first Philippine election not "influenced" in any major way by the American occupiers.

★

PHILIPPINES

Foreign Relations under Martial Law. [. . .]

The United States government was kept closely informed on martial law and other policies of President Marcos. In many ways, President Marcos gave special preference to American security and economic interests. At first, the United States continued to operate 23 military bases on 180,000 acres of land leased for 99 years without rent. Clark Air Base became one of the world's largest air bases, and Subic Bay became the largest naval base in Asia. American military aid to the Philippine Armed Forces doubled from $60 million in 1970–72 to $118 million in 1973–1975. Due to American military advice and training, the Philippine military adopted inhuman Vietnam-style tactics in fighting insurgents in Mindanao.

On January 7, 1979, the Philippines and the United States reached a new military bases agreement, the first since the 1947 arrangement. The new agreement affirmed Philippine sovereignty over the bases, the installation of a Filipino commander in each base; significant reduction of the base areas for American use; Philippine security for the base perimeters; unhampered military operations for the U.S.; and a thorough review of the agreement every five years. In conclusion, the U.S. pledged $500 million in military aid and $700 million in economic aid and loans for five years, which the Philippine government considered a "rental".

Contrary to the 1973 Constitution's termination of the parity rights granted to American citizens and corporations by 1974 and various Supreme Court decisions affirming this termination, President Marcos allowed Americans to continue to retain property and dominate natural resources development in the Philippines. U.S. multinational assets rose to over $2 billion, and half of the 50 largest firms were American-owned. American investment comprised 80% of the total foreign investments in the Philippines.*

End of the Aquino Era

On May 11, 1992 the Philippines held its general elections under the 1986 Constitution. For the first time in the history of elections in this country, there were so many candidates and political parties who campaigned for the government positions. Some 80,000 candidates ran for the 17,000 posts from the presidency down to municipal councilors. Thus the 1992 general election was the most extensive and hotly contested election in the country's history.

---

* Zaide, Sonia M. *The Philippines: A Unique Nation.* Quezon City: All-Nations Publishing, 1999, 389.

The election came at a turning point in our history. For the first time, the United States, a former colonial power, had little influence on the results. After the Mt. Pinatubo volcanic eruption (situated near the U.S. Bases) and defeat in the Philippine Senate of a new bases treaty, the Americans dismantled and pulled out their largest overseas military bases in Clark, Pampanga and Subic, Zambales.*

* Zaide, Sonia M. *The Philippines: A Unique Nation.* Quezon City: All-Nations Publishing, 1999, 405.

47

Cuban-American Relations

Over a decade after the collapse of the Soviet Union, the U.S. and Cuba remain locked in a stalemated "cold war," which is reflected in the strident tone of Cuban textbooks to this day. In this selection, plant and human epidemics suffered on the island are attributed to U.S. foreign policy.

★

CUBA

Biological warfare—Among the most criminal aggression that the US has carried out against Cuba [was] the spreading of toxic substances and germs over the island, causing the outbreaks of diseases that have affected people, plants, and animals. Only a deliberate enemy action could [have] caused these epidemics in a country whose high level of public health care and flora and fauna protection is recognized by the most competent, specialized regional and international organizations.

As early as January 1965 Cuban authorities discovered near Santiago de Las Vegas, in Havana province, a balloon that in breaking spread an unknown white substance. Then in September 1968, a foreign expert hired by the CIA introduced a virus that destroyed coffee plantations. In 1971, an African Swine Fever epidemic wreaked havoc on the porcine cattle of the western Cuban provinces.

But the biological warfare intensified after 1979. That same year, a third of all Cuban sugar cane plantations [were] affected by an epidemic of **sugar cane rust,** while **blue mold** infested 90 percent of the tobacco fields. These were both diseases Cuba had eradicated many years before.

In 1981, an epidemic of **hemorrhagic dengue** spread across the island, affecting more than 35,000 people in a few months, and causing the death of 150 of them, mostly children. Other infectious diseases, like **hemorrhagic conjunctivitis,** have also strangely proliferated.

Aside from the victims that this criminal activity has caused among the population, and its great damages on the country's basic crops, Cuba has had to make [super]human efforts, dedicate huge resources, and take extreme measures to stop and eliminate those epidemics, and recover from the considerable losses they have brought for the national economy.

All these forms of aggression have been systematically taking place along the 37 years of revolutionary power.*

---

* Navarro, José Cantón. *History of Cuba: The Challenge of the Yoke and the Star.* Havana: SI-MAR, 2000, 235, 236.

48

The Middle East

Aside from a brief mention of the formation of Israel after WWII, the first real mention of the region in most U.S. history texts typically comes in the context of the Nixon administration, when OPEC cut back on oil production in retaliation for U.S. support of Israel. Throughout these textbooks, students are likely to see the Middle East discussed in sections with titles that have decidedly negative connotations: "Economic Problems," "World Trouble Spots," "Violence in the Middle East," "Iran Hostage Crisis," Religious Conflict in the Middle East," "Terrorism," and "Problems in the Middle East." The only positive mention comes when the U.S. tries to broker a peace settlement between Arabs and Israelis, with the requisite photo of a U.S. President standing between two enemies shaking hands. As the U.S.'s role in the Middle East has increased, sharply divergent accounts of its regional role may be found in the textbooks of Middle Eastern countries. Nowhere else, perhaps, is the politics of history textbook writing so apparent.

★

SAUDI ARABIA

For this Saudi text, the establishment of the Jewish presence in Palestine by the United Nations was a serious blow to Muslim unity in the Middle East. (Israel is still unrecognized by the Saudi government.) The U.S. played a principle role in the affair by diplomatically recognizing Israel and supporting the new Jewish state, thus allowing them to overcome Arab resistance.

The Jews managed during WWI to obtain the Balfour Declaration in 1336 AH/1917 CE* which stipulated the establishment of a national home for the Jews in Palestine. The Balfour Declaration contradicted the promises made by the English to Sharif Hussein Bin Ali to the effect that Syria, including Palestine, would belong to the Arabs following its liberation from the Ottoman Turks. When Sharif Hussein asked the English about that, they sent to him somebody who reassured him that the settlement of the Jews in Palestine did not contradict the Arabs' independence in that country. The deception was effective on Sharif Hussein.

In the peace conference that was convened in San Remo, Italy, in 1339 AH [1920] Britain was entrusted with the mandate over Palestine, on condition that it would take upon itself to carry out what had been provided for in the Balfour Declaration regarding the establishment of a national home for the Jews in Palestine. [Britain] appointed the Zionist Jew Herbert Samuel as a first British High Commissioner in Palestine. Britain began to change the Arab-Muslim character of Palestine, and the flood of Jewish immigration began to pour into Palestine. That was organized by the Jewish Agency which was established in 1339 AH [1920], and which is the largest Jewish organization in the world today, to take care of their interests. The Jewish Agency was given vast authority and Britain cooperated with it to the highest degree. It operated in Palestine as if it were a

* The Muslim calendar was created by Caliph Umar I in 639 AD. Since it dates from the *Hijrah*, it is labeled as AH from the Latin *Anno Hijrah* (in the year of the Hijrah). Dates are written according to the Muslim calendar and are translated within brackets to correspond to the Julian calendar for the reader. CE here represents the Common Era, which corresponds to the commonly used AD (*Anno Domini*—in the year of our Lord).

state within a state. It established Jewish colonies in Palestine and built there storehouses for weapons and ammunition. Jewish money flowed into these colonies.

In the year 1365 AH [1946] the Zionists blew up the King David Hotel in Jerusalem, the seat of the English imperialist government in Palestine. The disturbances by the Jews increased and Britain thought it advisable to submit the Palestine question to the General Assembly of the United Nations. In 1366 AH [1947] the General Assembly of the UN adopted by a majority of 33 votes, among them the USA, the former Soviet Union and France, a resolution for partitioning Palestine into two states, Arab and Jewish, with the internationalization of Jerusalem. Thirteen states opposed this resolution, among them the Arab states, Turkey and Pakistan. Britain abstained.*

Immediately following the adoption of the partition resolution in the UN, the Jews announced that they accepted it while the Arabs rejected it. Britain announced that it would withdraw from Palestine in 1367 AH [1948]. British Imperialism, which imposed the Jewish immigration on Palestine during the Mandate period, thus enabled them to increase numerically and become a third of the inhabitants of Palestine in 1368 AH [1948] while their proportion did not exceed 1/12 of the Palestinians at the beginning of the Mandate period in 1339 AH [1920].

Palestine's coming under British rule following WWI was an opportunity for the realization of the Jews' hopes. Britain facilitated their immigration to this precious homeland and provided them with the possibility to organize themselves and to train themselves in using arms. The Palestinians tried to stand up against the Jews and their helpers, and their Jihad almost succeeded, had it not for the American government's inclination towards the Jews' side and its pressure on Britain to permit the entry of more than a hundred thousand Jews into Palestine in one year.†

---

* *Biography of the Prophet and History of the Muslim State,* Grade 10. Kingdom of Saudi Arabia: Ministry of Education, 2001, 113–15.

† *History of the Saudi Arabian Kingdom,* Grade 6. Kingdom of Saudi Arabia: Ministry of Education, 2001, 58.

★

GREAT BRITAIN

Palestine Mandate

Palestine proved a problem too difficult even for as tough and skilful a negotiator as Bevin. The problem was to a considerable degree created by his predecessors. Previous British governments had not only promised the Jews that they could make Palestine their national home but also offered guarantees to the Arabs already living in Palestine that their rights would be safeguarded. The Nazi persecution of the Jews brought an increase of immigration to Palestine immediately before and after the Second War. Violence between the Israeli (Jewish) and Arab communities escalated. British troops tried to keep order but antagonized both sides. In 1947, Bevin decided that Britain was in a no-win situation and handed the problem over to the United Nations. Almost immediately an Arab-Israeli war erupted, which led—after a decisive victory by the Israeli army—to the creation of the state of Israel in 1948.*

★

WARS

FRANCE

The United States is described here as an ally and supporter of Israel, especially in times of conflict. Here, the Six Day War not only marked the decline of Egypt's Nasser, but also marked the ascendant star of Saudi Arabia, the new Arab ally of the United States.

A Permanent State of War

• Between 1948 and 1982, Israel had five wars and conducted numerous military operations in the region. If the Jewish State had to face the

---

* Roberts, Martin. *Britain 1846–1964: The Challenge of Change.* London: Oxford University Press, 2001, 280.

hostilities of the Arab States in the region, it could count on the support of the United States, its principal ally, beginning in the 1960s. The Six Day War, June 1967, had significant consequences: Israel, the victor, conquered and occupied new territories. The question of the occupied territories divided the political classes. Considered by some as temporary political pressure on the Arabs, the supporters of a Great Israel—the "hawks"—hoped for their annexation and colonization by the Jews and opposed the partisans of a negotiated settlement to the Palestinian problem—the "doves."*

[. . .]

June 6, 1967, the Jewish State launched a preventative attack against Egypt, Syria and Jordan. The Israeli troops crushed the humiliated Arab troops. **Israel, victorious, occupied vast territories:** the Sinai Peninsula, the Gaza Strip, the West Bank and the Golan Heights. On November 22, the UN Security Council adopted resolution 242 calling for the withdrawal of Israeli troops from the occupied territories. A terrible military defeat for the Arab states, the Six Day War was also a serious political defeat for Nasser and marked the beginning of division in the Arab camp. Nasser's influence, backed by the USSR, faded next to that of Arabia, supported by the United States.†

★

SAUDI ARABIA

This Saudi text identifies four main confrontations between Israel and the Arabs since 1948. It is important to consider the language of the text, as it is published by the Ministry of Education and is the only history textbook offered to students in Saudi Arabia.

There were four military confrontations between the Arabs and the Jews since the ending of the British Mandate over Palestine:

---

* Lambin, Jean-Michel. *Histoire—T^{ales}*. Paris: Hachette, 2001, 262.
† Lambin, Jean-Michel. *Histoire—T^{ales}*. Paris: Hachette, 2001, 264.

The First Confrontation

The war of Palestine was in 1368 AH [1948]. Seven Arab states participated in it, namely Egypt, Syria, Lebanon, Iraq, Saudi Arabia, Yemen and
Trans-Jordan, in addition to the forces of the Palestinian Jihad fighters and
the non-Palestinian Arab and Muslim volunteers. Although the Jews were
very competent militarily and had military equipment in great quantities,
the Arab armies succeeded in inflicting upon them shocking defeats. The
Arab artillery bombarded Tel Aviv and the Arabs' victory appeared to be
close at hand. But the great powers resorted to deception and asked, in response to Israel's wish after it had been struck by panic, to conclude a truce
two weeks after the fighting had begun. During that truce Israel acquired
great quantities of military equipment, especially aircrafts, tanks and heavy
artillery, in addition to large numbers of volunteers from western countries.
[Then] Israel proceeded to usurp new lands. Nothing was left of Palestine
except the Gaza Strip, which came under Egyptian administration, and the
West Bank, which was annexed by King Abdullah to Jordan.

The Second Confrontation

It took the form of a treacherous tripartite aggression on Egypt and the
Gaza Strip on the part of Israel, France and Britain in 1376 AH [1956].
Thus, the forces of Imperialism, Crusadism and Zionism cooperated in
pouring their hidden malice on the Arabs and the Muslims. What irritated
[both] the English and French was the nationalization of the Suez Canal
in 1376 [1956]. France was [also] irritated by Egypt's help to the Algerian
revolt in weapons and by training the [Algerian] Jihad fighters. Israel was
angry at Egypt for the latter's closure of the Gulf of Aqaba for vessels making their way to Israel, whatever their type was. England and France resorted to methods of military invasion of the nineteenth century. Planes
hit Port Said with bombs while Israel swept through the Sinai Peninsula.
The Security Council asked the aggressor states to withdraw. UN emergency forces were deployed on the border of the Gaza Strip, on the Egyptian-Israeli border and along the Gulf of Aqaba.

The Third Confrontation

In the year 1387 AH/1967 CE Israeli planes attacked the Egyptian air-fields, and the Egyptian air force was destroyed in a few hours. Then, enemy forces swept through the Gaza Strip and Sinai up to the Suez Canal, and then—through the West Bank down to the River Jordan, occupying Jerusalem. During the other three days the enemy swept also through the Syrian heights (the Golan Heights) and occupied the town of Quneitra. In accordance with the request of Egypt, Syria and Jordan a ceasefire took place. The Suez Canal was closed and shipping there stopped. The Israelis put loudspeakers on the armored cars in the rest of the Palestinian cities and asked the inhabitants to leave the country or else their safety would not be guaranteed. They warned them that their houses would be blown up over their heads. Thus, large numbers of Palestinians departed from their country because of fear and inevitable destruction. The Jews built a defensive line alongside the Suez Canal on the Sinai side and named it Bar-Lev Line so that it would prevent any attack from the direction of Egypt against Israel. They began boasting of it [saying] that it would become a graveyard for anyone who dreamed of its crossing.

The Fourth Confrontation

In the war of the tenth of Ramadan 1393 AH (sixth of October 1973) the Egyptian and Syrian forces surprised the Israeli enemy with a violent offensive, which brought about God's victory for the Egyptians who crossed the Suez Canal, crushed the Bar-Lev Line and the legend of Israeli superiority, while the Syrians managed to advance on the Golan Heights. The UN intervened and asked the warring parties to stop fighting after the Egyptians had advanced in the Sinai Peninsula. Following the negotiations conducted by the US in order to end the 'problem of the Middle East' the Syrians got back Quneitra from Israel while the Israeli forces withdrew from Sinai to the international border. Israel still occupies the Gaza Strip, the [West] Bank and the Golan Heights in Syria and has not yet recognized the Palestinian people's right of self determination on its land and soil.*

*Biography of the Prophet and History of the Muslim State, Grade 10. Kingdom of Saudi Arabia: Ministry of Education, 2001, 116–18.

★

ISRAEL

On the morning of October 6th, Yom Kippur, it was clear that the Syrians and Egyptians were about to start a multi front attack in the next few hours. Chief of Staff David Elazar proposed to start a preventive air strike. However, due to an international relations policy Golda Meir rejected the proposal. Later, that same morning Israel began calling up reserves—at first only partial call up, and then a general one. Urgent contact with the Americans, and through them with the Soviets, was meant to prevent an escalation; but to no avail. At 13:50 on the Southern front, and five minutes later in the Golan Heights, the Egyptian and Syrian forces began their strike. The Yom Kippur war—"The Ramadan War" according to the Arabs—had begun.

In the South, 70,000 Egyptian soldiers crossed the Suez Canal with about 1000 tanks. During two days of bitter fighting the Bar Lev line was conquered—i.e. 30 positions with roughly 600 fighters. In the North, 40,000 Syrian soldiers and about 800 tanks washed over the Golan Heights. The close proximity of the Galilee settlements created an alarming situation.

Despite the stubborn Israeli resistance against ratios of 1:20, the Arabs won a significant advantage in this stage of the fighting. The element of surprise and the lack of preparation by the Israeli forces were major factors, as well as the wide use of new weaponry that complicated the operations of the air force and tank forces: missiles against air craft and missiles against tanks that were operated by ground forces. During the third day of the fighting the Egyptians fortified themselves along the Eastern bank of the canal in a strip 5 to 10 km wide. The Syrians took over half the Golan Heights—including the Hermon, a strategic location of vital importance that was well fortified although defended by a small force of 50 fighters.

The reserve units arriving at the front and the American Airlift that renewed Israel's weapon supply changed the balance of forces. The IDF displayed its known advantages: air superiority, daring, speed of movement and a preference for fire power. In the beginning the effort was concentrated mainly along the northern front. The counter attack started along three main routes and succeeded, after two days of difficult fighting, in reconquering territory that was lost. On the 11th of October the IDF began to enter Syrian territory. An Iraqi division, a Moroccan regiment, and two Jordanian regiments that came to re-enforce the Syrian army were destroyed. On October 15 the front was stabilized. One week prior to the cease-fire taking effect, the Hermon was re-captured in a face to face battle.

On October 23 a cease fire was achieved. From the Syrian perspective the war effort ended in disaster. Not only did the Golan remain in Israel's hand, but the IDF took over an additional 500 square kilometers of Syrian territory and its tanks were threatening Damascus. Even worse, heavy bombing in the heart of Syria heavily damaged the economic infrastructure. Refineries, power plants and oil pipe lines were destroyed. The IDF wanted to quickly cripple Syria so it could focus its forces on Egypt; but the commanders did not hide their desire to teach the Syrians a bitter lesson for the future.

The IDF could now focus on the Egyptian front. During the third day of fighting the Egyptian advance was blocked thanks to the reservists recently called up, but a northern counter attack in the direction of Al Kantara failed. On October 14 the Egyptian forces tried to force their way through Israel's line across the front. At the end of a stubborn day-old battle, 200 damaged tanks were left and the Egyptian bank was exposed. The general staff now turned its attention to a hidden plan that would alter the course of the war.

On the night between October 15 and 16 a paratrooper force crossed the canal north of the big Bitter Lake, the "soft belly" of the Egyptian defense, in the line between the second and third Army. The head of the bridge quickly deepened and with extended arms everywhere it was able to destroy the surface-to-air missiles. The Israeli Air Force regained control of the air. On October 19, 20,000 soldiers and hundreds of tanks were already operating in the western bank of the canal, up to 30km into Egyptian territory.

The Egyptians and Soviets now demanded what they refused at the beginning of the fighting, an unconditional immediate cease-fire. On October 22 the Security Council accepted a Soviet-American proposal for a cease fire within 12 hours. The decision (number 338) also demanded the full implementation of decision 242 from November 22, 1967 and called on both parties to open a dialogue to bring about "a just and permanent peace in the

Middle East." For the first time the UN called for direct negotiations in the Middle East and for the first time Egypt and Syria, and in a suggestive way, got the message of direct negotiations with Israel.

In the meantime the battles continued. Both sides blamed each other for serious violations of the cease-fire. The Third Army desperately tried to break the blockade. Trying as much as they could to enlarge their territorial gain, the Israelis were stopped at the height of their counter-attack and reluctantly accepted the cease fire. On October 24 they were able to completely surround the Third Army. Nearly 25,000 Egyptian with about 300 armored vehicles were left at the mercy of the Israelis who now controlled close to 1,700 square kilometers along the western bank of the canal.

During the same morning the UN Security Council adopted the new Soviet-American proposal. The decision again demanded an immediate ceasefire, and the withdrawal of the forces to the line of October 22. Also there was a decision to send the UN Emergency Forces (UNEF). This time the ceasefire was respected, but Israel refused to relinquish the strategic advantage it gained during the 36 hours between the two decisions of the Security Council. In the long process of the "separation of forces" along the southern front, these advantages would prove to be of great importance.

The Yom Kippur War resulted in a very heavy price for Israel: 2,365 killed, 6,400 wounded, and for the first time hundreds of prisoners of war. Per capita, in 18 days Israel lost the same number of fighters that the US lost during 10 years in Vietnam! This war also taught Israel some bitter lessons. Most of all, Israel was reminded of its vulnerability which it had forgotten after the swift victory of the Six Day War. Israel's belief in the power of the IDF also blinded it in the **"conception"** phase on the eve of the war. Still, militarily speaking, Israel won this war, just like the preceding ones. This achievement was particularly great, when considering the tough odds during the opening rounds of the Arab assault. That the IDF, despite the odds, found themselves controlling new territory demonstrated the limitations of the Arab military option.*

---

* Barnavi, Eli and Eyal Naveh. Semanim moderim: historyah la-hativah ha-'elyonah, *Modern Times*, Tel Aviv: Sifre Tel Aviv, 1999, 301–304.

★

THE PEACE PROCESS

When the world speaks of the peace process in the Middle East it has long meant the negotiations for peace between Israel and its Arab neighbors since 1948. Egypt's recognition of Israel in the Camp David Accords of 1978 and the Oslo Peace Accords of 1993 are the most recent significant milestones for peace. Most U.S. history textbooks portray the United States as a peacemaker in the region. They describe men such as Anwar el-Sadat as showing "courageous initiative" in offering peace to Israel. Pictures of Carter, Sadat, and Begin (1978) and Clinton, Rabin, and Arafat (1993) shaking hands can be found in almost every U.S. textbook.

★

FRANCE

France's presence in the Middle East as a colonizer dates back to the end of World War I, when the Ottoman Empire was carved up. France received a mandate over Syria and Lebanon, while Britain was allowed to occupy Jordan, Palestine, and Iraq. The French historically have been more sympathetic toward the Palestinians, in part because most of the displaced Palestinians from 1948 moved into neighboring Syria and Lebanon.

Egypt Withdraws from the Arab-Israeli Conflict

- Facing pressing social and economic problems in Egypt, **Saddat decided to end the 30 years of ruinous conflict with Israel.** He went to Israel in 1977 with this goal in mind. In September 1978 with President Carter presiding, he signed the *Camp David Accords* in the United States along with Israeli Prime Minister Begin. Egypt recognized Israel, which in return left the Sinai Peninsula. This agreement cost Egypt its membership in the Arab League. On October 6, 1981 Muslim fanatics assassinated Saddat.
- The Egyptian withdrawal left the door open for other Arab states.
- Syria and Iraq proved the most intransigent.
- Saudi Arabia, pro-Western and anti-Soviet, favored more moderate

support for the Palestinian cause but at the same time supported those calling for a return to Islam, the Islamists.

Confrontation between Arab Nations

• In 1979, the Iranian revolution constituted a new factor of tension in the Middle East. The pro-Western regime of the Shah of Iran was overthrown by an Islamist revolution directed by Khomeini. The price of oil reached record highs; it was the second oil crisis. Iranian support for the *Shiites* of Lebanon raised fears of **the spread of the Islamist revolution in the Middle East.** These fears were revived when Iran and Iraq entered into war in September 1980. Supported by the moderate Arab nations, Iraq attacked Iran, which resisted. A bloody war which claimed more than 800,000 lives lasted until 1988.

• Division between the Arab powers showed itself in **Lebanon** which was partially occupied, by Israel in the south and by Syria in the north. Between 1975 and 1990, the country was torn apart by a long **civil war.** There were several facets to the conflict: Israelis against Palestinians, a civil war between Muslims and *Lebanese Christians,* confrontations between Palestinians and Syrians and between Iraq and Syria involving Shiite militia. In 1991, **the Gulf War,** provoked by Iraq's invasion of Kuwait, saw the Arab nations react once again in a variety of ways. Syria joined the coalition of oil monarchies supported by the Americans and their allies while PLO and Jordan—officially neutral but in reality favorable toward Iraq—supported Iraq and were isolated on the international scene.

A Hope for Peace?

• In 1991, after the Gulf War, there appeared a hope for peace. **The end of the Cold War** and the disappearance of the USSR, the intense diplomatic activity of the Americans in the Middle East, and the rise of an intense peace movement in Israel all created a favorable climate. After mutual recognition between Israel and the PLO in 1992, a peace accord was signed in Washington by Rabin and Arafat—September 13, 1993—completed by the Oslo Accords: **the Palestinians had an autonomous territory** comprising the Gaza Strip and the territories of the West Bank.

An embryonic Palestinian state was created, but the presence of Israeli settlers in West Bank made cohabitation between Jews and Palestinians difficult.

- The construction of peace between Israel and the PLO was halted by the **religious fanatics in both camps** and by terrorist acts. The assassination of Rabin by a Jewish extremist in November 1995 and the attacks carried out by the Islamic extremists of Hamas—hostile to Arafat—in Israel reinforced the partisans of the conflict. At the end of the 1990s, the hope for peace seemed to have receded.*

☆

ISRAEL

In the summer of 1977 the Egyptians and Israelis began to inquire about direct channels of communication. Begin promised Romanian President Ceaucescu that if a meeting between him and Sadat took place "everything would be open to negotiations." Dayan, then foreign minister in Begin's government, secretly visited Morocco and suggested to one of Sadat's senior advisors a meeting between the two leaders. A few days later in Washington, Dayan put together a document in which Israel directly recognized the existence of a singular Palestinian problem and the possibility that the Palestinians would directly participate in discussions pertaining to their future.

But the decisive event took place on November 9th 1977. "In order to achieve peace and to spare the life of a single Egyptian soldier," Sadat declared before the Egyptian national convention, "I am willing to go to the ends of the earth and even the Knesset in Jerusalem." Begin took hold of the extended hand and formally invited the Egyptian President. On the 16th of November, Sadat repeated his intention to visit Jerusalem, this time in an interview with a US television network. Three days later he landed at Ben Gurion Airport.

A wave of enthusiasm washed over Israel. The astonished TV viewers saw before them a scene from political fiction: the leader of the most important Arab country was welcomed as a formal visitor by the leaders of

---

* Lambin, Jean-Michel. *Histoire—terminale*. Paris: Hachette, 2001, 268.

ᴏstracized "Zionist entity." Before negotiations even started, the dramatic gestures by the Rais* refuted one of the deeply rooted axioms in Israeli politics: "there is no one to talk to." More importantly, Sadat recognized the existence of Israel, not only in the land of Israel, but in its capital, and even in the Knesset.

It turned out that the depth of hatred that separated the two people was less profound than people thought. Just four years after the bloody war, Sadat was quite surprised by the warm welcome he received from the people in Israel.

The dialogue that was set out in Jerusalem was eventually successful, but only after a year and a half of intense negotiations. Shortly after the speeches of Begin and Sadat deep conflicts were revealed. The Rais stated that he did not come to Israel to sign a separate peace treaty. What he asked for in response to his recognition was what Egypt had always demanded: complete withdrawal of territory conquered during the 1967 war and self determination for the Palestinians, in particular the right to establish an independent state.

Sadat could not have demanded less if he expected to remain relevant in the Arab world. But his individual performance deeply hurt Egypt's position in the Muslim-Arab world. Very quickly a "refusal front" was organized by the traditional extremists: Libya, Iraq, the Leftist section of the PLO, Southern Yemen, Algeria, and the first and foremost, Syria, who Egypt had tried to persuade on the rightness of its way. Sudan, Tunisia, and Morocco, supported this initiative. The Saudis, whose money was so important to Egypt, and the Jordanians, who were directly affected by the process, chose to fill their mouths with water. In Egypt the people usually supported the President's initiatives, but among the politicians and the intelligentsia bitter voices were heard. The Rais needed quick and positive results in order to ensure his image, his rule and his own physical safety.

Menachem Begin thought differently. He also had had internal problems. The supporters of the vision of greater Israel were expecting him to act according to the principles of his party and his personal political vision. To be sure, Begin warmly welcomed his Egyptian counterpart and sincerely desired peace with him, but he was not prepared to abandon those things for which he fought all his life.

---

* Rais is a word for president or leader in Arabic.

At the end of December the Ismalia convention created two separate committees: military and political. After a short honeymoon, positions hardened and everything that was achieved on the 19th of November was now in danger. It was here that the Americans entered the picture.

Sadat's initiative surprised the Carter administration, but after some reserve the President and his advisors decided to join the process. Its failure would have resulted in disastrous consequences between those directly involved with the process, but a failure would also have jeopardized the US position in the region and the world. From this point foreword the United States took on a principle role in the process. It was the United States that made the signing of the first peace agreement between Israel and her Arab neighbors possible.

On the 15th of January 1978 at the Aswan, Sadat and Carter put together the wording of an agreement that had very little chance of being accepted by the Israeli government. It spoke of the Palestinian problem "from all sides", of the recognition of the legal rights of the Palestinians and of the need to allow the Palestinians to be involved in determining their future. It was already clear that the United States would put heavy pressure on Israel. At the end of March during Begin's visit to Washington, relations between Cairo and Jerusalem were already moving toward a heavy crisis. In response to the attack by "Black September"* along the shore road, the IDF operated in South Lebanon (Litani Operation). Begin ignored American pressure, which led to a crisis in the relations between Israel and its sole ally.

Only in July, at the Lids conference, where the foreign ministers of the three powers participated—Israel, Egypt, and the United States—were there clear signs of a compromise. Two months later, Begin and Sadat together with their American host, Jimmy Carter, met behind closed doors at the presidential vacation site at Camp David. Among the Israel team two participants stood out; they were the architects of the communication with Egypt, Moshe Dayan, and Ezer Weitzman. These 13 days of closed diplomatic meetings were full of crisis, surprises, heavy pressure, and partial rifts; but the efforts bore fruit. The final signed peace agreement was the result of many factors working together: Carter's determination, the desire of the participants to not miss out on an historic opportunity, and

---

* Black September was a Palestinian militant group.

ʒar that the only ones who would enjoy the failure of the process ould be the Soviet Union.

On Sunday, the 17th of September 1978, Anwar Sadat and Menachem Begin—with Jimmy Carter as a "witness"—signed two documents. The one described "the framework for establishing a peace agreement between Egypt and Israel," the other, "a framework for peace in the Middle East".

The second document constituted a basis for an overall peace in the Middle East, in particular the Palestinian problem (Clause 4). The major component was the granting of self determination to the population of the West Bank of Jordan and the Gaza Strip for a period of five years. The Israeli civilian and army government would be removed and their responsibilities would be transferred to an autonomous body "the self determination authority"—that would be elected through free elections among the people. For the first time the Israeli government recognized the fact that the ending of the conflict involved honoring the "legal rights of the Palestinian people and their rightful demand." In the meantime, in order to guarantee the security of Israel, the IDF would retain a minimal presence at predetermined points. Internal security and the public order would be handed to a police force that could also include Jordanian citizens. The borders of the autonomous region would be secured jointly by the Palestinian police and Israeli units. The final status of the lands would be discussed during this transition period, by Egypt, Israel, Jordan, if it so desired, and a delegation from the local Palestinian population.

The document also described the general principles on which peace between Israel and Egypt (clause 2) would be based as well as between Israel and the rest of its neighbors (clause 3). It also included a prohibition against the use of force to solve the problems between the sides and plans for a normalization in relations, reciprocal recognition, the canceling of economic sanctions and mutual cooperation—everything in accordance with the international guarantees that are derived from the UN charter.

The Camp David agreements were presented to the world by President Carter as a huge victory. "Beyond all hopes" the President was probably right. But those who saw problems with the agreement were also right. And indeed, the ink had not yet dried on the September agreements when difficult problems arose, including the fate of the settlement at the entrance of Rafiach, the future of the oil wells in Sinai, American monetary support that was to allow Israel's redeployment in the Negev; and above all, the realization of Palestinian autonomy. Only on the 26th of March

1979, at the end of another set of crises, exhausting diplomatic exercises, and American pressure, was the peace agreement between Egypt and Israel signed in Washington.*

★

SYRIA

Syria has a very large population of Palestinians. Most of them were displaced by the war of 1948. Egypt's recognition of Israel's right to exist in 1978 was a serious blow to Arab unity, especially after Egyptian President Nasser had inspired so much pride in the region after the Suez Canal Crisis. Instead of following Egypt in its new policy, most Arab nations, like Syria, rejected Egypt's leadership in the Arab world.

The following excerpts come from a history textbook published by Syria's Ministry of Education. Like many other countries in the Middle East, the government produces the curriculum and the resources for its public schools. This text represents the only history textbook available to students.

"We should believe that any hand extended for peace with the aggressors is a criminal hand that must be cut off, because that is an open treason against Islam and the Muslims. On this basis we judge the position of the conspiring agent, who violated his nation's will and his religion's instructions, [Egypt's late President] Anwar Sadat, as well as what he did, beginning in the disgraceful and treacherous visit to Israel and ending in his despicable and shameful negotiations."†

"Anwar Sadat signed with the Zionist entity the so-called "Egyptian-Israeli peace treaty." It called for alleged peace between the Zionist entity, on the one hand, and the Egyptian regime and the Arab countries neighboring the Zionist entity, on the other hand. This is another treacherous step on the road to ending the Arab-Zionist struggle in the interest of the enemy, imposing surrender solutions, relinquishing occupied Arab land and neglecting the national rights of the Palestinian Arab people."‡

* Barnavi, Eli and Eyal Naveh. *Modern Times Section B 1920–2000,* Tel Aviv: Tel Aviv Books, 1999, 305–307.

† *Islamic Education,* Grade 8. Ministry of Education, 1999/2000, 88.

‡ *National-Socialist Education,* Grade 12. Ministry of Education, 1989/1990, 57–58.

ne Arab-Socialist Ba'ath Party . . . has called for the . . . rejection of ace, negotiations and recognition of the Zionist entity." *

"The Arab-Socialist Ba'ath Party under the leadership of the Fighting Leader Hafez Assad rejected the treacherous conspiracies as well as the surrender treaties and agreements which the Egyptian regime had concluded with the Zionist entity and looked for ways to oppose them." †

"Syria . . . contributed to the establishment of the [Arab] Steadfastness and Opposition Front, following the visit by [Egypt's president Anwar] Sadat to Jerusalem [in Nov. 1977]." ‡

"The Syrian-Arab country, under the leadership of the Arab-Socialist Ba'ath Party and its Secretary General the Fighting Comrade Hafez Assad, managed to annul the submissiveness agreement [signed between Israel and Lebanon in May 1983, under the auspices of the US]." §

"Israel tries to mislead world public opinion by its acceptance of the negotiation with the Arabs and by its desire for peace, but a peace in its own special sense which means the Arabs' surrender, without [Israel's] implementation of the resolutions of international legality. The Fighting Leader Comrade Hafez Assad described Israel's game regarding the peace process saying: In spite of its claim that it wants peace, Israel is doing the opposite in word and in deed." ‖

"Israel shall not give up its expansionist ambitions and shall not change its mentality of control and expansion. Therefore, we must prepare for the defense of our land and homeland and not to place much hope in the possibilities of peace, because Israel is a state of invasion and aggression. It pursues them rather than pursuing peace." #

"The Arab people of Syria took upon itself the greatest burden in the confrontation and offered great sacrifices in both lives and property for the sake of the Arab nation's honor and dignity. Syria is now conducting a political battle stronger and more ferocious than the armed battle in order to

---

* *National-Socialist Education,* Grade 12. Ministry of Education, 1989/1990, 66.

† *National-Socialist Education,* Grade 12. Ministry of Education, 1989/1990, 58.

‡ *Modern History of the Arabs,* Grade 9. Ministry of Education, 1999/2000, 160.

§ *National-Socialist Education,* Grade 12. Ministry of Education, 1989/1990, 59.

‖ *National-Socialist Education,* Grade 8. Ministry of Education, 1999/2000, 107.

President Hafez Assad. *National-Socialist Education,* Grade 8. Ministry of Education, 1999/2000, 109.

recover the Arabs' rights for the sake of the Arab nation's future and progress . . . That is the battle of peace." *

"The facts of the present phase of our Arab history, especially regarding our confrontation with the Zionist enemy, stress the importance of Arab cooperation, whether in war or in the battle of peace." †

"Our nation still continues its struggle against the Zionist invasion, accommodating its circumstances and the recent struggle methods while emphasizing international legality as embodied in the UN resolutions 338, 242, 425 and the exchange of land for peace. Just and comprehensive Peace." ‡

"Liberating the Arab land that Israel has occupied . . . Establishing just and comprehensive peace that will return the Arabs' right . . . Supporting the struggle of the Palestinian Arab people for the recovery of its rights and the establishment of its independent state with Jerusalem as its capital." §

"Syria has gained an international standing, thanks to its leader's wise way and instructions which take inspiration from the interest of Syria and the Arabs, especially regarding the peace process which the Leader Assad described, saying: peace means equal dignity to all." ‖

"Syria has obtained the respect and support of the European states, the Great Powers and the international community because of its position regarding the peace process, that battle which it [Syria] wages presently with utmost courage and firmness for the recovery of the Arabs' right in return for spreading security and peace in the region." #

"Syria has agreed to enter the peace process in the region in response to the international initiative and on the basis of the implementation of the Security Council resolutions 242, 338, 425—which stipulate the withdrawal of Israel from the occupied Arab lands, and on the basis of the land-for-peace principle. All the developments and events in the region have emphasized that it is impossible to reach a real, just and comprehen-

---

* *National-Socialist Education*, Grade 9. Ministry of Education, 1999/2000, 65.

† *National-Socialist Education*, Grade 8. Ministry of Education, 1999/2000, 53.

‡ *National-Socialist Education*, Grade 10. Ministry of Education, 1999/2000, 148.

§ Goals of the Syrian regime under Hafez Assad, *National-Socialist Education*, Grade 7. Ministry of Education, 1999/2000, 64–65.

‖ *National-Socialist Education*, Grade 7. Ministry of Education, 1999/2000, 60.

National-Socialist Education, Grade 8. Ministry of Education, 1999/2000, 132.

sive peace in the region without Syria. That is what the Fighting Leader, Comrade Hafez Assad, has often called for, namely, that Syria is heading towards peace provided that it is just and comprehensive, which would return the land and the rights to their owners, remove injustice and put an end to occupation and aggression. This is the peace of the brave which will open the horizons of progress and prosperity for the region." *

"[Homework:] Extract from the following statement by the Fighting Leader Comrade Hafez Assad, the importance of achieving the peace which we are pursuing. [The statement:] We want peace indeed. We see and understand that everyone has an interest in that peace. But we also oppose anyone who tries to turn peace into a monopolized interest of his. We oppose him. No one will ever be able to make peace with Syria without Syria's consent, since it holds on to its interests and rights, and first and foremost—its occupied land . . . We have a right that we cannot relinquish. Giving up any part of the homeland means giving up the [whole] homeland . . . [It means] submission at the expense of [our] rights, destiny and future." †

"We are for peace [which is] in accordance with the UN resolution. It is the peace that accomplishes the return of the land and the return of the usurped rights." ‡

★

THE WEST AND THE MIDDLE EAST

In this Saudi Arabian selection, any U.S. interest in the Middle East comes across as manipulative. From the treatment of Muslim society in the Western academic community—called "Orientalism"—to the attempted conversion of Muslims by Christian missionaries, the West is guilty of attempting to undermine and ruin the Muslim world.

---

*National-Socialist Education, Grade 9. Ministry of Education, 1999/2000, 66.

† National-Socialist Education, Grade 9. Ministry of Education, 1999/2000, 68–69.

‡ President Hafez Assad, National-Socialist Education, Grade 10. Ministry of Education, 1999/2000, 83.

★

SAUDI ARABIA

It is possible to sum up the bad side, or the damage inflicted by Imperialism on the Muslims' homelands as follows:

- Tearing Islamic unity to pieces and spreading division among sons of the same country, by stimulating religious and sectarian chauvinism between various communities.
- Spreading harmful social habits, which are forbidden by [Islamic] religious law, such as drugs, alcohol, games of chance, playing cards and other kinds of wicked entertainment.
- Encouraging wanton and vulgar literature and art in order to kill the Muslims' conscience, invade them intellectually and destroy their morals.
- Directing the mass media such as the press, television, radio and cinema in a non-Muslim direction by instilling [in them] corrupted concepts and by attacking Islam's leaders under the guise of civilization and scientific objectivity.
- Emptying education of its Islamic content and giving it a secular direction in order to create a separation between the Muslims and their religion.
- Striving to keep the Muslims in a state of ignorance regarding the affairs of their [fellow] Muslim societies in the world, so that the Muslims will not grasp the extent of their human and material resources worldwide and become aware of the importance of their unity and solidarity.

This way, Imperialism's departure from the country does not necessarily mean the disappearance of its bad impact, for it tries to keep exercising its influence indirectly, by way of intellectual invasion (cultural imperialism). That is how the so-called Neo-Imperialism came into being.

Orientalism

Orientalism [Istishraq] means the study by Westerners of the civilization of Eastern nations—their languages, literatures, sciences, faiths and their peoples' customs and traditions. From this definition it becomes clear to us that the orientalists' works renders undeniable services to the Eastern civilizations, including our own Islamic civilization. But the Muslim nation has been greatly damaged as a result of the orientalists' work, from which one could infer their goal and the methods they have used to attain it. The real goal pursued by the orientalists through their study of Islamic culture in its various stages is shaking Islam's highest values in the minds of its sons, on the one hand, and affirming the superiority and power of Western civilization, on the other hand. For this end they strive to present any call for holding to Islam as a reactionary and backward one. They also strive to defeat the Muslims spiritually and intellectually, by eliminating the spirit of pride in Islam in the Muslim's heart and by dissolving his Islamic personality, so that he will become a stranger in his own society, secular in his way of thinking and a Westerner in his orientation.

The orientalists have applied one of two means in order to attain their goals: Either as members of religious institutions for which they worked, in harmony with missionary plans, or by working in cooperation with political institutions in order to realize for the latter imperialistic goals and political activities aimed at strengthening the influence of a certain state.

The methods and lies used by orientalists for fighting Islam may be summarized as follows:

1. Holding that the Qur'an is man-made and that Muhammad composed it.
2. Challenging the [authenticity of] the noble Prophetic sayings [the Hadith].
3. Their intentional distortion of Islamic texts in many cases and their [intentional] misapprehension of the phrases when they do not find room for distortion.
4. Depicting Muslim civilization in an image that is much less than its real one, in order to belittle its significance and look down on its achievements.
5. Accusing Islam of backwardness and stagnation.
6. Depicting Islamic society in the various ages as fragmentized and presenting its great men as selfish.

7. Having a low opinion of Muslim personalities, scholars and leaders.

8. Being selective regarding the sources from which the orientalists draw their accounts.

Christianization [Christian Missionary Work]

Christianization is an organized Crusader movement aimed at spreading Christianity among the Muslims and others. The Christianization movement is closely connected with modern European Imperialism.

Samuel Zwemer, the head of the Christianization associations, announced at the Jerusalem congress for Christianizers which was held in 1354 AH [the early 1930's]: 'The Christianization mission, for the fulfillment of which in the Muhammedan countries the Christian states have appointed you, is not done by bringing Muslims into Christianity. Your mission is rather bringing the Muslim out of Islam, so that he will become a creature with no connection with God, and hence, with no connection with morality, on which [all] nations rely in their life. Therefore, by this work of yours, you are the pioneers of the imperialist conquest in the Muslim countries. By that, the Muslim younger generation will conform to what Imperialism has wanted it to conform to, that is, not having an interest in major issues [but rather] becoming fond of comfort and idleness and aspiring to fulfill its desires by any means, until desires become its goal in life.' The extent of the malice harbored by Islam's enemies towards the True Religion is made clear by that.

Main Fields of Christianization [Activity]

In the field of medical care, hospitals and clinics have been spread in the Muslim countries. They have been provided with doctors who use the medical profession as a guise behind which they hide their true intentions. One of the female Christianizers said, while giving advice to a doctor who was going on a Christianization mission: 'You must seize these opportunities to reach the Muslims' ears and hearts and repeat the Gospels to them. Beware not to miss the opportunity of medical practice in the clinics and hospitals, for it is the most precious one ever of [all] these opportunities. The devil may want to tempt you and will say to you that your duty is medical practice only, and not Christianization. Do not attempt to listen to him.'

Education is a vast field for Christianization. Moreover, most Christianizers agree that it is the best field for transforming the Muslims' sons into Christian followers. For this reason only, most of the foreign schools in the Muslim countries have been connected with the Christianization missions. Because of that, the Jesuit Christianizers say: 'The primary Christianizer is the school.' School textbooks, which are written by the Christianizers, are usually employed for discrediting Islam, distorting the Muslims' history, accusing them of blind fanaticism, [claiming] that Islam was spread at the point of the sword, and fiercely attacking Islam's regulations regarding marriage and the family. Until recently the foreign Christianizing schools used to force all their students—Muslims, Christians and others—to enter the church once every day. Female Christianizing schools are very important in the eyes of the Christianizers, especially boarding schools, because they make the personal connection with the female students stronger and because they snatch them from the religious influence of the Muslim home. Christianizing schools and colleges are bent on presenting their graduates with every possible support, so that they will occupy leadership positions in society.

In the sphere of politics the Christianizers follow different paths, such as [the following]:

1. Stirring up dissension and unrest among the national minorities and religious communities. One of these was the riot in Syria in Ottoman times in 1860 CE, as well as the [Christian] Assyrians [riot] against the Iraqis after WWI.
2. Casting doubts on, and discrediting, the leading personalities in the Muslim world.
3. Supporting the trends that oppose Islam. The Christianizers in the Levant [Sham] were an effective force in reviving the Arab nationalist movement in order to separate it from the Islamic religion.
4. Cooperating with oppositionist elements in the country in order to stage military coups.
5. Preparing for imperialist invasions. Christianizers set about initiating provocations in the country. As the government intervenes against them, the Christianizers stir up in their turn public opinion in their [home] state to intervene in order to save them. Such was the intervention of Czarist Russia in the reign of Catherine the

Great for the protection of her Christian subjects in the Ottoman State and the [ensuing] outbreak of war between the two countries in the eighteenth century.

There are other fields the Christianizers have exploited, such as the humanitarian services rendered by the Christianizing societies, in addition to informative newspapers and magazines and various propaganda publications.*

Here we are today witnessing another experience that leads to another deterioration: The Western civilization, which has lost the meaning of spirituality, finds itself in its turn on the verge of an abyss. It is a civilization on its way to dissolution and extinction.†

---

* *Biography of the Prophet and History of the Muslim State,* Grade 10, Kingdom of Saudi Arabia: Ministry of Education, 2001, 119–121.

† *Biography of the Prophet and History of the Muslim State,* Grade 10, Kingdom of Saudi Arabia: Ministry of Education, 2001, 71.

49

Nuclear Weapons in North Korea

In 1993, the Clinton administration held talks with North Korea over the issue of its nuclear reactors. The Democratic People's Republic of Korea (DPRK) stepped up nuclear production in order to strengthen its hand at the bargaining table. In the end, the North Koreans agreed to limit production of nuclear material in exchange for energy resources. This event rarely receives mention in U.S. textbooks. The North Koreans, however, see it much differently: that they were able to wrest an agreement from the United States, the most powerful nation on earth, is a source of national pride.

★

NORTH KOREA

The year 1993 found the Korean peninsula in a nuclear crisis because of the "suspicion about the DPRK's nuclear development", which the United States prompted the International Atomic Energy Agency (IAEA) to raise.

After signing the Nuclear Safeguards Accord with the IAEA in 1992 in pursuance of its policy against nuclear weapons and for peace, and on the precondition that the parties to the Nuclear Non-Proliferation Treaty (NPT) would not deploy nuclear weapons on the Korean peninsula and would refrain from nuclear threat against Korea, the DPRK received ad hoc inspections by the IAEA, the transparency of its peaceful nuclear activities being proved in the course of these.

However, at a meeting of its Board of Governors held on February 25, 1993, the IAEA, at the instigation of some cliques in its Secretariat and some of its member states, and supported by the groundless information provided by a third party, passed a "resolution" forcing the DPRK to accept a "special inspection" of military facilities unrelated to its nuclear activities. Accepting the unjust inspection, which was outside the scope of the Nuclear Safeguard Accord and of the authority of the IAEA, would have meant justifying the espionage work of the United States, the other belligerent party, and opening the door to all its military sites.

Simultaneously, the United States made public that it would resume the joint military exercise "Team Spirit" that year in south Korea, an annual nuclear war exercise which it had suspended temporarily, on a larger scale than ever before. This was an absolute infringement upon the DPRK's sovereignty and a hostile act intended to demolish the socialist system in the north. It was as good as an ultimatum. The West predicted that the DPRK would put up the white flag as the odds were against it.

On March 8, the DPRK declared a semi-war state throughout the country and warned that no one could touch an inch of its land or even a blade of its grass. The world at large claimed that this was a "military countermeasure, a move outpointing [sic] the United States".

Four days later, on March 12, the DPRK Government issued a statement saying that it was compelled to withdraw from the NPT as a measure to safeguard its interests. This was a "bombshell" to the West. The US administration, which regards nuclear control as a major lever for implementing its foreign policy, was shocked.

A formal withdrawal from the NPT becomes effective 60 days after its declaration, a provision which provided a way out for the United States. It gave up its military blackmail against the DPRK and proposed negotiation.

On May 29, three days before the planned opening of the historic first round of DPRK-US talks, the DPRK test-fired its new-type missiles. It was in no way duty bound to notify the United States of the test-firing, but it did so intentionally. Three missiles were fired and, as notified, they hit their targets under the eyes of the United States, clearly showing that the DPRK was a powerful opponent that could not be underestimated.

The first round of DPRK-US talks, held in New York from June 2, elicited a US commitment to refrain from threatening the DPRK with nuclear weapons, respect the political system of the DPRK and support the peaceful reunification of the north and the south of Korea. The commitment was made on June 11, just one day before the DPRK's withdrawal from the NPT would become effective. As a result, the DPRK's withdrawal from the NPT was shelved and the situation on the Korean peninsular eased.

DPRK-US relations, however, soured again the following year.

The United States came up with preconditions for the third round of the talks, demanding that the DPRK should accept the IAEA's inspections and resume talks with the south of Korea. It threatened to apply "sanctions" against the DPRK unless the latter accepted the inspections by February 21, 1994, when the meeting of the Board of Governors of the IAEA was to be held. Japan, south Korea and the Western countries joined hands with the United States.

DPRK-US relations were further aggravated due to problems related to the change of fuel rods within the graphite-moderated reactor of the atomic power station in the DPRK. At that time, the fuel rods of the graphite-moderated reactor had to be replaced in line with scientific and technological requirements.

The replacement is required to be undertaken under the supervision of the inspection team of the IAEA, as the plutonium that is obtained in the course of replacement can be used for manufacturing nuclear weapons. Proceeding from this requirement, the DPRK requested the IAEA to send its inspection team for supervision of the undertaking.

The IAEA, however, did not send its inspection team, instead threatening that if the fuel rods were replaced without its supervision, it would ask the UN to take "sanctions" against the DPRK.

Now that the replacement of fuel rods could no longer be deferred, the DPRK undertook the replacement and declared its immediate withdrawal from the IAEA through the statement of a spokesman of its Foreign Ministry dated June 13.

It was at this time that the former US President, Jimmy Carter, came to the DPRK. In his long meetings with President Kim Il Sung on June 16 and 17, Carter expressed his full agreement with the attitude of the DPRK towards breaking the deadlock in DPRK-US relations with regard to the nuclear issue.

Afterwards, the United States stepped back from its intention to discuss the matter of "sanctions" against the DPRK at the UN Security Council and came to the third round of DPRK-US talks. On October 20, 1994, Clinton sent Kim Jong Il a letter of assurance in which he promised to fulfil the commitments made in the DPRK-US Agreed Framework.

On the following day, the DPRK-USA Agreed Framework was adopted in Geneva, an agreement the gist of which is as follows: According to the US president's letter of assurance, the United States would take action to provide the DPRK with "light-water reactors with 2,000,000-kw" generating capacity by 2003 and deliver to the DPRK 500,000 tons of heavy oil annually until the completion of the light-water reactor plant No. 1, in order to compensate the latter for its energy loss due to the freezing of its graphite-moderated reactor and other relevant facilities. Provided that it was assured by the United States on the delivery of the LWRs and heavy oil, the DPRK would freeze its graphite-moderated reactor and other relevant facilities and dismantle them eventually. Three months after the signing of the agreement, both sides would lift their sanctions against one another, including restrictive measures against postal services and financial settlement. With the solution of the historical and other practical problems, both sides would open liaison offices in each other's capital city and, with the progress in the solution of issues of much concern, upgrade their bilateral relations to ambassadorial level. The United States would neither use nuclear weapons against Korea nor threaten it with nuclear weapons, and the DPRK would remain as a party to the NPT and fulfill its commitments to the safeguards accords as required by the NPT. This was a remarkable event in the history of DPRK-US relations. That day *The New York Times* carried an article, under the headline *Score: Who Is the Winner in Bargain with Korea?*, in which it declared Kim Jong Il as the "winner".*

---

* Am, Jo, An Chol Gang (ed), and Kim Yong Nam (trans), et al. *Korea in the 20th Century: 100 Significant Events.* Pyongyang, Korea: Foreign Languages Publishing House, Juche 91 (2002), 185–89.

50

A New World Order

France, an imperial power eclipsed by the United States after WWI, has struggled with the reality of a US-dominated world. As we move into a new, uncertain century, the questions posed by this selection might well be pondered by students everywhere. Are we in an era of *Pax Americana?* Can we hope for peace and prosperity worldwide? Whose values should we espouse? Here, as always, it is worth asking what lesson we can learn from a broader perspective on our own history.

★

FRANCE

A New World Order

• At the end of the 20th century, could a new world order be born? **The United States remains the only superpower** culturally and economically as well as politically and militarily, which the Gulf War of 1990–1991 clearly proved. They exert a global influence but the superpower is hardly all-powerful; it has its limits. It cannot, or will not, impose its will everywhere. At its side, the European Union, Russia, Japan, China and perhaps India are regional powers that intend to maintain an important role.

• **Globalization progresses.** Whether it involves the population explosion, the protection of the environment (the Rio Earth Summit in 1992), the interweaving of economies or cultural attitudes, the world constitutes one immense village. But these developments also strike fear. Far from disappearing, nation-states continue to multiply, dispute their territories and resources, and attack one another in bloody confrontations. From Latin America to the Indian Ocean, conflicts, massacres and genocides feed the news. Only Western Europe and North America enjoy a peace envied by the people of the Balkans, Caucuses, Africa and the Middle East. However, terrorist attacks continue to ravage these lands in the name of nationalist claims (Irish Republican Army—IRA—in Great Britain) and religious extremists, as in France in 1995–1996 during the wave of attacks by the *Groupes islamiques armés* (GIA).*

• The Cold War is finished but it still remains to construct a new international order. Despite the UN, NGOs like Doctors Without Borders and Catholic Charities, and innumerable treaties signed between states, the law of the jungle prevails.†

---

* Armed Islamic Groups.
† Lambin, Jean-Michel. *Histoire—T^{ales}*. Paris: Hachette, 2001, 252.

BIBLIOGRAPHY

Agoncillo, Teodoro A. *History of the Filipino People*. Quezon City, Manila: Garotech Publishing, 1990.

Alvaro, Ana Lorena Orozco, and Efren Molina Vega. *Estudios Sociales 10*. San José: Santillana, 1999.

Am, Jo, and An Chol Gang (ed), Kim Yong Nam (trans), et al. *Korea in the 20th Century: 100 Significant Events*. Pyongyang, Korea: Foreign Languages Publishing House, Juche 91 (2002).

Bahr, Frank, et al. *Grundkurse Geschichte*. Darmstadt: Winklers Verlag, 1998.

Barnavi, Eli, and Eyal Naveh. *Modern Times section B 1920–2000*, Jerusalem: Tel Aviv Books, 1999.

Barr, Janis, et al. *Twentieth Century Canada*. Calgary: Wiegl, 1996.

Baylac, M.-H., et al. *Histoire—1re*. Paris: Bordas, 1997.

Berstein, Serge, and Pierre Milza. *Histoire du XIXe siècle*. Paris: Hatier, 1996.

———. *Histoire du XXe siècle: 1945–1973, Le monde entre guerre et paix*. Paris: Hatier, 1996.

———. *Histoire du XXe siècle: 1973 à nos jours, La recherche d'un nouveau ordre*. Paris: Hatier, 1996.

———. *Histoire du XXe siècle: 1900–1945, la fin du 'monde européen'*. Paris: Hatier, 1996.

———. *Histoire—1re*. Paris: Hatier, 1997.

———. *Histoire—T^ales*. Paris: Hatier, 1998.

Biography of the Prophet and History of the Muslim State, Grade 10. Kingdom of Saudi Arabia: Ministry of Education, 2001.

Bourel, Guillaume, et al. *Histoire—2de*. Paris: Hatier, 2001.

Brockie, Gerard, and Raymond Walsh. *Focus on the Past*. Dublin: Gill and McMillan, 1994.

Brom, Juan. *Esbozo de Historia de México.* Mexico City: Grijalbo, 1998.

Bumsted, J.M. *A History of the Canadian Peoples.* Toronto: Oxford University Press, 1998.

Claypole, William, and John Robottom. *Caribbean Story, Bk. 2: The Inheritors.* Kingston: Carlong, 1994.

Cook, Chris, and John Stevenson. *The Longman Handbook of Modern British History: 1714–2001.* London: Longman, 2001.

Dawson, Ian. *Challenging History: The Tudor Century.* Cheltenham: Thomson, 1993.

Díaz, Julio Montero. *Historia de España contemporánea.* Madrid: Luis Vives, 1996.

Domke. *The World and the Jews in the Past Generations: Part B, Volume 6: 1920–1970.* Jerusalem, 1995.

Dorel-Ferré, Gracia, et al. *Histoire—2de.* Paris: Bréal, 1996.

Drago, Marco, and Andrea Boroli (dir). *Storia.* Novara: Instituto de Geografico de Agostini, 1998.

Eliassen, Jørgen, et al. *Spor i Tid: verden før 1850.* Oslo: H. Aschehoug and Co., 1997.

Emblem, Terje. *Norge 1: Cappelens historieverk for den videregaende skolen.* Oslo: Cappelens, 1997.

Facilitating the Rules of the Arabic Language. Grade 9, pt. 1. Kingdom of Saudi Arabia: Ministry of Education, 1998.

Finkel, Alvin, et al. *History of the Canadian Peoples: 1867 to the present, v. 2.* Toronto: Copp Clark Pittman, 1993.

Francis, Daniel, and Sonia Riddoch. *Our Canada: A Social and Political History.* Scarboroug: Pippin, 1995.

Frank, Robert and Valéry Zanghellini. *Histoire—1ère.* Paris: Bélin, 1997.

———. *Histoire—2de.* Paris: Bélin, 1996.

Golecki, Von Anton, et al. *Deutsche Geschichte Zwischen 1800 un 1933—Geschichte der Supermächte.* Bamberg: C.C. Buchners Verlag, 1998.

Groiss, Dr. Arnon (ed). *Report: Jews, Zionism and Israel in Syrian Textbooks.* New York: Center for Monitoring the Impact of Peace, 2002.

———. *Report: The West, Christians and Jews in Saudi Arabian Schoolbooks.* New York: Center for Monitoring the Impact of Peace, 2003.

Heater, Derek. *Presenting the Past, Bk. 3: Reform and Revolution.* Oxford: Oxford University Press, 1991.

History for Iran in the Modern Age—4th Year. Tehran: Ministry of Education, 1996.

History of Russia: XXth Century. Moscow: Drofa, 1998.

History of the Revolution of our Great Leader Kim Il-sung: High School. Textbook Publishing Co., 1999.

History of the Revolution of our Great Leader Kim Il-sung: Junior High. Textbook Publishing Co., 2000.

History of the Saudi Arabian Kingdom. Kingdom of Saudi Arabia: Ministry of Education, 1998.

Islamic Education. Grade 8. Syria: Ministry of Education, 1999/2000.

[Islamic] Jurisprudence, Grade 10. Kingdom of Saudi Arabia: Ministry of Education, 2001.

Jager, Dr. Wolfgang, et al. *Kursbuch Geschichte.* Berlin: Cornelson, 2000.

Japan in Modern History. Tokyo: International Society for Educational Information, 1994.

Kim, Doojin. *Korean History: Senior High.* Seoul: Dae Han Textbook Co., 2001.

Kim, Hongsoo. *Korean History: Junior High.* Seoul: Dae Han Textbook Co., 2000.

Kirbyson, Ronald C. *Discovering Canada: Developing a Nation*. Scarborough, Ont.: Prentice Hall, 1992.

Lam, Dinh Xuan, et al. *Lich Su 12: tap hai*. Vietnam: Nha Xuat Ban Giao Duc, 1997.

Lambin, Jean-Michel, et al. *Histoire—terminale*. Paris: Hachette, 2001.

López, José de Jesús Nieto, et al. *Historia 3*. Mexico: Santillana, 2000.

Martell, John. *A History of Britain from 1867*. London: Thomson, 1988.

Martin, Howard. *Challenging History: Britain in the Nineteenth Century*. Surrey: Thomson, 1996.

McDonough, Frank. *The British Empire 1815–1914*. London: Hodder and Stoughton, 1994.

Mendes de Matos, Margarida, et al. *História, 10°ano, 2°volume*. Lisbon: Texto Editora, 1994.

Mlambo, A.S. *Focus on History: A Secondary Course for Zimbabwe, Book 4*. Harare: College Press Publishers, 1997.

Modern History of the Arabs. Grade 9. Syria: Ministry of Education, 1999/2000.

Murphy, Derrick, et al. *Britain: 1815–1918*. London: Collins, 1998.

National-Socialist Education, Grade 7. Syria: Ministry of Education, 1999/2000.

National-Socialist Education, Grade 8. Syria: Ministry of Education, 1999/2000.

National-Socialist Education, Grade 9. Syria: Ministry of Education, 1999/2000.

National-Socialist Education, Grade 12. Syria: Ministry of Education, 1989/1990.

Navarro, José Cantón. *History of Cuba: The Challenge of the Yoke and the Star*. Havana: SI-MAR, 2000.

Newest History of Foreign Nations: XXth Century. Moscow: Vlados, 1998.

Newman, Garfield, et al. *Canada: A Nation Unfolding*. Toronto: MacGraw-Hill, 2000.

Omolewa, Michael. *Certificate History of Nigeria*. Lagos, Nigeria: Longman Group, Ltd., 1991.

Palacios, Mario Alfonso Rodríguez, et al. *México en la historia*. Mexico: Trillas, 1992.

Pinto, Ana Lídia, et al. *Temas de Historia: história, ensino secundário, 10° ano, v. 2*. Porto: Porto ed, 1996.

Postlethwaite, T. Neville (ed). *International Encyclopedia of National Systems of Education, 2nd ed*. New York: Pergamon, 2001.

Rémond, René. *Histoire des États-Unis*. Paris: PUF - Que sais-je?, 1992.

Roberts, Martin. *Britain 1846–1964: The Challenge of Change*. London: Oxford University Press, 2001.

Romero Vargas, Dr. Germán. *Nuestra Historia*. Managua, Nicaragua: Editorial Hispamer, 1995.

Sauvain, Philip. *The Modern World: 1914–1980*. Cheltenham: Stanley Thornes, 1998.

Scott-Baumann, Michael (ed). *Years of Expansion: Britain 1815–1914*. London: Hodder and Stoughton, 1999.

Sibanda, M., and H. Moyana. *The African Heritage: History for O'level Secondary Students, Book 3*. Harare, Zimbabwe: Zimbabwe Publishing House (Pvt) Ltd., 1999.

Silva, Fransisco de Assis. *História do Brasil: Colônia, Imperio, República*. São Paulo: Moderna, 2002.

Smith, Simon C. *British Imperialism: 1750–1970*. Cambridge: Cambridge University Press, 1998.

Stumpo, E. Beniamino. *Il nuovo libro di storia: per i nuovo programmi*. Firenze: LeMonnier, 2001.

Traynor, John. *Challenging History: 1890–1990.* Surrey: Thomson, 1991.

Vargas, Dr. Germán Romero. *Nuestra Historia.* Managua: Editorial Hispamer, 1995.

Vasquez, Josefina Zoraida. *Historia de México: origenes, evolución y modernidad del pueblo mexicano: tercer grado.* Mexico: Trillas, 1999.

Vicento, Cládio. *História geral.* São Paulo: Scipione, 2002.

Villari, Rosario. *Storia Contemporanea.* Bari: Laterza, 1990.

Webb, R.K. *Modern England: From the Eighteenth Century to the Present.* London: Unwin Hyman, 1989.

World in the XXth Century, The. Moscow: Prosveshchenie, 1999.

Zaide, Sonia M. *The Philippines: A Unique Nation.* Quezon City: All-Nations Publishing, 1999.

PERMISSIONS

Excerpts from *Historia de España contemporánea* by Julio Montero Diaz. Copyright 1996 by Luis Vives. Reprinted with permission from Luis Vives.

Excerpts from *History of the Saudi Arabian Kingdom* Kingdom of Saudi Arabia: Ministry of Education, 1998. Copyrighted translation in *The West, Christians and Jews in Saudi Arabian Schoolbooks* by the Center for Monitoring the Impact of Peace, 2003. Reprinted with permission from CMIP.

Excerpt from *Il nuovo libro di storia. Per i nuovi programmi*, vol. 3 by Stumpo, E. Beniamino. Copyright 2001 by LeMonnier. Reprinted with permission from Le Monnier.

Excerpts from *Islamic Education, Grade 8* by the Syria Ministry of Education, 1999/2000. Copyrighted translation in *Jews, Zionism and Israel in Syrian Textbooks* by the Center for Monitoring the Impact of Peace, 2002. Reprinted with permission from CMIP.

Excerpts from *Modern History of the Arabs, Grade 9* by the Syria Ministry of Education, 1999/2000 Copyrighted translation in *Jews, Zionism and Israel in Syrian Textbooks* by the Center for Monitoring the Impact of Peace, 2002. Reprinted with permission from CMIP.

Excerpt from *The Modern World: 1914–1980* by Philip Sauvain. Copyright 1989 by Stanley Thornes. Reprinted with permission from Philip Sauvain.

Excerpts from *National-Socialist Education, Grade 7* by the Syria Ministry of Education, 1999/2000 Copyrighted translation in *Jews, Zionism and Israel in Syrian Textbooks* by the Center for Monitoring the Impact of Peace, 2002. Reprinted with permission from CMIP.

Excerpts from *National-Socialist Education, Grade 8* by the Syria Ministry of Education, 1999/2000 Copyrighted translation in *Jews, Zionism and Israel in Syrian Textbooks* by the Center for Monitoring the Impact of Peace, 2002. Reprinted with permission from CMIP.

Excerpts from *National-Socialist Education, Grade 9* by the Syria Ministry of Education, 1999/2000 Copyrighted translation in *Jews, Zionism and Israel in Syrian Textbooks* by the Center for Monitoring the Impact of Peace, 2002. Reprinted with permission from CMIP.

Excerpts from *National-Socialist Education, Grade 10* by the Syria Ministry of Education, 1999/2000 Copyrighted translation in *Jews, Zionism and Israel in Syrian Textbooks* by the Center for Monitoring the Impact of Peace, 2002. Reprinted with permission from CMIP.

Excerpts from *National-Socialist Education, Grade 12* by the Syria Ministry of Education, 1989/1990 Copyrighted translation in *Jews, Zionism and Israel in Syrian Textbooks* by the Center for Monitoring the Impact of Peace, 2002. Reprinted with permission from CMIP.

Excerpts from *The Philippines: A Unique Nation* by Gregorio F. Zaide and Sonia M. Zaide. Copyright 1999 by All-Nations Publishing Co. Inc. Reprinted with permission from All-Nations Publishing Co. Inc.

Excerpts from *Presenting the Past, Bk. 3: Reform and Revolution* by Derek Heater. Copyright 1991 by Oxford University Press. Reprinted with permission from Oxford University Press.

TRANSLATIONS

This project would not have been possible without the tireless efforts of the many translators who read the texts, gave their input, explained nuances, and in the end provided the useful translations you read here. Their remarkable work demonstrates a keen understanding of the bigger picture envisioned in this project and a desire to share that bigger picture with the next generation of historians. The Arab texts were generously provided by the Center for Monitoring the Impact of Peace (CMIP), a not-for-profit organization which has published several reports detailing the contents of textbooks in the Middle East, in both Israel and the Arab nations. Their full reports can be viewed at www.edume.org.

We wish to express our gratitude to the following individuals who translated the excerpts from the countries indicated:

BRAZIL: *Emilia Beatriz Ribeiro Rocha Laranjeira*
CHINA: *Dr. Daniel Fried*
COSTA RICA: *Dana Lindaman*
CUBA: *English edition provided by the publisher*
FRANCE: *Jérôme Viala-Gaudefroy, Dana Lindaman*
GERMANY: *Dr. Rebecca Bennette*
ISRAEL: *Jason O'Connor*
ITALY: *Lia Brozgal, Anna Skubikowski*
JAPAN: *English edition provided by the publisher*
MEXICO: *Dana Lindaman*
NICARAGUA: *Dana Lindaman*

NORTH KOREA: *Roger Kim*
NORWAY: *Dr. Dawn Tommerdahl*
PORTUGAL: *Juvenil Damaceno, Jr.*
RUSSIA: *Boris Granovskiy*
SAUDI ARABIA: *Dr. Arnon Groiss (Center for Monitoring the Impact of Peace)*
SOUTH KOREA: *Roger Kim*
SPAIN: *Dana Lindaman*
SYRIA: *Dr. Arnon Groiss (Center for Monitoring the Impact of Peace)*
VIETNAM: *Narquis Barak*

INDEX